Tennessee's New Deal Landscape

Tennessee's
NEW DEAL
Landscape

A GUIDEBOOK

Carroll Van West

THE UNIVERSITY OF TENNESSEE PRESS / KNOXVILLE

Copyright © 2001 by The University of Tennessee Press / Knoxville.
All Rights Reserved. Manufactured in the United States of America.
First Edition.

All photographs are by the author unless otherwise noted.

The paper used in this book meets the minimum requirements of
ANSI/NISO Z39.48-1992 (R 1997) (Permanence of Paper).
The binding materials have been chosen for strength and durability.

Library of Congress Cataloging-in-Publication Data

West, Carroll Van, 1955–
Tennessee's New Deal landscape : a guidebook / Carroll Van West.— 1st ed.
    p. cm.
Includes bibliographical references and index.
ISBN 1-57233-107-0 (cl.: alk. paper)
ISBN 1-57233-108-9 (pbk.: alk. paper)
1. Historic buildings—Tennessee—Guidebooks. 2. Historic buildings—Tennessee—
Pictorial works. 3. Public buildings—Tennessee—Guidebooks. 4. Public buildings—
Tennessee—Pictorial works. 5. New Deal, 1933–1939—Tennessee. 6. Architecture,
Modern—20th century—Tennessee—Pictorial works. 7. Tennessee—Guidebooks.
8. Tennessee—Pictorial works. 9. Tennessee—History, Local. I. Title.
F437 .W47 2001
917.6804'54—dc21   00-009686

Contents

Preface: Using This Book   *xi*

Acknowledgments   *xiii*

Introduction: The New Deal Landscape of Tennessee   1

1. State Offices and County Courthouses   29
2. Federal Courthouses and Post Offices   46
3. Community Buildings and Institutions   77
4. Schools   96
5. Housing   128
6. Parks, Memorials, and Museums   149
7. Dams to Privies: A New Deal Foundation for Modern Tennessee   212

Notes   255

A Note on Sources   263

Index   269

Illustrations

Figures

Park Headquarters, Big Ridge State Park, Union County	4
Central Staircase, Madison County Courthouse, Jackson	6
PWA-sponsored Football Field, Union City	7
Rustic-Style Dwelling at Norris, Anderson County	10
TVA System, Interpretive Marker, Norris Dam West Overlook, Anderson County	11
CCC-constructed Gazebo, Forest Service Road 77, Cherokee National Forest, Polk County	12
PWA-constructed Building No. 1, Alvin C. York Veterans Administration Medical Center, Murfreesboro	15
Postcard of the Davidson County Public Building and Courthouse, Nashville	16
WPA-constructed Dam and Spillway, Standing Stone State Park, Overton County	20
WPA-constructed Bohannon Building, Livingston	21
NYA-constructed Liberty School, Sequatchie County	23
"Agriculture" Mural by Dean Cornwell, Davidson County Public Building and Courthouse, Nashville	32
Tennessee (John Sevier) State Office Building, Nashville	34
Franklin County Courthouse, Winchester	37
Lake County Courthouse, Tiptonville	39
Lauderdale County Courthouse, Ripley	40
Madison County Courthouse, Jackson	41
Polk County Courthouse, Benton	44
LaFollette Post Office, Campbell County	51
On the Shores of the Lake by Dahlov Ipcar (1938), LaFollette Post Office	51
Newport Post Office, Cocke County	53
Postcard of Nashville Post Office, Davidson County	55
People of the Soil by Edwin Boyd Johnson (1938), Dickson Post Office, Dickson County	57

Milan Post Office, Gibson County	59
Great Smokies and Tennessee Farms by Charles Child (1941), Jefferson City Post Office, Jefferson County	63
Jefferson City Post Office, Jefferson County	64
Electrification by David Sloane Martin (1940), Lenoir City Post Office, Loudon County	66
U.S. Post Office and Courthouse, Columbia	68
Maury County Landscape by Henry Billings (1942), U.S. Post Office and Courthouse, Columbia	68
Dayton Post Office, Rhea County	71
Dresden Post Office, Weakley County	73
Gleason Post Office, Weakley County	74
Gleason Agriculture by Anne Poor (1942), Gleason Post Office, Weakley County	75
Parrotsville Library, Cocke County	82
Hancock County School Library and Shops, Sneedville	83
Tiptonville Public Library, Lake County	85
Columbia Armory, Maury County	86
Loyd Campbell Boy Scout Lodge, Etowah, McMinn County	87
Union City Armory, Obion County	88
Obion County Public Health Building, Union City	89
Veterans Administration Hospital, Murfreesboro, circa 1950	91
Dunlap Community Building, Sequatchie County	93
Kingsport Civic Auditorium and Armory, Sullivan County	95
Caryville School, Campbell County	99
West End High School, Nashville	104
Johnson County High School Shops, Mountain City	110
Corryton School, Knox County	111
Obion County High School Gymnasium, Union City	115
Alpine Gymnasium, Overton County	117
Oak Grove School, Overton County	118
Gentry School, Putnam County	119
Bristol Tennessee High School, Sullivan County	124
The Stone Castle, Bristol Tennessee High School, Sullivan County	125
Homesteads Tower, Cumberland Homesteads, Cumberland County	132
Cheatham Place, Nashville	137
College Hill Courts, Chattanooga	139
Haywood Farms Dwelling, Douglass Community	140

Foote Homes, after 1998–99 Renovations, Memphis	*144*
Riverview Apartments, Kingsport	*148*
CCC Cabin, Norris Lake State Park, Anderson County	*153*
Lodge and Tearoom, Norris Lake State Park, Anderson County	*154*
Whitehead Family Dwelling, Cades Cove, Great Smoky Mountains National Park, Blount County	*158*
Cove Lake State Park, Campbell County	*160*
War Memorial, Campbell County Courthouse Grounds, Jacksboro	*162*
Sagamore Lodge, Chickasaw State Park, Chester County	*164*
Postcard of the CCC Bridge, Cumberland Mountain State Park, Cumberland County	*165*
WPA-constructed Entrance Gate, Old Hickory Boulevard, Percy Warner Park, Nashville	*167*
Grundy Lakes State Park, Tracy City	*170*
Booker T. Washington State Park, Hamilton County	*171*
Picnic Shelter, Pickwick Landing State Park, Hardin County	*173*
CCC-constructed Trail, Pickwick Landing State Park, Hardin County	*173*
Fairfield Gullies, Natchez Trace State Park, Henderson County	*175*
Lodge, Natchez Trace State Park, Henderson County	*177*
Check-In Station, Reelfoot Lake State Park, Lake County	*179*
Guest Cabins, Standing Stone State Park, Overton County	*183*
Amphitheater, Standing Stone State Park, Overton County	*184*
Trail Shelter, Pickett CCC Memorial State Park, Pickett County	*186*
Nature Center, Pickett CCC Memorial State Park, Pickett County	*187*
Postcard of the Laura Spellman Rockefeller Memorial, Great Smoky Mountains National Park, Sevier County	*192*
Sugarlands Administration Building, Great Smoky Mountains National Park, Sevier County	*194*
Memorial to Edward Meeman, Meeman-Shelby Forest State Park, Shelby County	*196*
Reconstructed Chucalissa Village, T. O. Fuller State Park, Shelby County	*200*
Swimming beach, Rock Creek Recreation Area, Cherokee National Forest, Unicoi County	*204*
"The Beach," Big Ridge State Park, Union County	*205*
CCC cabin, Big Ridge State Park, Union County	*206*
Loy Cemetery, Big Ridge State Park, Union County	*207*

Postcard of the Cane Creek Falls, Fall Creek Falls State Park, Van Buren County	209
Cedar Forest Lodge, Cedars of Lebanon State Park, Wilson County	210
TVA System, c. 1960	215
PWA Public Utility Marker, Marshall County Courthouse Grounds, Lewisburg	217
Norris Dam, Anderson County	220
Rice Grist Mill, Norris Lake State Park, Anderson County	221
Stone Dwelling, Norris Village, Anderson County	224
Postcard of Norris Dam—Before and After, 1937	225
WPA Crew Installing Sidewalks in Woodbury, 1937, Cannon County	228
Postcard of Berry Field, Nashville	229
Postcard of "Florida Sunbeam Crossing Tennessee River Bridge, Chickamauga Dam," Hamilton County	234
Postcard of Pickwick Dam, Hardin County	236
Cherokee Dam, Jefferson County	238
Postcard of Fort Loudon Dam, Loudon County	241
Ocoee Dam No. 3, Polk County	246
Watts Bar Dam and Highway Bridge, Rhea County	248
Douglas Dam, Sevier County	251

Maps

East Tennessee	26
Middle Tennessee	27
West Tennessee	28
Cherokee National Forest, South Unit	188
Great Smoky Mountains National Park, Blount and Sevier Counties	191
Cherokee National Forest, Unicoi Area	202

Preface: Using This Book

Tennessee's New Deal Landscape: A Guidebook identifies over 250 important, representative historic properties and places from the New Deal era of 1933 to 1942. The guidebook begins with a thematic overview of Tennessee's New Deal period, highlighting political trends and the ten primary federal agencies involved in creating the state's New Deal landscape. Next come seven chapters that inventory New Deal historic places according to their general property types. These chapters present representative examples of state offices and county courthouses, federal courthouses and post offices, community buildings, schools, housing, parks, and public improvements, with the latter including the dams and reservoirs of the Tennessee Valley Authority. The chapters are organized by county, in alphabetical order, and each inventory entry identifies the New Deal agency or agencies involved in the project and gives the property's address. The vast majority of places are open to the public, but a few are private properties not open to visitors; these noted locations should be viewed from the roadside or sidewalk. Each inventory chapter also has brief introductions about political, cultural, and social patterns that shaped the places listed in the chapter. These analytical sections provide readers with context and perspective on why, where, when, and in what way an individual New Deal project was undertaken.

While the book identifies historic properties from all sections of Tennessee, all extant buildings and places associated with the New Deal era are not included. The inventory instead contains representative examples from all three Grand Divisions as well as examples of the major architectural types, building projects, and social programs of the Depression decade. Many inventory listings are architectural landmarks of the craftsmanship associated with such agencies as the Civilian Conservation Corps (CCC), the National Park Service (NPS), and the Public Works Administration (PWA), but just as many properties may have little aesthetic value. They are included due to their historical and social significance. The book also includes examples of the "other side" of the New Deal legacy—the population displacement and the destruction of existing historical places, rural landscapes, buildings, and urban fabric due to well-meaning but sometimes ill-conceived New Deal projects.

As a book about architecture and history, *Tennessee's New Deal Landscape: A Guidebook* is meant to be of value to a broad range of readers and travelers who are interested in the Depression decade but have lacked a book that identifies specific properties in almost every Tennessee county. Since its inception, the Tennessee Valley Authority has established visitor centers and printed brochures about its facilities—in this book, the other significant New Deal agencies in Tennessee receive their fair due and recognition. Indeed, if there is any one lesson contained within the pages of this book, it is that the New Deal landscape of Tennessee owes much to TVA but that many other agencies and individuals left their own marks, and their own significant legacies. Taken together, New Deal agencies transformed the state's public landscape, leaving in their wake the infrastructure for the emergence of a modern—and different—Tennessee in the second half of the twentieth century.

Acknowledgments

Many individuals and institutions have encouraged and assisted me in the research and fieldwork of this book. I thank the Tennessee Historical Commission for its support of research on Tennessee's county courthouses built between 1865 and 1940; that project first introduced me to the wealth of extant buildings and significant local resources from the New Deal era across the state. Staff, county, and town officials at the various public buildings were always valuable sources of information, and their pride in their historic public buildings became contagious. The courthouse project was part of a multiple-property nomination to the National Register of Historic Places, with funding from both the state and the National Park Service. The commission also has assisted and funded various local National Register projects that are related to the research of this book, including projects in the counties of Bledsoe, Campbell, Claiborne, Dickson, Dyer, Moore, Obion, Tipton, and Wilson. These also resulted in nominations to the National Register of Historic Places.

In conducting these projects, several of my graduate students in historic preservation or public history at Middle Tennessee State University produced helpful National Register nominations, theses, and research papers. I again thank Lauren Batte, Trina Binkley, Margaret Binnicker, Kate Carothers, Jeff Durbin, Brian Eades, Megan Dobbs Eades, Chris Hetzel, Robbie Jones, Jennifer Martin, Judi McIntyre, Ruth Nichols, Anne-Leslie Owens, Nathan Poe, Ginger Ramsey, Holly Rine, Steve Sadowsky, Blythe Semmer, Leslie Sharp, Rebecca Smith, Harrison Stamm, Amanda Wild, Greg Phillipy, Sean Reines, and Leslie Draper Stalcup for their scholarship and friendship.

As is true in almost all of my work in Tennessee history, collaboration with local historians and interested citizens is very important. Many of the state's ninety-five county historians have given me valuable guidance and suggestions. Perhaps even more important is the quality research by historic site professionals, historians, and historic preservationists who work in such agencies as the Tennessee Department of Transportation, Tennessee State Parks, Tennessee State Library and Archives, Tennessee Division of Archaeology, and

Tennessee Valley Authority. Robert Leighninger of Louisiana State University was most kind to share his research on New Deal agencies, especially a list of Public Works Administration projects in Tennessee.

Finally, scholarship developed for the *Tennessee Historical Quarterly* and the *Tennessee Encyclopedia of History and Culture*, both administered and published by the Tennessee Historical Society, has greatly assisted this book. I thank Ann Toplovich, the society's executive director, for her support and encouragement of my various Tennessee history projects.

Introduction

The New Deal Landscape of Tennessee

The Great Depression was the greatest economic dislocation of the twentieth century. Coming on the heels of the general prosperity of the Roaring Twenties, the crash of the New York stock market in October 1929 and the deflating economy of the winter of 1929–30 shocked, then scared millions of Americans. But early on in the South a sunny optimism prevailed; as late as September 1930 the editorial writers of the *Nashville Tennessean* even boasted that the state had no depression, despite dire matters in the northeast and west.

In Tennessee the depression really made its presence felt in early November 1930, when the failure of the Bank of Tennessee, controlled by the Nashville-based financial giant Caldwell and Company, led to an immediate run on other Caldwell-controlled banks across Tennessee and six other states. By the time the dust had settled a week later, Caldwell and Company filed for bankruptcy; soon thereafter, another 120 banks in some seven states declared bankruptcy. Thousands of Tennesseans saw their savings literally disappear overnight while businesses lost valuable capital. Unemployment in the private sector began to rise quickly, and state government could do little to break the slide, since the Caldwell failure had crippled its finances.

Millions of dollars in government funds had been deposited at the Caldwell bank due to the company's political connections with the Democratic party, especially Luke Lea, publisher of the *Nashville Tennessean*, and Gov. Henry Horton. Approximately seven million dollars were now gone. Angry state legislators, urged on by Memphis political boss Edward Hull Crump (who wanted to eliminate Lea and Horton to pursue his own political agenda), investigated the matter and brought impeachment charges against Governor Horton. But rural legislators feared the power of the Crump machine more than a disgraced governor. The state house of representatives refused to vote Horton out of office.

Henry Horton survived the Caldwell debacle, but his state and many of its citizens did not. When the specter of depression first stalked the land, few looked to government for solutions, but in 1931–32, as money tightened, credit disappeared, banks failed, and millions searched for work, more and more Americans turned to their governments—local, state, and federal—for help. In the South, state and local governments had never done that much for public relief, outside of a limited program of county poorhouses, public work projects, and welfare programs, which private charities and foundations had largely supported. In Tennessee, local governments in many counties had taken advantage of state initiatives to expand and upgrade their schools and road systems during the mid- to late 1920s. State government also had drastically increased spending. Faced with paying those construction bonds and debts in depressed times, most state, city, and county officials felt that additional public debt was out of the question, no matter how great the need. Nor were the resources of local charities, social organizations, and churches of much help, as demands in 1931–32 quickly overwhelmed these traditional outlets of public welfare.

Widespread hard times were the result. By 1932 no one was claiming that Tennessee was free of the depression. In that year 578 businesses failed, while all segments of the economy were in steep decline. Farm products were worth $313 million in 1929—they were valued at a mere $132 million in 1932. Between 1929 and 1934, 106 banks in Tennessee closed their doors. Unemployment reached an estimated 25 to 30 percent.

With private, local, and state resources exhausted, many Americans waited for the federal government to step forward. But President Herbert Hoover, a progressive Republican, steadfastly opposed any major federal involvement, out of both philosophical and financial concerns. Like many opinion makers and government leaders, he thought more government spending would actually impede economic recovery. A few federal programs, however, brought public works jobs in communities across Tennessee. From 1930 to 1932 a major Treasury Department initiative to fund modern, architecturally impressive post offices led to new facilities being built in Chattanooga, Knoxville, Rogersville, Huntingdon, McMinnville, and other Tennessee county seats, while Memphis received a major expansion of its downtown post office and customs building. Nationally, the Bureau of Reclamation continued its program of building dams and irrigation projects, with Hoover Dam on the Colorado River being the most famous; in Tennessee, the bureau carried out initial planning for a dam on the Clinch River.

Once the depression threatened the stability of the financial structure of American capitalism, Hoover decided to act. In late 1931 he proposed the creation of the Reconstruction Finance Corporation (RFC) in order to restore confidence in the nation's private money markets and to revive credit.

The RFC became law on January 22, 1932, and soon went into business. President Hoover expected a rather quick response from the banks and credit markets, but banks continued to fail, and credit continued to shrink. On July 21, 1932, Hoover reluctantly agreed to sign the Emergency Relief and Construction Act, which provided $300 million for RFC relief loans to the states and created a pool of $1.5 billion for loans on public works projects that would generate enough income to pay the money back.

The RFC in 1932 and early 1933 had a limited effect on the worsening depression in Tennessee, but the Depression decade's legacy of public works began with the agency's projects of 1932 and 1933. Initial public works projects during the fall of 1932 included sewers, electricity distribution, and toll bridge and road construction, since these were income producing. Knoxville had the first recorded project, beginning on October 29, 1932. To qualify for the relief money, the state created a state relief committee, which in turn selected five-member county committees. Many members of this administrative structure would soon serve on various state and local New Deal committees. Most relief money went to the cities, where the numbers of needy were highest, but in time all counties benefited in some way from the RFC money; by early 1933, according to the count of historian John Dean Minton, some fifty thousand Tennesseans received RFC money. Newly inaugurated Gov. Hill McAlister told the Tennessee General Assembly on February 28, 1933: "I do not see how destitute people of our state could have been cared for during this winter without this federal aid, and it will be a matter of serious concern to Tennessee if for any reason it should be withdrawn."[1] For the rest of the decade, all of Tennessee's governors could have said the same thing—federal aid kept many Tennesseans afloat in the Depression decade.

In the early to mid-1930s, state government did little to support relief, recovery, or reform efforts outside of approving necessary legislation to allow federal programs to proceed at the state and local levels. Strongly supported by the Crump machine, which preferred low taxes and little government spending, McAlister's administration from 1933 to 1937 moved away from promoting the progressive spending on highways and education found in prior administrations. When possible, however, state departments often found ways to provide matching dollars, labor, and support to assist federal projects. Despite contributing few dollars of its own, state government soon became an active, at times even enthusiastic supporter, of the New Deal, especially during the administrations of Gordon Browning (1937–39) and Prentice Cooper (1939–45) in the second half of the New Deal period. The state, for example, established the Department of Conservation, the State Planning Commission, and the Department of

Institutions and Public Welfare in order to better administer programs such as Social Security and the new state parks and forests.

But the initiative for recovery and reform during the Depression decade lay almost entirely with the federal government. President Franklin D. Roosevelt's inaugural promise of a "New Deal" to bring the nation out of the poverty and despair of the Depression found a receptive audience among reformers of all persuasions, with Tennessee being no exception. In March 1933 Roosevelt's "New Dealers" quickly began a whirlwind of activity and change that left few sectors of the society or economy untouched over the next nine years.

Attention first went to the region's ailing financial institutions, beginning with the bank holiday of March 1933. Roosevelt chose to continue and soon expand the RFC. Under the New Dealers, the agency assumed a mission of saving capitalism from itself, according to historian James Olson, becoming "most symbolic of the New Deal and the state capitalism it fostered."[2] For instance, in Tennessee, a RFC subsidiary, the Commodity Credit Corporation, helped local banks increase loans to consumers who wanted to buy appliances powered with electricity from TVA. Funds from RFC also underwrote such popular New Deal programs as the Civilian Conservation Corps (CCC). A comprehensive inventory of historic properties associated with the federal government's initial response to the Great Depression would include many his-

Park Headquarters, Big Ridge State Park, Union County.

toric bank buildings and financial institutions that were propped up by RFC support, as well as the Treasury Section's post offices of 1930 to 1932.

But this book focuses instead on the massive federal response orchestrated by the administration of President Franklin Roosevelt, especially "alphabet" agencies created by the New Dealers between 1933 and 1937 to solve the depression and reform the nation's economy and culture. When most Tennesseans think of the New Deal, they also think of the letters TVA, CCC, WPA, and PWA. Since Roosevelt's inauguration in 1933, commentators, historians, and political scientists have debated the pros and cons of this massive, and in some cases unprecedented, level of federal involvement in all aspects of American life, from banking to day care and from dairy production to symphonic concerts. Whatever one's ideological viewpoint, period newspapers, letters, diaries, and oral interviews indicate no doubt that Tennesseans in the 1930s understood, to different degrees of course, that the New Deal changed their relationship with the federal government. They were exchanging local control and traditions for federal money and expertise. People of the Depression decade realized they were experiencing change—some of it good, some of it indifferent, and some of it for the worse. The impact was pervasive and often the change was profound—no wonder many Tennesseans of that generation still have strong feelings about the 1930s.

Historians have debated whether the New Deal aimed at recovery or reform. But in Tennessee, an appraisal of the purpose and function of the New Deal's building projects, along with the actual numbers of dollars spent and numbers of people employed in these projects, makes it evident that reform and recovery typically went hand-in-hand. If there was to be a lasting recovery in this backward southern state, New Dealers believed, federal programs had to modernize the state's public improvements as they also reformed citizens to function better in a modern world.

In Tennessee at the height of New Deal spending, over two-thirds of federal dollars were invested in public infrastructure—roads, water and sewer systems, bridges, land reclamation, reforestation, and public utility systems—projects that represented the creation of a new public landscape of better roads, land, and municipal services in this southern place. In 1940, the state released a report that listed by county the amount of New Deal money spent between 1935 and 1938. A handful of counties—such as Hamblen in East Tennessee and Stewart in Middle Tennessee—avoided dollars for New Deal public works. But most took the money, with the great bulk of it always going for the construction of highways, bridges, roads, and airports and/or the establishment of public utilities. In Moore County, for example, over

$92,000 went to transportation and utilities while a mere $3,000 were spent on other projects. In Macon County, over $187,000 was spent on transportation improvements, while only $3,800 went to small education and recreation projects. Tipton County counted $671,000 for roads and utilities and only $81,000 for public buildings. The disparity in Scott County was even greater—$425,000 for transportation and utilities, but a mere $6,892 for a football field and agricultural school building at Oneida. All four counties were rural and impoverished; the New Deal spending gave them a better chance of joining the nation's economic mainstream by way of improved, paved roads while the newly available and inexpensive public utilities would prove attractive, in theory at least, to new industrial investment.

The above totals do not count the huge investments in the engineered landscape represented by the Tennessee Valley Authority—underscoring just how much money was poured into a new public infrastructure in Tennessee.

Central staircase, Madison County Courthouse, Jackson.

"The New Dealers," as Jordan A. Schwarz aptly summarizes, " sought to create long-term markets by building an infrastructure in undeveloped regions of America,"[3] and foremost among these undeveloped regions, in the words of the president himself, was the Tennessee Valley. The need was for more than better roads, land, community institutions, and modern utilities; the new foundation for a modern Tennessee also called for new credit mechanisms, better-educated citizens, and a reinvigorated community spirit.

Thus, Tennessee benefited significantly from the New Deal. Within a decade, it received thousands of miles of new roads, thousands of acres of restored land and forests, new lakes, huge new parks, hundreds of new schools, modern airports, many new buildings for community revitalization, and a modern electrical production and distribution network. Several of these projects (the agricultural diversification programs, roads, bridges, and airfields) were clearly linked to improving markets and market access in the state. But even when the project was just a new school, for example, that new building typically had electricity, a library, a lunch room for hot meals, sanitary restrooms (or privies in rural areas), and physical education facilities. The building was a demonstration of the amenities, and the necessity of modern technology, for a productive life. Reformers assumed that this new public infrastructure would almost automatically produce better-educated, more worldly consumer participants in an expanded regional and national

PWA-sponsored football field, Union City.

economy. But these changes did not happen overnight; typically local residents gladly accepted the new buildings and programs but adapted them to their own needs and concerns. Recovery and reform were not exclusively one-way exchanges between New Dealers and the citizens of Tennessee.

Unfortunately, few officials were interested in eliminating or even diminishing the power of Jim Crow segregation, a true albatross to change and improvement in the South. Race was a very real limiting factor to the impact of reform in Tennessee. Public utilities were built but not extended to African American neighborhoods, which were often outside of the legal city limits. Even when they used the new courthouses and community buildings, blacks were still relegated to the basements and rear entrances. In rural counties, New Deal funding meant that paved roads became more common, except for those that served black farm families. Federal farm policies were of limited value to tenants. The New Deal often provided some benefits to African Americans, but in general it left Tennessee blacks with a raw deal.

Politics and politicians further shaped Tennessee's New Deal experience. In applying for and receiving federal dollars, the state benefited from several political leaders well positioned in Washington. Kenneth D. McKellar was a senior member of the Democratic delegation in the U.S. Senate; he chaired the committee that oversaw the U.S. Postal Service. Toward the end of the New Deal era, McKellar gained even more clout as the chair of the Senate Appropriations Committee. More importantly, McKellar often served as eyes and ears for Edward "Boss" Crump in Memphis. Crump dominated Memphis politics—and that of the state Democratic party—like no other politician of the twentieth century. Elected to the U.S. House of Representatives in 1933, Crump used his term in Washington to learn more about the system and to ensure that Memphis and Shelby County would receive enormous amounts of federal dollars throughout the New Deal years. Much good came of these dollars, but Crump wanted the grants, loans, and jobs largely to extend his power in the city and the state. Another powerful Tennessean in Washington was Nashville congressman Joseph W. Byrns, who served as House Majority Leader in 1933 before becoming Speaker of the House of Representatives from 1935 to 1936. Finally, Roosevelt's high-profile secretary of state, Cordell Hull, was a native of Tennessee and a former Tennessee congressman.

The New Dealers created many significant institutions to implement wide-ranging and sometimes confusing programs. In establishing Tennessee's new landscape of public buildings, parks, and public improvements, the following ten agencies are of particular importance.

Tennessee Valley Authority

Congress established the Tennessee Valley Authority on May 18, 1933, as part of Roosevelt's "First One Hundred Days" of legislation. The new agency took an earlier idea of Sen. George Norris of Nebraska, who had envisioned a regional development project evolving from the federal government's ammunition works at Muscle Shoals, Alabama, and expanded it into a regional development project of unprecedented scope and imagination. TVA's goals included flood control, improved river navigation, increased fertilizer production, better agricultural practices, natural resource conservation, industrial promotion, and the generation of public electrical power throughout the seven states of the Tennessee Valley.

To administer the agency, Roosevelt picked three directors—all men of ability and vision. The chair was Arthur S. Morgan, a progressive educator and engineer who was the authority's visionary. Morgan was most in tune with Roosevelt's goal of regional planning for the purpose of rural uplift and reform. David Lilienthal, a Wisconsin progressive who had successfully fought for public power, was the authority's spokesperson for cheap electricity and grassroots activism. The one Tennessean among these directors was actually a native of Canada—Harcourt Morgan, the president of the University of Tennessee. Due to the success and popularity of the university's agricultural extension program, rural and small-town Tennesseans viewed Harcourt Morgan as their man among the directors, the one who would look after their agricultural interests and needs.

Roosevelt's choices, on paper, were complementary, seemingly the perfect blend of expertise and interests for the Tennessee Valley. But differences soon emerged over creating new cooperative ventures (Arthur Morgan's vision) versus working within existing markets (Lilienthal and Harcourt Morgan) and over the value of public power (Arthur Morgan again stood alone) versus private power. Add personal quibbles and personality conflicts to these policy differences, and Roosevelt had a recipe for disaster. By 1937, the three directors were at each other's throats—with Arthur E. Morgan generally receiving the blame from historians today—and their often personal bickering diminished the effectiveness of the authority. Still, the backgrounds of the three original directors indicate that TVA was more than a generator of electricity; it also was to be an agent of reform, especially for farm families and town residents throughout the Tennessee Valley. Long before the first dams and hydroelectric plants were finished, TVA employees were covering the state, bringing expertise and advice on progressive farming, home economics, economic development, and recreational development to farm families and local business owners.

The first TVA dam project was at Norris, in Anderson County (see chapter 7). TVA took earlier plans of the Bureau of Reclamation, adapted both them and the site, and immediately began construction on its model demonstration project. Norris Dam opened in 1936. But by that time TVA's public power critics had the agency in court. Although the U.S. Supreme Court ruled in *Ashwander et al. v. Tennessee Valley Authority* (1936) that the authority was constitutional, another court in December 1936 granted an injunction against TVA dam construction and power distribution. That injunction was not lifted until 1938. The following year, the private Commonwealth and Southern sold its large private power interests, including the Tennessee Electric Power Company, to TVA. One of the new facilities acquired in this deal was the Great Falls Hydroelectric Plant and Dam at Rock Island, on the border between Warren and White Counties. By 1939, with the acquisition of most of the private hydroelectric plants in the region, together with its own dams at Norris, Pickwick, and Chickamauga, TVA had become an extremely powerful economic player in the Volunteer State. From 1939 to 1943, due to perceived military needs and then wartime demands, additional dams

Rustic-style dwelling at Norris, Anderson County.

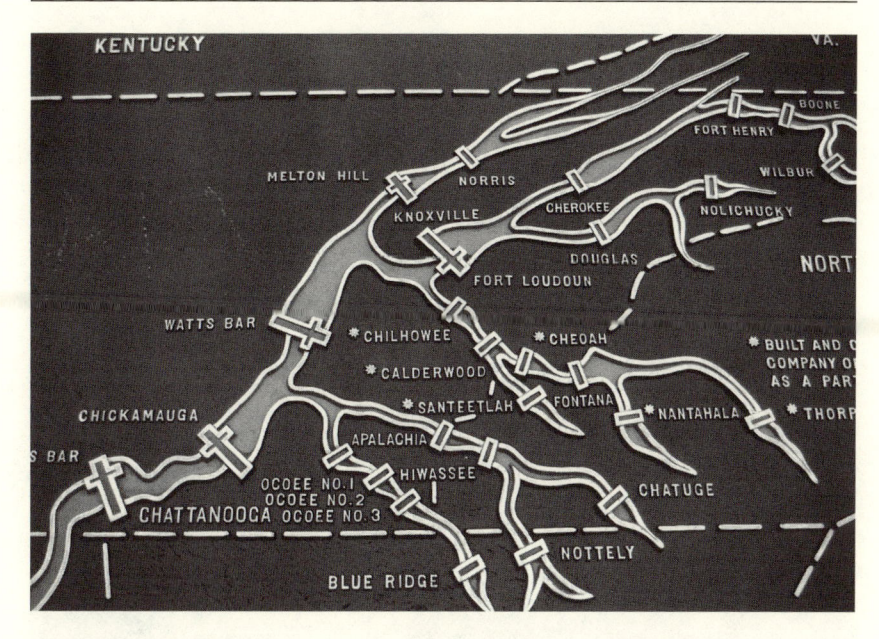

TVA system, interpretive marker at Norris Dam West Overlook, Anderson County.

and plants were built at Cherokee, Douglas, Fort Loudon, Watts Bar, and Ocoee No. 3. By 1944, Kentucky Dam, built along the Tennessee River in western Kentucky, was finished; it flooded large portions of Tennessee bottomland in Henry and Stewart Counties. According to a 1946 count, TVA could produce 2.5 million kilowatts of power and serviced some 668,000 households in the Tennessee Valley.

Along with TVA's engineered landscape, however, there were often individual landscapes of broken dreams, left by the families who were forced to leave their farms in the interest of the greater good and the name of flood control. In 1946, TVA owned over 1.1 million acres—and had removed 72,000 people from that land. Never before nor since had such a massive forced dislocation occurred in the valley.

Civilian Conservation Corps

The Civilian Conservation Corps (CCC) built a public infrastructure for tourism and recreation as well as rebuilding the land of Tennessee itself. Established by Congress as the Emergency Conservation Work program on March 31, 1933, the CCC soon became the most popular of the New Deal's alphabet agencies.

CCC-constructed gazebo, Forest Service Road 77, Cherokee National Forest, Polk County.

(When the agency was reauthorized in 1937, the ECW name was dropped in favor of CCC.) Overgrazing, the lack of crop rotation, clear-cutting of timber, and harsh mining practices had severely eroded the state's land—conditions many Tennesseans recognized and decried by the Depression era. Communities eagerly sought the acquisition of a CCC camp—Johnson City offered one hundred acres in April 1933, a figure matched by officials in Clarksville the following month. The first CCC camp, however, was in Unicoi County. Camp Cordell Hull was established near Limestone Cove and worked in the Cherokee National Forest. "The entire project is one which appeals tremendously to the imagination as well as to common sense," proclaimed the *Knoxville Journal* on August 12, 1933. "Its work is well worth doing. It accomplishes the relief of families in need and the rehabilitation of jobless and discouraged men."

Administratively, Tennessee was part of the CCC's Fourth Corps, District C. The state had eleven district headquarters with another fifteen branch headquarters located in county seats or near large project areas. While the Department of Interior's National Park Service directed CCC work at national, state, and local parks and recreation areas, two other federal bureaus directed the many conservation and reclamation projects. From 1933 to 1935 the Soil Erosion Service of the Department of Interior supervised the projects, while after 1935, directing such projects became a responsibility of the Soil Conservation Service of the Department of Agriculture. The number of CCC camps in Tennessee ranged from thirty-three in 1933—with most in East Tennessee—to seventy-seven in 1935, the program's highest number. The various projects reflected both need and political considerations. Since federal officials estimated that over a six-month period a CCC camp would spend about eighteen thousand dollars, state representatives and senators with influence made sure that their districts received their share of the money and jobs.

A project superintendent directed the work of each CCC company, with supervision coming from traveling federal inspectors. Companies that built parks sometimes employed engineers and architects while they hired skilled local carpenters and artisans. These positions were few compared with the many for the enrollees, or the CCC "boys," as they were called then. Selected for service by the Labor Department through the state relief program, which confirmed individual eligibility, the enrollees were young, single unemployed men, aged between seventeen and twenty-eight from 1933 to 1937; thereafter, the age limits were redefined as between seventeen and twenty-three. Enrollees signed up for six-month terms, with most serving about one year. In exchange, the men received a typical military life: they lived in barracks, dressed in uniforms, and followed typical military-style routines and regimentation led by the uniformed camp commanders. "An undeniable martial atmosphere prevailed in CCC camps," observes historian James C. Steely, including "Army field kitchens and mess halls for hearty camp food, surplus World War uniforms for initial CCC enrollee clothing, plus wartime tent and barrack designs for housing."[4]

Enrollees received thirty dollars month, but twenty-five dollars were sent home to help their families. And, if they desired, they could improve themselves with various education programs held at the camps. CCC national director Robert Fechner, a native of Tennessee, sought to implement regulations that required all enrollees to know how to read and write before they were honorably discharged. Fechner never succeeded, but many CCC men gained some educational benefits from their service. In an interview in the Murfreesboro *Daily News Journal* of August 17, 1999, Allen Byford of Cannon County recalled of his six months at a Kingston camp: "I didn't know how to write my name until I went there. We had a school teacher teach us there, and he learn't me how. That's how I knowed how to sign my check."

The camps were typically composed of tents and prefabricated buildings. Enrollees sometimes built other camp structures, using locally available materials. A typical camp included barracks, a kitchen and mess hall, officer quarters, recreation building, school, hospital, and an office. At CCC installations after 1937, it became more common to use tents and other impermanent buildings. The Tellico Plains Ranger Station was once a CCC camp.

Historians have long praised the CCC's contribution to state and local parks, but a count of corps activity on June 30, 1938, suggests that the agency also made crucial contributions to rebuilding the state's lands and forests and to fire prevention. At that time, five CCC companies were at work in the national parks, five were in state parks, and two toiled at TVA parks. But in conjunction with the state forestry division and TVA, the corps also placed four companies in the national forest, four in state forests, eleven in TVA and forest service projects, and six in Soil Conservation Service projects. From April 1933 to July 1938, some 46,900 Tennesseans were employed in CCC camps; a final estimate is that 70,000 Tennesseans had served in the corps by the time Congress disbanded the program in 1942.

Public Works Administration

Tennesseans both in the 1930s and today often confused the Public Works Administration (1933–39) with the later Works Progress (or Projects) Administration (1935–42). For example, a PWA official in 1938 ordered the erection of signs at the huge Veterans Administration hospital outside of

PWA-constructed Building No. 1, Alvin C. York Veterans Administration Medical Center, Murfreesboro.

Murfreesboro to correct the public perception that the hospital was a project of the WPA, since that agency was providing labor for the hospital's construction. The PWA was organized in June 1933 under Title II of the National Industrial Recovery Act and operated with the formal name of the Federal Emergency Administration of Public Works (FEAPW). Many metal plaques on PWA-funded buildings today have the FEAPW designation.

The goals of the PWA were to put people to work and to stimulate the depressed construction industry. Headed by Harold Ickes, the agency also wanted to fund the construction of large-scale, well-designed projects that would be of service for years after the Depression.

The Tennessee PWA director was Kenneth Markwell, who maintained offices in Nashville. During its six years of existence, the agency undertook approximately 555 projects, worth a total of ninety-nine million dollars, of which some sixty million came from PWA grants and loans. The agency "not only provided wages for thousands of depression-weary Tennesseans but had enhanced significantly the physical portrait of the Volunteer State," concluded historian Thomas H. Coode.[5]

The PWA initially placed emphasis on road construction, allocating almost $9.5 million to Tennessee for this purpose in June 1933. The result was hundreds of miles in new roads, new bridges, paved city streets, and improved railroad crossings. The agency further supported local governments

Postcard of the Davidson County Public Building and Courthouse, Nashville.

in building eight modern courthouses, while providing additional millions for state office buildings, hundreds of public schools, model public housing projects, large hospital projects in Memphis and Murfreesboro, and public utilities for towns and cities. For most of these projects, the PWA usually provided outright federal grants for 45 percent of the project cost, coupled with loans on extremely favorable terms for the remaining 55 percent. State PWA director Markwell took particular pride in the PWA schools, calling them "the most worth-while projects in which any community can invest—both from the standpoint of permanent value to its young citizens and the job-giving value to those employed in the construction processes."[6]

Agricultural Adjustment Administration

The Agricultural Adjustment Administration (AAA), a division of the U.S. Department of Agriculture established in the spring of 1933, was one of the key New Deal agencies in Tennessee. Headed initially by George Peek, the agency employed a brilliant staff, which unfortunately had difficulty deciding whether AAA was a reform agency or a cooperative effort to lower farm production and raise farm prices. But soon the agency's effort to reduce the size of targeted crops such as cotton and tobacco had a marked effect on the Tennessee landscape. Once productive fields were left fallow, and then were later restored through various AAA conservation programs, while thousands of tenant houses stood empty as a rural peasantry searched vainly for new jobs and homes. An exodus from farm to town was underway, leaving in its wake abandoned rural communities, rural schools, and declining rural churches. The AAA strongly supported the agricultural extension service of the University of Tennessee and, due to federal funding, many counties hired extension agents and home demonstration agents for the first time. The extension and home demonstration agents, in turn, promoted new agricultural practices, buildings, and technologies both in the fields and in farmhouses that further gave a new look to the state's rural landscape.

Rural reform, however, floundered when it came to poor farmers, sharecroppers, and tenants, many of whom were African Americans. "The entire AAA bureaucracy," noted historian Roger Biles, "reflected a vested interest in landlords' welfare, and no one spoke for the usually inarticulate and frequently illiterate sharecroppers."[7] Price support programs rarely benefited agricultural workers, and, due to thousands of acres taken out of cultivation, tenants found themselves worse off than before the New Deal. A purge of agency reformers in February 1935 merely made public the obvious: AAA was a conservative, pro-landlord New Deal program.

Civil Works Administration

Another of the major 1933 programs is the little-known and underappreciated Civil Works Administration (CWA). The Roosevelt administration planned for the CWA to be a short-lived relief program, getting the nation through the winter of 1933–34. Headed by C. C. Menzler, who administered the Tennessee State Relief Administration, the Tennessee CWA effort began on November 20, 1933, and the program officially ended on March 31, 1934. In these short four months, however, the CWA expended some $12.7 million of federal money, matched only by $916,000 in state funds, and employed almost 60,000 people in 1,150 relief projects. The key to success was the level of local support and sponsorship. "Without the cooperation of civic organizations, usually eager to supply plans for improvement or repair, the Civil Works Administration could not have operated," concluded historian Forrest A. Walker.[8] CWA funds improved and repaired roads and bridges, built schools, and repaired all sorts of public buildings. Public health projects were also important, with the agency counting some fourteen thousand sanitary privies constructed that winter. "Sewing rooms, school lunch programs, office work, research, and teaching were among the projects established for the employment of women," according to historian John Dean Minton.[9] The

CWA's Public Works of Art project began the state's New Deal arts programs. Another CWA project produced a valuable statewide survey of farm families. The variety of programs supported by the CWA set a precedent for the later broad public improvement efforts of the WPA, especially such women-focused work projects as canning, community gardens, and sewing.

Tennessee Emergency Relief Administration

The Federal Emergency Relief Administration began on May 22, 1933, with Harry L. Hopkins as administrator. In the Volunteer State. the agency was known as the Tennessee State Relief Administration (TSRA). It directed both direct relief and work relief until December 1933, when work relief passed to the newly created Civil Works Administration. On April 1, 1934, the Tennessee Emergency Relief Administration (TERA) assumed the programs of both the CWA and the TSRA. TERA completed many of the CWA's eleven hundred projects in Tennessee. It also initiated hundreds of new public works projects, such as a brick school at Gentry in Putnam County. After 1935, the WPA finished many other TERA-initiated projects.

TERA's relief program supplied an estimated 80,000 Tennessee families with surplus commodities, including beef and cheese from the Midwest. The cattle program brought some 75,000 head of midwestern cattle to several places in the state—like the large Crain estate in Warren County—where they were then distributed to needy rural families. Urban and rural families both benefited from canned goods from other Tennessee counties in addition to various surplus commodities supplied by the federal government. TERA's Rural Rehabilitation Division relocated farm families from submarginal land and provided loans to other needy rural families. In little more than a year, TERA spent over thirty million dollars in Tennessee, with almost 98 percent of the money coming from the federal government. With the general assembly and Governor McAlister providing very little public funds for relief, TERA kept thousands of citizens from homelessness and starvation in the early years of the New Deal.

Resettlement Administration and Farm Security Administration

Created by executive order in 1935, the Resettlement Administration (RA) assumed control of earlier federal rural rehabilitation and resettlement programs. Headed in Washington by Rexford Tugwell, who was never popular with conservatives, the controversial RA continued major projects in all three Grand Divisions of Tennessee, including large land-use projects involving thousands of acres and hundreds of farm families. In 1937, Congress passed the Bankhead-Jones Farm Tenancy Act, which transferred RA projects to the newly created Farm Security Administration (FSA). The FSA also offered loans to poor and tenant farm families so they could either purchase land or improve their meager plots.

Also active in rural communities was the Soil Conservation Service (see chapter 7), another important Agriculture Department program established in 1935. The SCS supervised CCC conservation and reclamation projects throughout the state between 1935 and 1942. Its greatest impact on Tennessee, however, came after World War II as counties established their own SCS committees and programs and more individual farm families participated in various conservation programs.

Works Progress Administration

The Works Progress Administration (WPA) brought New Deal benefits to almost every town and village in Tennessee. Established in May 1935 and headed by Roosevelt favorite Harry L. Hopkins, the WPA employed nationally over eight million workers in a wide variety of tasks between 1935 and 1943. Between 1935 and 1939, its formal name was the Works Progress Administration; after 1939 this changed to the Works Projects Administration. State WPA administrator Col. Harry S. Berry, a veteran of World War I and former state highway commissioner, established offices in Nashville in July 1935. In its first three years, the WPA spent seventy million dollars, with an estimated 60 percent of its money going to road and bridge projects, while millions more went to airports (a personal favorite of Berry's), public parks, and public utilities. The WPA also provided workers for the building projects of other federal agencies while funding the construction and repair of hundreds of schools and public buildings.

WPA administrators always wanted the bulk of federal money to go to wages, so Berry and division administrators sought local project sponsors to provide materials and cash for individual projects. In fact, Tennessee was more successful in this regard than most other states—sponsors provided almost 32 percent of the total costs of projects, compared with a national average of approximately 17 percent.

Critics laughed that the agency's letters really stood for "We Piddle Around," and national administrator Harry Hopkins admitted that his

WPA-constructed dam and spillway, Standing Stone State Park, Overton County.

agency's primary role was to put people to work, with the purpose of the project being a secondary concern. But community leaders and government officials found need almost everywhere. The WPA not only constructed buildings, bridges, and roads; it also made important contributions to the arts of the Volunteer State. Its programs gave employment to artists, musicians, architects, writers, photographers, librarians, and museum professionals. One of the agency's lasting historical legacies is *The WPA Guide to Tennessee*, prepared by the agency's Federal Writers' Project and published in 1939.

State educators took pride in new schools but also praised WPA efforts to bring reform projects to existing school systems. In White County a WPA garden and canning project provided 44,696 pounds and 28,241 quarts of vegetables and fruits for the county's program of hot lunches, which were served daily by fifty-five WPA women workers and one National Youth

WPA-constructed Bohannon Building, Livingston.

Administration woman worker. "In many cases," admitted county school superintendent Quill E. Cope, "this meal is the only real meal that the child gets during the day. The psychological effect that a hot lunch has on a child when compared to soggy biscuits, cold fried eggs, and greasy cold bacon can be easily seen."[10] Cope found this relatively inexpensive, easy-to-administer program one of the most effective New Deal efforts in White County. In rural communities school lunch programs were often the most popular of all of the various projects carried out by the WPA's Women's and Professional Projects division. Other communities, most notably Clarksville and Montgomery County, established large adult-education programs. From serving hot lunches to building state parks, the WPA employed thirty to forty thousand Tennesseans a year during its existence.

All of these WPA workers—ripe for coercion due to their dependence on public coffers—were too much of a temptation for some Tennessee politicians. Patronage had a long tradition in the state's political culture; unfortunately, some WPA positions were filled not by the needy but by those with the right connections. By the late 1930s, the WPA was mired in political controversy. Gov. Gordon Browning charged that the Crump machine used WPA relief money and WPA-funded patronage to help defeat him in the all-important Democratic primary. Browning was not above using patronage for his own ends, but this time he was right about his enemies. A congressional investigation of the Tennessee case, along with those of several other states, found that the complaints about Crump and his cronies had merit. In 1939 Congress passed the Hatch Act, which forbade federal employees from working in national elections.

Despite the political controversy, WPA remained an extremely active public program, even as war clouds began to gather in 1941 and 1942. Prentice Cooper, governor of Tennessee from 1939 to 1945, used WPA funds to launch a large state program aimed at improved war preparedness. One of the agency's last major programs was the construction of large brick and masonry national guard armories along the state's major highways.

National Youth Administration

President Roosevelt established the National Youth Administration (NYA) on June 26, 1935, as part of the administration's implementation of the Emergency Relief Appropriations Act of 1935. At the state level, Tennessee had a NYA state director, Bruce Overton, who supervised district and local directors. The administration saw NYA's primary value as providing funds and work scholarships to keep needy students in high school and college under its Student Aid program. By December 1938 students at about 600 high schools and 45 colleges in Tennessee had received some $1.5 million in NYA aid. These benefited both black and white students. In 1936, the president of Morristown College, an all-black private high school and college in Hamblen County, reported that the program kept needy students in school and helped the college keep its doors open for all students. Overton estimated that NYA's student aid benefited approximately 3,080 college students and 8,460 high school students each year in Tennessee.

The NYA established an almost equally large Works Projects program, which received $1.38 million in funding from 1935 through 1938. This NYA division was to teach students a permanent trade and result in the construction of educational, recreational, or community buildings. Construction projects became especially common in Cumberland Plateau counties. In Jackson County, NYA workers constructed eleven masonry buildings. In Spencer, the seat of Van Buren County, the NYA undertook the construction of the county's first public high school, Van Buren County High School, after Burritt College closed in 1938. Using the locally popular building material of Crab Orchard Stone, the students constructed the high school's main classroom building along with the woodworking shop from 1938 to 1939. As was the case in other NYA construction projects, local sponsors, such as the county board of education, provided materials and heavy equipment for the work. The county also acquired a stone quarry where the students cut the stone, moved it to the school site, and constructed the buildings. (None of these buildings survive today.) Industrial arts buildings and school recreational buildings were common NYA projects, since students could learn new skills to make themselves more attractive to industrial employers or enjoy positive, constructive after-school activities. One of the most innovative industrial training projects was at Dickson, where in the fall of 1940 NYA administrators worked with government, education, and business leaders to establish a Resident Work Center. On thirty acres, the project built industrial training buildings, a school, dormitories, and other educational and recreational structures. Students selected for the program lived in the dormitories, attended school for four hours a day and worked in the industrial shops for another four hours as they made goods to support the center. Reformers believed that these new educational environments held great potential for rural and urban youth who had been buffeted by the Depression. In May 1941 President Roosevelt announced a supplementary appropriation of $22.5 million to expand the program to approximately 300,000 teenagers nationwide.

At the end of May 1941 a state report estimated that 12,865 black and white students had participated in NYA programs in Tennessee. But in less

NYA-constructed Liberty School, Sequatchie County.

than a year, the successful and popular agency was scaled back significantly as wartime demands for soldiers and labor expanded. By December 1942 Tennessee educators learned that only $104,000 would go to Tennessee NYA programs, with the money split between black and white high school students, according to their respective percentages in the 1940 census. The state no longer had its own director but reported to a regional director based in Atlanta. More importantly, any NYA building project had to be geared toward the war effort. The era of NYA and public improvements in Tennessee was over.

So too was the era of public building and improvements associated with the New Deal in Tennessee. From 1933 to 1942 New Deal agencies had pumped hundreds of millions of dollars into the Volunteer State. In his study of the New Deal and the South, historian Roger Biles concluded that the New Deal transformed southern agriculture from a plantation-dominated system to modern agribusiness, dependent more on capital and technology than on sharecropping and tenancy. It created a foundation for the region's tourism industry and spurred larger industrial investments due to the region's improved transportation and utility systems. These years spurred urban growth and established the first large public housing projects in the cities. The New Deal, however, did little directly to challenge or replace the ethos of Jim Crow segregation. Historian Dewey W. Grantham observed: "The South welcomed federal programs and economic assistance as long as such intervention did not interfere with its traditional system of race relations and the existing structure of political and economic power in the region."[11] But New Deal programs and ideals did give important forums and opportunities to southern reformers as they also galvanized leaders in the African American community, who took important first steps toward the modern Civil Rights Movement.

Those who witnessed and participated in the New Deal in Tennessee understood the decade of change had been significant and profound. In 1933, Chattanooga journalist and businessman George Fort Milton perceived Tennessee as "the setting for a great social as well as economic experiment, possibly the most far-reaching ever planned by the Federal Government." Six years later, Milton liked what had happened—the end of the plantation system, more industry, better education, and the promise of political change. He proclaimed that Tennessee and the South had "undergone more fundamental change that has any other section of the country."[12] Outsiders also noticed the difference. In *This I Remember* (1949), Eleanor Roosevelt, who often visited Tennessee projects such as TVA and Cumberland Homesteads, recalled her first visit to the region in 1932 when she saw firsthand the poverty and inner strength of Tennesseans. By 1940, "after the housing and educational and agricultural experiments had had time to take effect," she visited the TVA region again, "and a more prosperous area would have been hard to find. I have always wished that those who oppose authorities to create similar benefits in the valleys of other great rivers could have seen the contrast as I saw it."[13]

Today, many components of the New Deal landscape continue their contributions to Tennessee's society and economy. The mammoth dams and reservoirs of the Tennessee Valley Authority are merely the most obvious parts of the new public infrastructure of dams, electrical systems, public utilities, roads, and parks created between 1933 and 1942. The huge conservation landscape of the Great Smoky Mountains National Park and Cherokee National Forest along the mountains of East Tennessee is a New Deal legacy. So too are the popular state parks along the Cumberland Plateau and the Delta of West Tennessee. Many state and federal highways still follow the alignment created by New Deal workers. Hundreds of public employees work daily in New Deal courthouses, government offices, and community buildings. Thousands of children attend school in New Deal buildings. While utility systems have been upgraded since the 1930s, small to large towns alike still use water towers, sewage systems, sidewalks, and switchyards installed by New Deal programs.

All of these components together create a distinctive public landscape from a significant decade of the twentieth century. We often look for the quaint Colonial Revival–styled post offices and schools, or the Rustic-styled park buildings, when we want to explore the New Deal era. These are impressive architectural legacies of a distinctive era. But just as important to the landscape of New Deal Tennessee are the roads, the privies, the levees, the reforested hills, the open hills, and the new government offices situated in every county seat that suddenly served citizens' needs for social security, education, and welfare. Most importantly, these artifacts of the past, both large and small, help us to recall an era when ideals and hope were not empty words, a time when reform and a better life was there for the taking, by a generation courageous enough to grasp them.

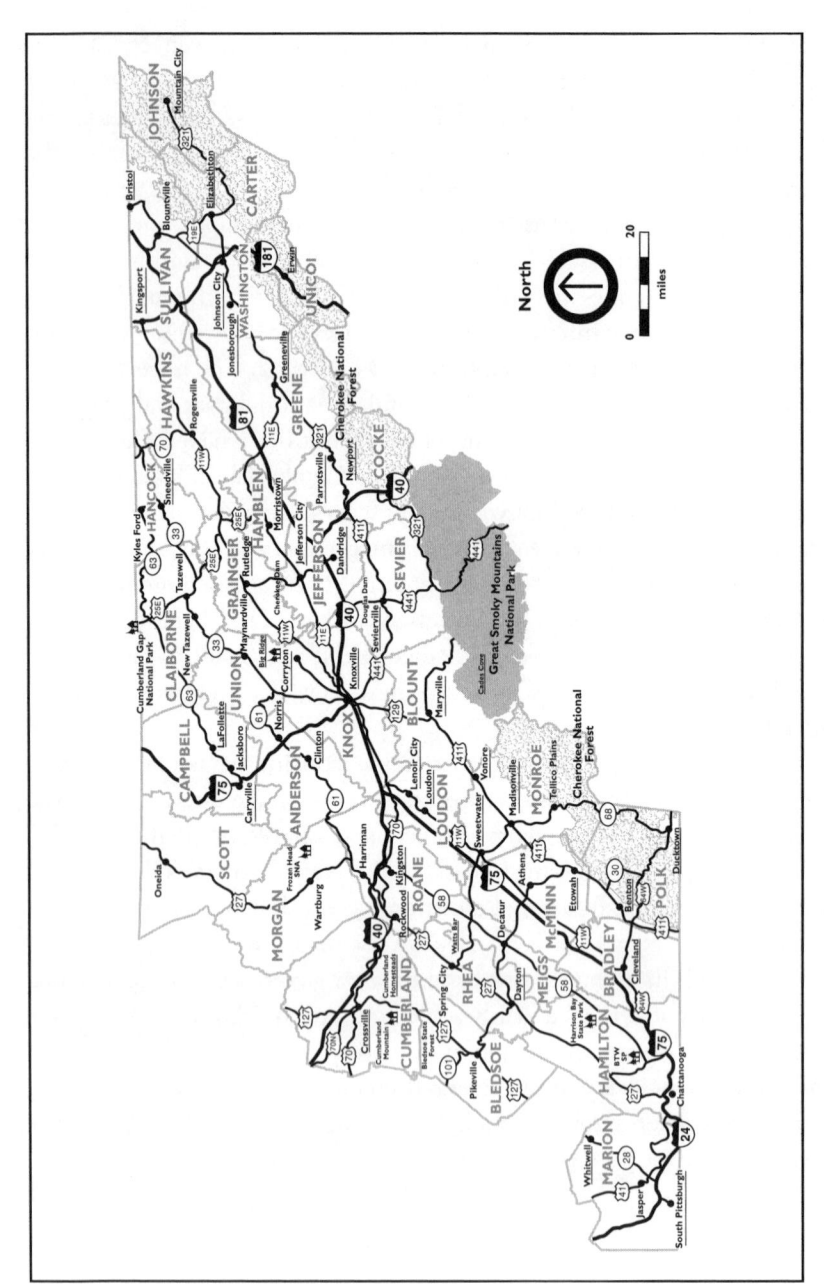

East Tennessee.

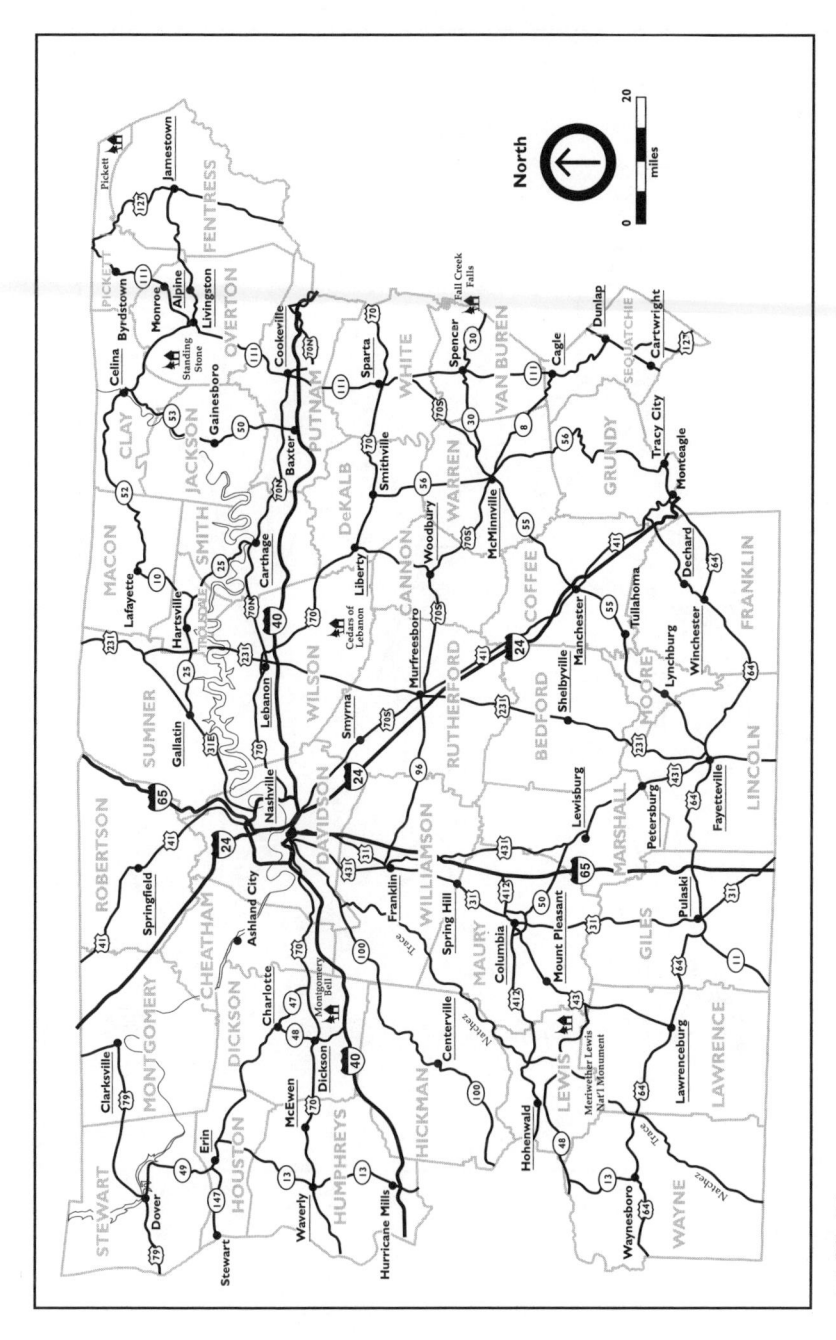

Middle Tennessee.

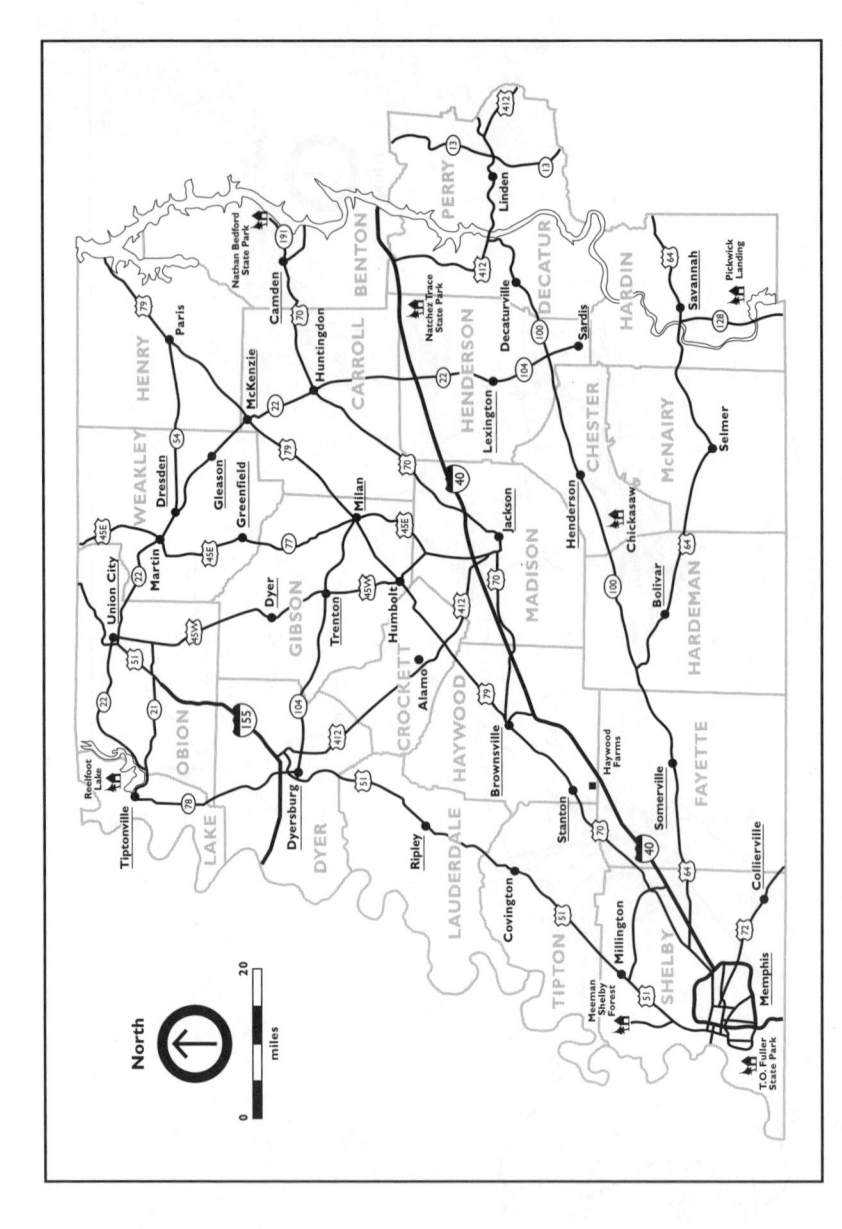

West Tennessee.

1

State Offices and County Courthouses

The Tennessee State Capitol, a monumental Greek Revival masonry edifice located on a prominent hill in the center of Nashville, had served as an architectural and cultural symbol of state government since the 1850s. Its solitary prominence, both within the political landscape of Tennessee and the built environment of Nashville, changed in the depression decade. By 1940 two other monumental structures—the Tennessee State Supreme Court Building and Tennessee State (now John Sevier) Office Building—flanked the state capitol. For decades the state capitol had held all branches of government; now the judiciary had left and a huge new building served the ever-expanding administrative divisions of the executive branch. The new buildings reflected the expansion of state government in response to federal programs of the New Deal era. They also expressed a changed relationship between state and federal government because both buildings had been built with federal funds, courtesy of the New Deal's Public Works Administration. The state capitol itself had been partially renovated and modernized with New Deal funding. The tie between the federal and state government had not been expressed so clearly since the 1860s, when federal troops occupied Nashville during the Civil War and covered Capitol Hill with their fortifications and tents.

Across county seats in Tennessee from the mid- to late 1930s, a similar enhanced federal presence was felt as many county courthouses received facelifts courtesy of New Deal agencies. For instance, the PWA gave grants for repairs to the courthouses in Loudon and Roane Counties. In 1933–34, the Civil Works Administration and the Tennessee Emergency Relief Administration undertook renovations at the Warren County Courthouse and the Overton County Courthouse. In Williamson County the WPA renovated the antebellum courthouse on Franklin's public square and built a new county jail in a restrained Art Deco style. Clay countians also witnessed WPA crews at work on their historic courthouse, built in 1871, and the courthouse grounds.

Renovations and repairs affected many other Tennessee courthouses, but the biggest federal impact came when the Public Works Administration funded the construction of eight new county courthouses between 1936 and 1940. The architecture of these buildings was both monumental and modern, an effect that architectural historians commonly classify as either PWA Modern or Classical Modern because the designs creatively merged the Classical Revival style found in early-twentieth-century American public architecture with elements from the faddish Art Deco style. Historians credit architect Paul Cret for originating this blending of classicism and modernism—Cret called the style "Starved Classicism"—and the Treasury Department quickly endorsed variations on the style for its new post offices in Knoxville, Chattanooga, and Nashville, constructed between 1931 and 1934.

The new buildings shared many characteristics: classical symmetry, flat wall surfaces, vertical window bands separated by fluted piers, and applied, stylized Art Deco elements. Five of the PWA courthouses were constructed with concrete and brick walls, which were then veneered with smooth limestone. Three others, however, had just brick exterior walls; all three—the Lauderdale, Polk, and Lewis County courthouses—were located in poor, rural counties. Interior elements were often very stylized but varied from one courthouse to another. Murals, relief sculpture, and mosaics reflected the history and culture of a given county. In the central hall of the buildings, there is often an engraved, metal-cast design outlining a map of the country. These maps depict towns, main highways, railroads, and rivers, giving some indication of the county's connections to a wider world.

The New Deal courthouses not only represented a new architectural era in Tennessee public buildings; they also symbolized an "evident commitment to the shift of government from neutral arbiter to social welfare activist."[1] Interior floor plans of the local courthouses reflected this change in government purpose. In rural counties, the new courthouses had offices for the county extension agent, the home demonstration agent, and such New Deal agencies as the Agricultural Adjustment Administration, the Soil Conservation Service, the WPA, CCC, and NYA. Federal welfare programs and the new Social Security Administration also operated out of the local courthouse. By participating in and supporting New Deal programs, county government officials made political decisions that actually diminished local autonomy over governmental affairs in exchange for federal funding and expertise.

County officials also worked in new buildings that centralized the functions of local government into one place more than before. County jails, once typically placed in a separate building behind the courthouse or on the square, were now located within the PWA courthouses. In other counties, where the older courthouse was renovated rather than replaced, New Deal agencies also funded the construction of modern jails, such as PWA projects in Bradley, Cheatham, Hamblen, and Lincoln Counties.

Despite their size, style, and materials, the new courthouses generally were compatible with the existing townscape. They replaced older buildings in the center of the town square; they were not placed in new locations, outside of the historic center of town, as some counties would do with new courthouses in the 1960s and 1970s. Together, the modernist exteriors and interiors of PWA courthouses, as well as their location, underscored an overall purpose of the New Deal: to find modern solutions to the crisis of the Great Depression while presenting the impression of more efficient government administration in which federal, state, and local officials worked together for public benefit. The buildings today remind their communities of a past cooperative effort between government and its citizens to enhance civic pride and dignity in the face of adversity.[2]

But as the design and function of the courthouses changed, the new buildings also maintained the status quo of Jim Crow segregation in southern public buildings. They contained separate, and smaller, basement rest rooms for African Americans. Some basement rest rooms even had exterior entrances only, meaning that blacks had to leave the building before they could enter a rest room. New Deal reform efforts rarely challenged the ethos of Jim Crow segregation in public facilities.

In the same years that the PWA funded courthouse construction across Tennessee, New Deal agencies also launched a more limited program to construct modern city halls and county office buildings in small towns. Most of the new buildings typically centralized all of city government, from the mayor's office to the police chief to the new public utility administrator, in an unadorned red-brick building. Other buildings were more architecturally prominent and used locally available stone in their construction. These buildings too are evidence of the growth of public services during the New Deal, even in some of the state's smallest towns and county seats.

CHESTER COUNTY
City Hall (1939), 121 Crook Avenue, Henderson

The WPA constructed this two-story, red brick building, which stood adjacent to the Chester County Courthouse. The PWA funded the project with a grant of $9,395. In 1999 residents began to explore ways to expand the city hall's facilities, but the building was demolished in 2000.

STATE OFFICES AND COUNTY COURTHOUSES

DAVIDSON COUNTY
Davidson County Public Building and Courthouse (1936–38), Public Square, Nashville

Architects Emmons H. Woolwine of Nashville and Frederic C. Hirons of New York designed this preeminent example of PWA Modern style in Middle Tennessee; the building was one of the few in the state for which the architect was chosen through a juried competition. John Clark of Woolwine's firm was the project architect. Featured in the PWA's book *Public Buildings* (1940), the courthouse combined the offices of city and county government, thus the unusual name. J. A. Jones Construction Company completed the steel, concrete, Indiana limestone veneer, and granite building in March 1938 for a total project cost of $2,167,911.

Commanding the south facade are twelve giant Doric fluted columns, which support a cornice that features carved animal heads by sculptor Rene Chambellan.

"Agriculture" mural by Dean Cornwell. Davidson County Public Building and Courthouse, Nashville.

The building was the city's first central air-conditioned building. Art Deco–influenced details abound throughout the building, from the central lobby's glass-and-bronze chandelier to the multicolored terrazzo floor. The central lobby also contains Public Works of Art Project–funded interpretive murals depicting in allegorical terms the themes of Industry, Agriculture, Commerce, and Statesmanship by artist Dean Cornwell. (For more on the Public Works of Art Project, see chapter 2.) Nudes were depicted in these allegorical representations, which led to vocal complaints from some members of the public who questioned the display of human anatomy, no matter how stylized, in a public building. A native of Kentucky, Cornwell (1892–1960) gained fame first as an illustrator, then later in his career as a muralist. Described as the "dean of illustrators" by his biographer, Cornwell received national recognition from his work at the Los Angeles Public Library and the Eastern Airlines Building at Rockefeller Plaza in New York City before accepting the Nashville commission.[3] Cornwell also painted federally funded historical murals—this time of fully clothed heroes from the state's past—at the nearby Tennessee State Office Building, another PWA project.

The construction of the Davidson County Public Building and Courthouse came at a high cost for Nashville's historic public square. The new building replaced a local Greek Revival icon by architect Francis Strickland (the son of architect William Strickland); federal projects also included the demolition of the historic city market and city hall. These projects were the first steps in what would become the almost total destruction of the city's Public Square landscape, leaving the courthouse in the isolated surroundings so noticeable today.

DAVIDSON COUNTY

Tennessee State (John Sevier) Office Building (1937–40), 400 Sixth Avenue North, Nashville

Woolwine and Hirons were also the architects of this large state office building, which stands immediately east of the state capitol. Opened as the Tennessee State Office Building in 1940, it was later renamed to honor John Sevier, the first state governor. The Sevier's combination of fluted pilasters, limestone veneer walls, classical entablature, and Art Deco–influenced detailing is another impressive PWA Modern design. Dean Cornwell executed the Public Works of Art Project murals in the first-floor lobby. *The Discovery of Tennessee* portrays important individuals from the settlement era of state history, centering on the commanding figure of John Sevier, the state's first governor, who gained most of

Tennessee (John Sevier) State Office Building, Nashville.

his popularity from military campaigns against Native Americans. *The Development of Tennessee* shows the next generation of leaders, with Andrew Jackson given center stage in the mural. Both murals reflect a typical treatment of history in New Deal art, in which the common folk and the great heroes are shown working together to build a community, a state, or the nation. From her study of New Deal–sponsored art, historian Sue Beckham observes: "what southerners in the 1930s wanted was to be freed from the burden for their unique history and to share the bountiful and victorious history of the rest of the country."[4] Art themes based on the southern frontier were the best way to achieve those goals.

DAVIDSON COUNTY

Tennessee State Supreme Court Building (1936–38), 401 Seventh Avenue North, Nashville

Featured in the PWA's *Public Buildings*, the new State Supreme Court Building is a four-story 140-by-87-foot Tennessee marble veneer building that rests on a granite base. Its total project cost was over $650,000, and it replaced several fine mansions from the mid- to late nineteenth century that had once been part of the Capitol Hill area. Chief Justice Grafton Green, due to crowded space in the capitol and the court's ever-increasing caseload, urged the state to take advantage of the PWA program and construct a separate building for the judicial branch.

The Nashville architectural firm of Marr and Holman produced a design that emphasized the building's horizontal massing, classically inspired pilasters, and Art Deco detailing. All these design elements became architectural signatures of the firm's later county courthouses, most of which were PWA funded. The interior featured two separate courtrooms, central air-conditioning, and a basement garage that used elevators to connect directly with the upper floors. Marr and Holman were both Nashville natives. Thomas Marr received his college education at Gallaudet College in Washington, D.C., and returned to Nashville, where he developed an architectural career. Joseph Holman was a much younger man who attended Vanderbilt University. They established the firm in 1913 and initially Marr did most of the design work while Holman administered the projects and solicited clients. But after Marr's death in 1936, Holman became the firm's primary designer.

DAVIDSON COUNTY
Tennessee State Capitol (1934–38), Capitol Hill, Nashville

Various New Deal–funded arts and architectural projects left an important legacy at the Tennessee State Capitol. In 1934, a team of architects employed by the Historic American Building Survey, a federal program initiated by Charles Peterson of the National Park Service and Secretary of Interior Harold Ickes to put unemployed or underemployed architects, historians, and draftspersons to work, conducted a thorough architectural investigation of the state capitol. The resulting working drawings, plans, and photographs proved invaluable when the state restored the capitol building in a historically appropriate manner some fifty years later in the late 1980s and early 1990s. Also in 1934 funds from the Civil Works Administration's Public Works of Art Project had an impact on public art at the state capitol and other government buildings in Nashville. The project commissioned Gilbert H. Switzer of Knoxville to design a commemorative bust of naval hero Adm. David Farragut. It also commissioned sculptor Belle Kinney to produce a bust of Adm. Albert Gleaves, a World War I naval hero. Kinney's commission was one of thirty-five given to artists in Tennessee in a program chaired at the state level by architect Edward E. Dougherty of Nashville. Kinney also produced models for bas-relief panels for the facade bays of the adjacent War Memorial Building, another state office building, while her husband, Leopold Scholz, produced a three-foot-high model of Athena, in hopes that it would be re-created in full size at the Nashville Parthenon. That recreation did not happen, but the model remained on display at the Parthenon until sculptor Alan LeQuire completed his full-sized statue of *Athena Parthenos* in the late 1980s.

With funds coming from either the CWA, WPA, or PWA, other Tennessee artists were commissioned to paint portraits of important Tennesseans, industrial and agricultural landscapes, and historic places and events. Several of these art works are now in the collections of the Tennessee State Museum in Nashville.

After the new Tennessee Supreme Court Building opened in 1938, the state's high court left its chambers and offices in the capitol. The firm of Emmons Woolwine, with John Clark as principal designer, received a commission to remodel both the governor's offices and the vacated supreme court offices. In the state's official historic structure report on the capitol, it is not clear what government entity funded the renovation. But newspapers credit the Public Works Administration. The new offices were designed in a Colonial Revival motif, with an obvious nod to such Georgian landmarks as Westover, an eighteenth-century Tidewater Virginia plantation house. For the Governor's Reception Room, New York artist George Davidson executed eleven panels depicting important events in Tennessee history. Kirayr H. Zorthian was commissioned to paint the designs "in a technique believed to correspond to the color and character of scenic wallpapers of the mid-nineteenth century."[5]

The reception room murals portray the chronological development of early Tennessee history, beginning with the Cherokee Indians and explorer Hernando de Soto, before showing such pivotal early settlement events as the establishment of Fort Prudhomme at Memphis, Fort Loudoun in East Tennessee, and Fort Nashborough at Nashville, along with the creation of the Watauga Association and the State of Franklin in upper East Tennessee. Nashville itself is prominent in the murals' storyline, from its Battle of the Bluffs in 1781 to an imaginative view of Nashville in 1854, near the time when the state capitol was completed. Two allegorical panels of Andrew Jackson's Hermitage plantation and of a steamboat represent the state motto of "Agriculture and Commerce." The murals interpreted the state's exploration, settlement, and early political history, themes of interest to the public and scholars alike in an era when the "frontier thesis" of Frederick Jackson Turner held sway in American historiography. When taken on the obligatory field trip to Nashville, generations of school children (including the author) received a brief lecture on the murals and their meaning during their capitol tour.

FRANKLIN COUNTY

Franklin County Courthouse (1936–37), One South Jefferson Street, Winchester

The Franklin County Courthouse was built with a $100,000 local bond issue and a grant from the PWA totaling $42,000. Marr and Holman of Nashville were the architects, while Niles Yearwood of Nashville was the contractor. Construction began in April 1936, and the building opened in April of the following year. At that time the county court officially proclaimed the courthouse as a "magnificent building—a monument within itself—erected by the people with pride and forethought who are ever looking forward toward progress and the betterment of Government."[6] Notable for its central clock tower—the only New Deal courthouse in Tennessee to have such a feature—the three-story limestone veneer building rests on a landscaped terrace that is about five feet above street level, emphasizing the building's prominence in the public square. The courthouse reflects PWA Modern style in its classical pilasters and low relief Art Deco details on both the exterior and interior. On the east elevation was the original outside entrance to the segregated African American rest room. This elevation was designed to serve as the service access to the building. It has no stairs leading to the top of the terrace, but it was the location of a loading ramp and coal chute.

Franklin County Courthouse, Winchester.

HAMBLEN COUNTY

Hamblen County Jail (1935–36), West Third Street at N. Jackson Street, Morristown

This two-story brick building, with a full-brick basement, is designed in an understated Art Deco style, characterized by its stylized concrete cornice. The initial project cost was just over forty-four thousand dollars, of which the PWA provided a grant of almost twenty thousand dollars.

HAMILTON COUNTY

Hamilton County Courthouse Addition (1937), Georgia Avenue at Sixth and Lookout Streets, Chattanooga

In 1937 the PWA commissioned R. H. Hunt Company to design a compatible rear addition to the Hamilton County Courthouse, a Beaux-Arts landmark, which had earlier been designed by the Hunt firm. The new wing substantially enlarged the building to its present T-shape.

HARDEMAN COUNTY

City Hall (1941), 150 Tippah Street North, Grand Junction

This two-story, hipped-roof, red-brick building, constructed by the WPA, has city offices and community meeting rooms. Grand Junction was an important West Tennessee railroad junction in the nineteenth and early twentieth centuries.

LAKE COUNTY

Lake County Courthouse (1936), 229 Church Street, Tiptonville

The core design of the Lake County Courthouse dates to 1905, when a two-story, frame Victorian-influenced building, complete with bay windows, was built as the county courthouse. In 1936, however, a major WPA-funded renovation occurred. Under the direction of H. J. McGuire & Co. of Memphis, the original frame building was given a brick veneer on all four sides. The contractor then removed an original Victorian tower from the facade and replaced it with a two-story Classical Revival–style portico. Other brick rooms were added to the rear; the courtroom was renovated; but the bay windows

STATE OFFICES AND COUNTY COURTHOUSES 39

Lake County Courthouse, Tiptonville.

were retained. The ninety-thousand-dollar WPA project not only added more office space for new government services; it also changed the building drastically in appearance, from the Victorian style to the Classical Revival.

LAUDERDALE COUNTY
Lauderdale County Courthouse (1935–36), 100 Court Square, Ripley

The first of Marr and Holman's PWA county courthouses to be completed in Tennessee, the Lauderdale County Courthouse was funded with local bonds totaling seventy-five thousand dollars and a PWA grant of fifty thousand dollars. The contractor was the R. M. Condra Company. WPA-funded workers demolished a courthouse dating from 1870 before construction began; many continued on as construction workers for the new building. Opened in December 1936, the courthouse tripled the space of the old one and included all county offices, rooms for the local WPA office, two courtrooms, the public library, rest rooms for whites and blacks, and a large community room (for whites only) with a kitchen and a dining room.

Its design is unique among Marr and Holman's PWA courthouses due to its use of buff-colored glazed brick as the main exterior material and its cruciform

Lauderdale County Courthouse, Ripley.

plan. Located at the center of the cruciform, in the first floor rotunda, is an inlaid terrazzo map of the country, showing its towns and transportation systems. The rotunda ceiling has coffered panels surrounding a ceiling medallion set within a central concave area. "Zig-zag–influenced angular Art Deco decorative elements," noted architectural historian Trina Binkley, enliven both the exterior and interior, "framing doors, doorways, windows, and at the ceiling line."[7] Plus, the new courthouse did not overwhelm the public square; new landscaping helped to highlight the building. A county historian remarked in 1957: "few prettier spots exist in the United States than the lawn about the courthouse, for here are a few of the ancient trees, and many new pecans, maples, locusts, and shrubs which sit of a carpet of green grass with squirrels playing."[8]

LEWIS COUNTY
Lewis County Courthouse (1939), Court Street, Hohenwald
The two-story Lewis County Courthouse differs from other PWA courthouses in that the architecture firm, Hart and Russell of Nashville, completed no other New Deal courthouses in Tennessee. The PWA supported the $84,501 project with a grant of $37,505. The courthouse's largely unadorned red-brick design lacks the PWA Modern monumentality found in other New

Deal buildings. Nor was the new building placed at the previous courthouse location. Instead, county officials put the new courthouse on a large lot once occupied by a public school. The result was the appearance of a courthouse square in a town that was not designed to have such a public space. Hohenwald was a late-nineteenth-century railroad town, initially settled by Swiss homesteaders. Like many railroad towns of that era, it is oriented to the tracks and depot and did not include a public square in its plan.

Five brick pilasters organize the building's projecting central block into five bays, with the large second-story windows providing excellent lighting and ventilation for the main courtroom. Two-story wings on either side of the central block contain staircases and additional offices. The county jail was installed in the southern wing, with an exercise area built on top of the roof. The building rests on a full concrete basement that contains additional offices and rest rooms.

MADISON COUNTY

Madison County Courthouse (1936–37),
100 East Main Street, Jackson

An excellent example of PWA Modern style from Marr and Holman, the Madison County Courthouse is a four-story, limestone veneer, concrete-and-steel building built for a project cost of $307,000, of which the PWA

Madison County Courthouse, Jackson.

provided $142,000. Foster and Creighton of Nashville undertook the demolition of the earlier courthouse as well as the construction of the new building, which also used WPA labor for the work.

Featured in *Public Buildings* (1940), the courthouse was described as "streamlined architecture at its best" in the local newspaper due to its blend of Art Deco elements and the classically inspired pilasters of its facade.[9] The interior was spacious, well appointed, and enhanced with terrazzo flooring, Tennessee marble wainscoting, and fireproof construction. Mrs. Alex Dancy, the newspaper's society editor, remarked: "such a beautiful building should be kept as such and be the object of great civic pride on the part of every citizen."[10] According to architect Joe Holman Jr., each floor served a specific purpose and audience. The basement contained county offices, the sheriff's office, segregated rest rooms, and storage space; the first floor was for elected county officials; the second floor was for local judges and courts; the third floor was for state judges and courts; and the fourth floor was a modern jail. Indeed, the Madison County Courthouse was unique in its dual function as a county and state courthouse. It had offices and courtrooms for the Western Division of the Tennessee Supreme Court and the West Tennessee Court of Appeals. The building also housed a large law library.

OBION COUNTY
Obion County Courthouse (1939–40), Public Square, Union City

Another Marr and Holman courthouse, completed in early 1940 for a project cost of just over two hundred thousand dollars, is this limestone veneer PWA Modern building in Union City. The new facility had been long sought by civic and business leaders in the county. A county history of 1941 recalled: "it took more than two years, the combined efforts of the County Court, the Chamber of Commerce and other local organizations, committee meetings, appointments with Senators and Representatives, volumes of letters and telegrams, editorial appeal, all for the proper presentation of facts and the exigencies of the case, together with the addition of personal and private effort and expense to pursue the work."[11] The end result was an almost instant modern landmark set squarely within the heart of the town. Art Deco details such as the frets on the architrave, the crenelated cornice, and "X" and star pattern of the exterior lamps are representative PWA Modern elements. The splashy interior had terrazzo floors, marble wainscoting, and Art Deco–styled ornamental metal. "Its modernist blending of Art Deco and Classicism," notes historian Holly A. Rine, "was at odds with the more conservative public and commercial architecture of the town."[12] Yet, it seems that the community eagerly embraced the new building. "Composition and general construction of the building are all definitely more substantial and complete than any other building project ever attempted in the county," observed the 1941 history. "As we view the new county courthouse building there appears no greater symmetry and harmony in general outline and contour to be found."[13]

OVERTON COUNTY
Bohannon Building (1936), Town Square, Livingston

The two-story Bohannon Building, constructed in Crab Orchard stone, features a low-key Art Deco facade, with its size and distinctive design making it a landmark in the otherwise vernacular-style commercial buildings of this small Cumberland Plateau county seat. Federal officials in 1933 pinpointed Overton County as having serious unemployment problems. Therefore, they instituted several different waves of public works, beginning with CWA and TERA projects at the adjacent county courthouse in 1933–34. Local builder and contractor M. H. Hankins supervised the work, which included adding vaults to offices, pouring a concrete floor on the first floor, adding a balcony to the court room, replacing windows, and painting the interior. Rather than replace the existing courthouse with a larger, modern building, WPA officials chose to build a new county office on the west side of the square. The Bohannon Building, named for County Judge C. B. Bohannon, contained first-floor spaces for commercial businesses, while the second floor was devoted to county offices. Public rest rooms were placed in the basement. Local builder M. H. Hankins supervised the project, which cost approximately eighteen thousand dollars. The building remained in public hands until 1971. Another WPA project on the town square was the construction of a post office, which is described in chapter 2.

POLK COUNTY
Polk County Courthouse (1937), Public Square, Benton

Designed by the R. H. Hunt Company of Chattanooga, the Polk County Courthouse exhibits a restrained PWA Modern design compared with the Marr and Holman courthouses in Tennessee. Its brick facade has a projecting five-bay central block, with flanking two-bay wings. The building retains

Polk County Courthouse, Benton.

many interior features, including terrazzo floors, vaulted plaster ceilings, Tennessee marble wainscoting, and much interior woodwork. Forcum Jones Company was the contractor; the total project cost was approximately one hundred thousand dollars, of which the PWA provided just over forty-nine thousand dollars. The new building replaced an early Colonial Revival–style courthouse that had burned on December 2, 1935; the stone wall that defines the courthouse lot is dated as circa 1880.

SUMNER COUNTY
Sumner County Courthouse (1940), Public Square, Gallatin
The Sumner County Courthouse, with its two-story fluted piers defining each side of the building, is an expressive statement of PWA Modern style set among the late Victorian and early-twentieth-century commercial architecture of Gallatin's square. Designed by Marr and Holman and built by W. R. Smith and Sons of Nashville, it is the last PWA courthouse to be constructed in Tennessee. The total project cost was $170,000; the PWA provided grant support of $78,750. Like in neighboring Davidson County, the new courthouse in Gallatin replaced an earlier Greek Revival style building, leading to some local controversy about the project.

WASHINGTON COUNTY
Jonesboro Town Hall (1938–39), Main Street, Jonesborough
The PWA provided a grant of almost $2,900 to support the construction of this one-story, red-brick Colonial Revival municipal building. Located a block from the Washington County Courthouse, the building is part of the Jonesborough historic district. Although the building now houses a commercial business, its earlier use as a combination public building is well conveyed by the extant garage door, which the fire department once used.

WEAKLEY COUNTY
Greenfield City Hall (1940), 222 North Front Street, Greenfield
This one-story stone building holds most city offices for this small West Tennessee railroad town. Except for modern replacement windows and doors, and a handicapped access ramp, its exterior has changed little in the last six decades. W. H. Whitis was mayor and John B. McAdams was city clerk when Greenfield officials used WPA funds and labor to build the facility.

2

Federal Courthouses and Post Offices

When President Franklin D. Roosevelt launched his New Deal in 1933, he depended on loyal support from southern Democrats, who had been suddenly thrust into congressional leadership roles as the Democratic party grabbed control of Congress after the 1930 elections. One of these congressional leaders was Tennessee Sen. Kenneth D. McKellar, who had served in the Senate since 1916. His seniority meant that he became the chairman of the Senate Committee on Post Offices and Post Roads as well as a ranking member of the Senate Appropriations Committee. Tennessee, thus, was well positioned politically to receive more than its fair share of new postal facilities to be constructed by the Treasury Department, often with the support of New Deal agencies, during the 1930s.

The scores of federally constructed post offices found in Tennessee's rural county seats and small towns are both the most obvious and the most lasting New Deal legacy across the state. Most are one-story, red brick, gable-roof buildings, with symmetrical five-bay Colonial Revival–style facades. The post offices reflected standardized designs produced by the Office of the Supervising Architect of the Treasury Department. For decades, the Office of the Supervising Architect was a powerful, independent agency, really the arbiter of federal design. In 1932, for instance, it had 750 employees. Its power to design in-house most federal buildings infuriated the members of the American Institute of Architects, and AIA criticism was especially loud during the Great Depression. In 1933, during a New Deal reorganization of the Treasury Department, the office lost its independent status and became part of the Public Buildings Branch of the Procurement Division of the Treasury Department. In another New Deal reorganization in 1939, the Supervising Architect's Office moved to the Public Buildings Administration within the Federal Works Agency, and the title of supervising architect was eliminated. Power over federal design shifted to regional offices, and private firms began to receive more commissions.

From 1933 to 1939, Louis A. Simon was the supervising architect of the Treasury Department, thus his name adorns the cornerstones of most of the Tennessee post offices. Simon was an MIT graduate, who had worked in the Supervising Architect Department since 1896. Prior to becoming department head, he was the superintendent of the architectural section from 1905 to 1933. The Treasury Department's post offices are still the best example of academic architectural style in many town squares. When compared with the modernist PWA county courthouses and massive TVA facilities, the small-town post offices make an intimate, conservative architectural statement about the presence and purpose of the New Deal and the federal government.

In addition to being small-town architectural ornaments, many post offices became local art museums in the late 1930s and early 1940s. The New Deal funded various federal arts projects to commission artists and sculptors to produce works for public buildings. According to a mid-1990s survey of twenty-eight extant Tennessee public art works by Howard Hull, a professor of art education at the University of Tennessee, the most important agency was the Treasury Department's Section of Painting and Sculpture, later the Section of Fine Arts. Between its creation in 1934 and its dissolution in 1943, it commissioned and funded most of the murals and art found at the post offices or at federal buildings which contained post office facilities. Its national leaders—Edward Bruce, Edward Rowan, and Forbes Watson—came from art backgrounds and its competitive juried selection process emphasized quality and diversity. In Tennessee, for example, eleven women artists received post office mural commissions.

Other important art agencies included the CWA's Public Works of Art Project, the Treasury Relief Art Project, and the WPA's Federal Art Project. The Public Works of Art Project only lasted for six months in 1933–34, although later federal agencies often took over its unfinished projects. Since funding came from a percentage of federal appropriations for new building construction, the Treasury Relief Art Project was much more substantial and lasted until 1939. The WPA's Federal Art Project was extremely varied, funding all types of visual arts as well as performance arts. In a limited way, its projects were even color-blind; African American sculptor Will Edmondson of Nashville, for instance, received WPA grants in 1937 and 1939. Women artists received commissions too. Laura Woolsey Daily, associated with the well-regarded arts program at the University of Chattanooga (now University of Tennessee at Chattanooga), produced a series of woodcuts depicting Hamilton County sites and landscapes, including the TVA's Chickamauga Dam. This collection is now at the Chattanooga Regional History Museum.

The arts project's diversity reflected the philosophy of director Holger Cahill: "it is not the solitary genius but a sound general movement which maintains art as a vital, functioning part of any cultural scheme. Art is not a matter of rare occasional masterpieces . . . in a genuine art movement a great reservoir of art is created in many forms both major and minor."[1]

These art commissions "were a uniquely American blend, combining an elitist belief in the value of high culture with the democratic ideal that everyone in the society could and should be the beneficiary of such efforts," observed historians Marlene Park and Gerald E. Markowitz.[2] In comments at the opening of the National Galley of Art in 1941, President Roosevelt remarked that for generations Americans had been taught that "art was something foreign to America and to themselves—something important from another continent and from an age which was not theirs—something they had no part in, save to go to see it in a guarded room on holidays or Sundays." But Roosevelt expressed pride in the recent work of American art—"some of it good, some of it not good, but all of it native, human, eager and alive—all of it painted by their own kind in their own country, and painted about things they know and look at often and have touched and loved."[3]

Most of this art could be classified as part of the American Scene movement, which historian Barbara Melosh defines as a "contemporary movement to express a distinctive national culture" by aiming "squarely for the artistic center, endorsing a representational style updated with modernist gestures."[4] That observation certainly holds true for the Tennessee mural art. The general theme of the Tennessee post office art is the significance and meaning of place in each individual community. In rural towns, scenes of early settlement and the frontier, where ordinary people are working together for mutual goals, represent this theme. In larger, more industrial towns, images of the past often are blended with those from technology and development to represent a community's sense of place and achievement.

Not all of the Tennessee murals survive; the mural in Clarksville was destroyed. Nor do all of the post offices survive. From the mid-1980s to mid-1990s, the postal service expanded and updated its facilities nationwide, abandoning and selling older New Deal era buildings. But, interestingly, in Clinton, Lewisburg, McKenzie, and Manchester, the postal superintendent had the mural moved to the new building due to the painting's local popularity. In Newport, a mural titled *TVA Power* was moved to a local museum administered by the Daughters of the American Revolution, while in Johnson City, the post office mural now adorns the lobby of the Culp Center Auditorium at East Tennessee State University.

New Deal art at the local level may also be viewed at various federal buildings constructed during the depression years, especially where the post office shared modern buildings with the federal judiciary. These combination post offices and federal courthouses range from the conservative Colonial Revival style to the most modern examples of "Starved Classicism" style. East Tennessee, due in part to the political pull of its Republican congressional representatives in the Hoover years, gained impressive landmark federal buildings in Knoxville and Chattanooga. In some sources, architect Paul Cret, who originated the "Starved Classicism" style, is credited with the design of the federal courthouse in Knoxville. The local firm of Baumann and Baumann was the project architect. Greeneville later saw its earlier federal building expanded and renovated by the PWA.

ANDERSON COUNTY
U.S. Post Office (1937), West Main Street, Clinton

Clinton's New Deal post office, built in 1937 with assistance from the WPA, is located in the town's historic business district. With its symmetrical five bays, central cupola, and classically influenced entrance, it is an excellent example of standardized interpretation of Colonial Revival style produced by the office of Louis A. Simon. After the new post office was built in 1988, the New Deal building became a private business, while its post office mural was installed in the new Clinton Post Office on Charles G. Seivers Boulevard.

Horace Day's *Farm and Factory* expresses how industry was transforming the traditional rural life of Anderson County. At the center is a huge horse-drawn hay wagon, with the hay stacked loose, not in bales from a machine. Around the wagon are modern-day scenes and machines, from an automobile, a railroad bridge and coal train, and the imposing brick walls of the Magnet Mills in Clinton, the town's primary employer for a generation. To the left of the wagon are two men with lunch boxes, representing factory workers. On the wagon's right is a man working in hay and a woman carrying a bucket of water, representing family farmers. Horace Day, then the director of the Herbert Art Institute in Augusta, Georgia, was the mural artist. In a June 1940 interview in the local newspaper, he explained that the inclusion of industrial scenes was to show the community's "progressive" character. Of course, no one that summer would have guessed that in less than two years Day's depiction of a rural place turning modern would be an understatement—the military's construction of the Clinton Engineering

Works and the town of Oak Ridge ushered the county overnight not just into the modern age, but into the atomic age as well.

BENTON COUNTY
U.S. Post Office (1936), Town Square, Camden

The Camden post office is an excellent example of the distinguished, conservative Colonial Revival design favored by Louis A. Simon. It is listed in the National Register of Historic Places. While the Supervising Architect's Office provided the design, local WPA work crews constructed the building. Two years after its opening in 1936, WPA workers installed the mural *Mail Delivery to Tranquility* by John Fyfe, who grew up in Tennessee and taught visual arts at Whitehaven High School in Shelby County. Fyfe's mural depicts the delivery of mail in frontier Benton County at an early settlement hamlet called Tranquility. This theme of frontier mail service was popular in the Treasury Section murals across the nation. At the Camden mural, men are its focal point, whether bringing or reading the mail. Women and children are in the background, standing near the dwelling, composed of adjacent single-pen log cabins. Fyfe interjects action into the moment through a young man using an axe to chop down a tree; Benton County was then, and still largely is, a forested region.

CAMPBELL COUNTY
U.S. Post Office (1936), 100 South Tennessee Avenue, LaFollette

The modernist design of the LaFollette Post Office, attributed to the office of Louis A. Simon, is in contrast to the typical Colonial Revival post office in Tennessee. Its symmetrical three-bay facade features a slightly projecting central bay that exhibits the "Starved Classicism" style associated with federal buildings during the 1930s. For LaFollette to receive the post office, local politics combined with federal patronage. Prominent community and business leader J. P. Miller lobbied Senator McKellar, an old ally, for the building. Miller's daughter, Irene, was its postmistress.

The Treasury Section mural, *On the Shores of the Lake* by Dahlov Ipcar, depicts bass fishermen at the recently completed Norris Lake, reminding locals that new recreational opportunities awaited them. Artist Dahlov Ipcar was the daughter of William and Marguerite Zorach, who also painted post office murals in Tennessee.

FEDERAL COURTHOUSES AND POST OFFICES 51

LaFollette Post Office, Campbell County.

On the Shores of the Lake *by Dahlov Ipcar (1938), LaFollette Post Office.*

CARROLL COUNTY
U.S. Post Office (1935), Town Square, McKenzie

Situated across from the city square, the historic McKenzie Post Office, well preserved on both its interior and exterior, is now a local museum about New Deal governor Gordon Browning, who was a progressive Roosevelt supporter during his 1937–39 administration (see the introduction for more on Browning). The building's style is Colonial Revival, but represents a variation of the standard design found in the state. The building is flat-roofed, with four symmetrical bays, and an off-center Federal-style entrance, complete with semi-elliptical fanlight and classical pilasters.

The post office's original mural, *Early United States Post Village* by Karl Oberteuffer (1938), was installed in 1938. It has been restored and moved to the city's modern post office on Highland Drive. The mural addresses the beginnings of postal service in West Tennessee, similar to the mural found in neighboring Camden. But this work also emphasizes westward migration: at the forefront are two men constructing a wagon, while another Conestoga wagon, identified as U.S. Post, and three frontiersmen are nearby. In the background is a postal building, a stage coach, and a solitary woman passenger. The artist was Karl Oberteuffer, whose parents were both respected painters. His mother, H. Amiard Oberteuffer, was once on the faculty of the Memphis Academy of Art.

COCKE COUNTY
U.S. Post Office (1937), 219 Broadway, Newport

The traditional style of the Newport post office, which is now used for private business, fit in well with the town's other Colonial Revival public buildings, such as the nearby Cocke County Courthouse. Compared with other Colonial Revival post offices of the New Deal era, however, the Newport building is almost plain in appearance. Its flat roof lacks a cupola; its symmetrical five-bay facade is restrained, with only the semi-elliptical fanlight, transom, and side lights surrounding the main entrance reflecting formal Colonial Revival style.

The original post office mural was one of the most famous in the state; in 1980 it was placed on display at the local Daughters of American Revolution museum at 805 Cosby Road in Newport. Titled *TVA Power*, it depicted the golden future envisioned by TVA planners, when traditional farming communities would be thrust by industry and electric power into the twentieth century. Muralist Minna Citron, a New York artist and teacher, inter-

Newport Post Office, Cocke County.

viewed local residents, TVA engineers, and civic leaders for several weeks before beginning her work.

Federal officials praised the resulting work of art. In an address at the opening of an exhibition of the mural by the Art Students League in New York City in 1940, TVA director David Lilienthal quoted from Carl Sandburg's poem "The People, Yes!" in praise of the mural. Eleanor Roosevelt was among the audience that evening. Lilienthal then used mural sketches as illustrations for his article "The TVA and Decentralization," which was published in the June 1940 issue of *Survey Graphic: Magazine of Social Interpretation*. "The new face of the TVA region. Farms and industries show the effect of cheap electricity, refreshed soil, local enterprise" read the caption for the mural in the article.

After the mural was installed at the Newport post office in the fall of 1940, the Newport mayor wrote Citron a letter of praise: "the whole town is loud in its praise of the manner in which you have shown the many activities of this section of the country. The TVA background is excellent, but what we like best is the way you have shown our industries and buildings of Newport."[5]

COFFEE COUNTY
U.S. Post Office (1940), North Spring Street, Manchester

With its hipped roof, cupola, and symmetrical five-bay facade, this WPA-constructed post office is a good example of the standardized Colonial Revival designs produced by the Supervising Architect's Office and is attributed to Louis A. Simon. Its location near the town square influenced the theme and content of artist Minna Citron's mural *Horse Swapping Day*, which is now installed at the modern Manchester post office. As she had with her Newport commission, Citron visited Manchester and interviewed local residents. Unlike Newport, which was an industrial railroad town, Manchester was mostly a rural county seat. Thus, Citron chose a rural theme centered at the town square for the mural. Three Tennessee walking horses, with at least one modeled after Gene Autry's horse, Champ Jr., dominate the scene. After her initial drawings for the mural received criticism from Treasury Section officials, Citron studied the Autry horse during a show at Madison Square Garden in New York City before coming up with her final composition.

CUMBERLAND COUNTY

Milo Lemert Memorial County Offices (1937), North Main Street, Crossville

In its cupola and five-bay symmetry, the Lemert office building, which is the former Crossville post office, is similar to other Colonial Revival designs from Louis A. Simon. However, its distinctive use of Crab Orchard stone—the signature building material of the New Deal's nearby Cumberland Homesteads project—makes it different than the traditional red-brick post offices found in other county seats. Indeed, the amount of mail generated by the Homesteads project was one reason why this small rural town received a new post office.

The building's mural dates to 1940, but was moved to the new city post office on York Highway (U.S. 127N) about fifty years later. Artist Marion Greenwood's *The Partnership of Man and Nature* is a dramatic portrayal of how traditional values and landscape could blend with the progressive promise of TVA's massive dam projects. At the center is a family group of a husband in overalls, a wife in a simple farm dress, and crawling child; to the right is a barn, silo, and plow. To the left, however, is a TVA dam. All three elements—family, nature, and modernity—exist in balance and harmony in the painting. The image represents "the human benefits of technology," according to Barbara Melosh.[6] Marion Greenwood was among the most accomplished and best-known New Deal muralists.

DAVIDSON COUNTY
U.S. Post Office (1934), 1100 Broadway, Nashville

From 1930 to 1933, the Treasury Department designed and constructed large modern post offices of "Starved Classicism" style in Knoxville and Chattanooga. In Nashville, Treasury Department officials commissioned architects Marr and Holman to design a new city post office, but construction did not begin until the New Deal years. In 1933–34, Marr and Holman worked with federal agencies to construct one of the state's best examples of a "Starved Classicism" building, enlivened with Art Deco exterior and interior details and emboldened with its facade's massive fluted colonnade. In its October 28, 1934, issue, the *Nashville Tennessean* gushed about the marble used in the building: "The exterior of the building is of white Georgia marble and granite, but the interior is finished principally in Fantasia Rose marble from East Tennessee and Monte Neva marble of warm grayish-brown color also from East Tennessee, and the Westfield marble from Pennsylvania which is dark, flecked with green. The first floor level of the stairway is of Royal Jersey green marble. The landing is of Verde Antique marble."

"I've always marveled," architect Charles Warterfield Jr. observed fifty years later, "that such a sophisticated and expensive building came out of the ground in the post-depression years"; the building reflects the "government's commitment to good architecture as a function of the recovery."[7] The paired American

Postcard of Nashville Post Office, Davidson County.

eagles at the building's entrance are a direct reference to both the federal government and the New Deal. New Deal iconography in 1933–35 heavily relied on the popular symbol of the American eagle. Nashville architects Marr and Holman used Tennessee and Pennsylvania marble extensively in the ornate interior design that features polychromatic marble floors and walls; aluminum grilles, doors, and staircases; and a plaster and marble ceiling. Plans have been underway since 1999 to convert this National Register–listed building into the Frist Center for Visual Arts, to open in the early twenty-first century.

DAVIDSON COUNTY

U.S. Post Office (1934), 1101 Donelson Avenue, Old Hickory

Old Hickory was a company town centered around the chemical factories of the DuPont Corporation. This one-story, red-brick, flat-roof restrained Colonial Revival design came from the Office of the Supervising Architect, Louis A. Simon. Its central entrance features four concrete Doric pilasters supporting a concrete dentilled cornice that contains the lettering "United States Post Office." The building is listed in the National Register as part of the Old Hickory historic district.

DICKSON COUNTY

U.S. Post Office (1936), 201 West College Street, Dickson

Rarely in Tennessee did the PWA fund the construction of a post office in a small county seat. The National Register–listed Dickson post office is a notable exception. Its distinctive "Starved Classicism" design came from Louis A. Simon's Office of the Supervising Architect. The Dickson facility "exhibits the classical elements reminiscent of early federal buildings and influences of the twentieth-century modern and International styles," observed architectural historian Christopher Hetzel. "The classical influences include the building's symmetrical design and the vertical emphasis of its exterior and fenestration. The modern influences are visible in the building's flat, virtually unembellished exterior and its simple design."[8]

Although a residence and studio today, the building still retains its fresco mural, *People of the Soil*, executed on-site by Tennessee artist Edwin Boyd Johnson in the fall of 1938. Johnson trained in art at Watkins Institute in Nashville and graduated from the Art Institute of Chicago. He was living in Chicago at the time of the commission. The mural portrays average frontier

People of the Soil *by Edwin Boyd Johnson (1938), Dickson Post Office, Dickson County.*

people doing commonplace things—standard thematic subjects for Treasury Section art. But within this group of pioneers, Johnson portrays an African American man and woman, a depiction of race that was a rarity for Treasury Section art in Tennessee.

The selection of Johnson's topic did not come easy. Section officials asked Johnson to present three possible drawings to the local postmaster, Hugh Reeves, so he could judge if any of the murals would offend the community. Reeves initially preferred a sketch titled *Rural Free Delivery*, a drawing that Johnson considered inferior to his own preference, *People of the Soil*. The artist complained to Treasury Section superintendent Ed Rowan: "It seems to me that if the Government desires to embellish it's [sic] buildings with the best works of contemporary painters and sculptors, the matter of selecting the designs should be left entirely to a jury of artists rather than to the layman whose appreciation of art is usually of the magazine, bill board or calendar cover caliber. I know that art appreciation in the South is not far advanced but we are not helping the situation by giving them the mediocre design they have chosen."[9]

Rowan asked the local postmaster to let Johnson make the final decision; the postmaster relented, and once the fresco was completed on December 18, 1938, it seems that everyone was pleased. "From all reports," Johnson told Ed Rowan, "the mural is well liked, and I think that the people of Dickson know just a little more than they did before about fresco painting." Postmaster Reeves reported to Rowan: "The Murial [sic] he installed is very satisfactory and we have quite a bit of comment from both white and colored patrons. It really adds very much to the beauty of the lobby."[10]

FRANKLIN COUNTY
U.S. Post Office (1939), 305 West Main Street, Decherd

Decherd, established as a railroad town in the 1850s, was one of the smallest communities to receive both a federal post office and Treasury Section artwork. The post office is a one-story, hipped-roof, red-brick building with five symmetrical bays. Over the entrance door is an American eagle, with its wings spread wide.

The wood carving, *News on the Job* by Enea Biafora, centers on a woodcutter, with his axe resting between his legs. On his right is a girl carrying a basket of food; she lays a comforting hand on the woodcutter's shoulder. On the left is a boy reading a letter from the mail. The scene, thus, is linked to the postal service and to the local timber industry. Artist Enea Biafora was born in Italy but became a naturalized U.S. citizen. During the New Deal, Biafora received several different commissions for works to decorate federal buildings.

GIBSON COUNTY
U.S. Post Office (1935), 382 South Main Street, Milan

In the designs for a post office in Milan, a rural trade center at that time, Treasury Department architect Louis A. Simon approved a design of Renaissance Revival style, a marked departure from the preference for Colonial Revival–styled post offices in West Tennessee. Obviously Simon's office chose an architectural style that directly reflected the town's name. It is a two-story masonry building, with five symmetrical bays. A Palladian pediment, with American eagle, supported by two classical pilasters defines the center entrance. The post office is listed in the National Register of Historic Places.

GIBSON COUNTY
U.S. Post Office (1935), 200 South College Street, Trenton

The post office in Trenton, the seat of Gibson County, is another distinctive building in West Tennessee because officials used a "Starved Classicism"

Milan Post Office, Gibson County.

design instead of the regionally preferred Colonial Revival style. The building's size and materials also were different in its red brick construction (rather than concrete) and one-story height. Its symmetrical facade has an off-center projecting entrance.

GREENE COUNTY
U.S. Post Office and Courthouse (1937, 1940), 101 West Summer Street, Greeneville

The historic U.S. Post Office and Courthouse in Greeneville is a two-story Colonial Revival structure first built in 1914. In the mid-1930s federal officials approved the building's expansion to hold additional courtroom space as well as offices for new federal agencies. By 1937 a two-story wing of compatible Colonial Revival design had been completed. Next, in 1940, a second-floor court room received two impressive teak wood sculptures from William Zorach, a well-established sculptor who was among the initial American modernists. At the time of the commission, Zorach was an instructor at the Art Students League in New York City; he carved the two works at his Maine studio. At first Treasury Section officials wanted Zorach to use aluminum as his medium; in order to save costs, however, Zorach convinced them to let him execute the carvings in teak wood. The sculptures were displayed at the Whitney Museum in New York City before their installation in Greeneville on March 9, 1940.

Man Power portrays a powerfully built male figure leaning on a shovel, with the image of Norris Dam in the background. *The Resources of Nature*, on the other hand, portrays a woman and child surrounding by flowing water, trees, and blossoming plants. In a press release, Zorach explained how the two sculptures complemented each other: "The two panels symbolize the forces that contribute most to the peaceful development of this country—Together the two panels express the importance of the family and labor in this development." In particular, *The Resources of Nature* "symbolizes the natural power and resources of America" while *Man Power* "symbolizes man's effort and his development of the possibilities of this country and the tremendous projects which his brain conceives and his labor brings into being."[11] Historian Barbara Melosh views the sculptures as showing "nature and technology as complementary, beneficent sources of power."[12] In 1998 construction began in downtown Greeneville on a new federal building and courthouse.

HAMILTON COUNTY
Solomon Federal Building (1937–38), 1110 Market Street, Chattanooga

The monumental Solomon Federal Building in downtown Chattanooga is an outstanding example of federal public architecture from the early 1930s. Planned in 1931 and built in 1932, the building was a collaborative effort between the local firm of R. H. Hunt Company and Shreve, Lamb, & Harmon of New York City as directed by the Office of the Supervising Architect of the Treasury Department. The building is the main downtown post office, as well as a federal courthouse and office building.

The Treasury Section of Fine Arts commissioned Hilton Leech of Sarasota, Florida, to paint *Allegory of Chattanooga*, which was installed above the judge's bench in an upstairs court room in 1937. As architectural historian Sara A. Butler has observed, Leech's "dramatic compilation of heroic figures alludes to specific moments in the Chattanooga past, promoting local pride and tying the federal courtroom into local history. The mural creates a 1930s image of an ideal world" while its "conjunction of images representing hard work in the past and contemporary technology reinforces the optimistic New Deal message that a bountiful future was still attainable."[13] The building also contains the bust statue of *The Mail Carrier*, which rests on a large marble pedestal. The Public Works for Art Project commissioned sculptor Leopold Scholz to design the piece, which was installed on the first floor in late November 1938.

HARDEMAN COUNTY
U.S. Post Office (1940), 118 East Market Street, Bolivar

The Colonial Revival style and red-brick material of the Bolivar post office, attributed to Louis A. Simon, complements the town's many historic, nineteenth-century buildings. WPA work crews erected the building in 1940.

Carl Nyquist's mural in the post office, *Picking Cotton* (1941), portrays the significance of cotton cultivation in Hardeman County. Seemingly endless rows of cotton stretch into the landscape. Small frame, unadorned tenant dwellings lay in the background, while a family of cotton pickers, including a young girl, toil in the fields. The pickers are all white. While Nyquist's portrayal is plausible, it was misleading in terms of its depiction of race and gender roles. According to sociologist Charles S. Johnson's *Statistical Atlas of Southern Counties* (1941), almost 70 percent of Hardeman County farm operators were tenants, and a black farmer was twice as likely to be a tenant than a white farmer. Treasury Section officials asked Nyquist to check to make sure there were white tenants in Hardeman. When the artist reported in the affirmative, he received approval for the design, but the fact remained that most Hardeman tenants were African Americans. Nyquist's depiction of tenant women in the mural is just as problematic. The young girl is well dressed, with combed hair and no head covering—far from the reality of child labor in the cotton fields. The adult women are shown as distracted and of little help to the men when the opposite was true: tenant women worked as hard in the fields as their husbands, brothers, or sons. To give the artist his due, however, his mural is the only extant one in the South to show a white woman actually picking cotton.

HARDIN COUNTY
U.S. Post Office (1939), 507 Main Street, Savannah

This Colonial Revival design, attributed to Louis A. Simon, differs from most other similarly designed post offices in that it has a one-story concrete portico entrance, with four Corinthian columns supporting the pediment. Savannah needed a new, larger post office after the nearby construction of

Pickwick Dam by the Tennessee Valley Authority. In circa 1952, officials extended the original five-bay building with a two-bay addition on the west side. The post office was converted in the early 1990s into the Tennessee River Museum, which interprets the river's impact on the land, people, and heritage of the Tennessee Valley.

HAYWOOD COUNTY
U.S. Post Office (1936), West Main Street, Brownsville

This one-story, brick, symmetrical five-bay Colonial Revival design from the office of Louis A. Simon is a block west of the county courthouse. In the late 1980s, it was converted into a private business once a new post office building opened.

HENDERSON COUNTY
U.S. Post Office (1937), South Broad Street, Lexington

The most impressive public building in this small West Tennessee county seat, the historic Lexington Post Office is a brick, symmetrical five-bay Colonial Revival building of standardized design, attributed to the office of Louis A. Simon. With a winning bid of $51,067, the Bonded Construction Corporation built the post office in 1937. L. E. Tull was the construction engineer. At that time Lexington was the administrative headquarters for the large Natchez Trace land-use project of the Agriculture Department.

Artist Grace Greenwood's mural in the post office, *Progress of Power* (1940), is a powerful composition of the transformation inherent in modern technology. It dynamically blends images of a horse, aircraft, power switch, turbine, and speeding locomotive, suggesting the dramatic shift from horsepower to electricity. The mural's two male figures portray the centrality of man's role in this new technological world. Lexington residents liked the mural. Postal clerk Henry B. Davenport reported: "The mural has caused a great deal of interest around here, and we have received many nice compliments from the general public. . . . [M]any local citizens call at my window and ask about the mural. I describe it to the best of my ability, and it seems that it is being well-liked by the people of this community, especially these civic-minded citizens who appreciate the finer things in life."[14] A new post office opened in Lexington in 1997; this Treasury Section and WPA landmark awaits its second life.

HUMPHREYS COUNTY
U.S. Post Office (1937), 113 West Main, Waverly

Now a commercial building, the former Waverly Post Office is a red brick, symmetrical five-bay, Colonial Revival–style building with a central cupola. The standardized design came from the offices of Louis A. Simon, and WPA workers helped to construct the building.

JEFFERSON COUNTY
U.S. Post Office (1939), 200 East Andrew Johnson Highway, Jefferson City

Although it shares the same brick material, symmetrical five-bay facade, cupola, and general Colonial Revival style of other post offices in Tennessee, the Jefferson City Post Office was a variation in the standard design that came from the offices of Louis A. Simon in the late 1930s. Its modernist, decorative fanlight over the double entrance door, along with the modernist

Great Smokies and Tennessee Farms *by Charles Child (1941), Jefferson City Post Office, Jefferson County.*

Jefferson City Post Office, Jefferson County.

grilles of the cupola and the wide concrete band of the cornice, show a more contemporary interpretation of Colonial Revival style.

In the early 1940s the Cherokee Dam project of the Tennessee Valley Authority forever changed the landscape of this rural East Tennessee county. Charles Child's *Great Smokies and Tennessee Farms* (1941) interprets the hayfields, rolling fields, farms, and mountains of East Tennessee before TVA, in a nostalgic look at a rapidly disappearing world due to the power plants and the new Great Smoky Mountains National Park.

LAUDERDALE COUNTY
U.S. Post Office (1937), 17 East Jackson Avenue, Ripley

Just off the town square and visible from the steps of the PWA's Lauderdale County Courthouse, the Ripley Post Office is a well-preserved example of the red brick, symmetrical five-bay, Colonial Revival–style building designed by the office of Louis A. Simon. This WPA-constructed building was listed in the National Register of Historic Places in 1988. Art historian Howard Hull called the post office mural, *Autumn*, by Marguerite T. Zorach, "perhaps the most modern looking of all post office murals in the state."[15] Artist and teacher Burton Callicot of Memphis installed the mural in 1939. Zorach depicts a frontier scene, with a woman and boy gathering nuts while two men and a pack of dogs are hunting. Creative in its mixture of fall colors, looseness of stroke, and its distortion of figures, the mural is modern in technique, yet traditional in theme. It documented the subsistence lifestyle still found in this rural county during the depression decade, linking both past and present in one forceful composition.

LAWRENCE COUNTY
U.S. Post Office (1935), 218 North Military Street, Lawrenceburg

Two blocks from the town square, across from the historic Crockett Theater, the Lawrenceburg Post Office differs from its New Deal counterparts in similar rural county seats. With Louis A. Simon as supervising architect and John W. Wolcott Jr. listed as architect, the symmetrical five-bay brick building has a flat roof and few stylistic elements, save for the concrete American eagle medallions that flank the filled-in fanlight of the double-door entrance. In the 1990s the Classical Revival–styled building was converted into a local library and archives.

LOUDON COUNTY
U.S. Post Office (1938), 217 East Broadway, Lenoir City

The Lenoir City Post Office is one of the state's most unadorned New Deal buildings as far as its exterior architectural style. Although the design is attributed to the office of Treasury Section architect Louis A. Simon, the building's hipped roof, symmetrical five-bay facade, and understated classical entrance merely hint at Colonial Revival style. The real marvel is the interior mural, *Electrification*, by prominent American illustrator David Stone Martin. Its straightforward, powerful interpretation of the impact of electrical power lines on the rural landscape is one of the era's most compelling artifacts of the transformation wrought by the Rural Electrification Administration and the Tennessee Valley Authority during the depression.

　· In 1939 the federal government and *Life* magazine joined to sponsor a national competition for public art, titled the "Forty-eight States Competition," with each state receiving a prize-winning painting in one selected city. Competition between artists for the awards, and resulting commissions, was fierce; the competition attracted 1,475 entries. Just as hotly contested was the fight between towns within each state; many places wanted a competition winner to

Electrification by David Sloane Martin (1940), Lenoir City Post Office, Loudon County.

grace their public buildings. *Life* published illustrations of all winners in its issue of December 4, 1939; the sketches were also displayed at the Corcoran Art Gallery in Washington, D.C. Martin's *Electrification* won the Tennessee competition, and in August 1940 it was installed in Lenoir City, an appropriate location since TVA was then constructing the mammoth Fort Loudon Dam a mere couple of miles away.

"What appeared on the wall of the Lenoir City Post Office," observed historian Sue Beckham, "was a mural of strong Tennessee men putting up power lines so that electricity and all that its presence implied were assured for the future." Its composition also implied that TVA was "a well-oiled machine" that would "serve the area long after the present workmen have departed."[16] As historians Marlene Park and Gerald E. Markowitz remarked, the "abstract patterns of the power lines are both the form and the content of the painting."[17]

Unlike some of the other states' competition winners, the local community praised Martin's mural. The local postmaster, Harry M. Calloway, wrote the Treasury Section to register his approval. Then in August 1940, the local Rotary Club hosted a banquet to honor Martin and his wife for their contributions to civic culture in Loudon County.

MARION COUNTY
U.S. Post Office (1934), 303 Elm Street, South Pittsburgh

New Deal programs often targeted hard-hit industrial communities for their initial projects. Such was the case in South Pittsburgh, Tennessee, where a new post office was constructed in 1934. It is a well-executed Colonial Revival design, from the office of Louis A. Simon, that features a hipped roof, understated classical entrance, 12-over-12 light windows, and brick quoins.

MARSHALL COUNTY
U.S. Post Office (1935), 121 1st Avenue South, Lewisburg

The historic New Deal post office in Lewisburg now provides offices for the local newspaper. The building has an attractive Colonial Revival design, attributed to the office of Louis A. Simon, with a fanlight over the entrance, keystones over the 16-over-16 windows, brick quoins, and hipped roof.

When the town's new post office was constructed on East Commerce Street, the original Treasury Section mural was restored and moved to the new building's lobby. Executed by Memphis native John H. R. Pickett, *Coming 'Round the Mountain* (1938) portrays a frontier scene of pioneers traveling over mountainous terrain, admittedly an odd choice of subject for a town located in the heartland of Middle Tennessee like Lewisburg. But Pickett viewed the commission as more than a painting for Lewisburg; he saw it as a tribute to his native state. Pickett wanted to portray, as he explained to Ed Rowan of the Treasury Section, "the spirit of the migration of the early settlers from North Carolina over the Cumberland Pass and around the mountains into Middle Tennessee."[18]

MAURY COUNTY
**U.S. Post Office and Court House (1940),
South Garden Street, Columbia**

This impressive four-story concrete building provided offices for federal programs, a courtroom for federal judges, and the local post office. Postmaster General James A. Farley dedicated the building during the city's annual Mule Day Festival in 1940. Architects Louis A. Simon and William Dewey Foster are credited with the building's understated PWA Modern design. Neal A. Melick was the supervising engineer. The facade features an eagle, sculpted by Sidney Waugh of Massachusetts in 1941, centered above its

68 FEDERAL COURTHOUSES AND POST OFFICES

U.S. Post Office and Courthouse, Columbia.

Maury County Landscape by Henry Billings (1942), U.S. Post Office and Courthouse, Columbia.

cornice. The American bald eagle was a favorite symbol for New Deal agencies, including the RFC and the NRA.

The first-floor entrance lobby features Henry Billings's mural titled *Maury County Landscape* (1942). Billings portrayed the recent transformation of the county's rural landscape, caused by phosphate mining, chemical companies, burley tobacco farming, and the arrival of TVA-generated electricity. Although the post office moved to new quarters in 1979, the building still houses courtrooms and offices.

MAURY COUNTY
U.S. Post Office (1940), 201 North Main Street, Mount Pleasant

With its blend of modernist elements within an overall symmetrical shape reminiscent of the state's other Colonial Revival post offices, the Mount Pleasant Post Office is the most distinctive New Deal postal facility in Middle Tennessee. The design is attributed to the office of Louis A. Simon. Projecting from its central entrance is a flat metal canopy on which is perched a metal American eagle. Flanking the entrance are Art Deco–styled light fixtures, while the windows of the five-bay facade are large metal casement windows, like those found in International style buildings.

If the exterior is modernist, the interior lobby mural, *Early Settlers Entering Mount Pleasant* (1942) by Eugene Higgins, is traditional in its execution and subject. Its "soft-edged representational look," according to Howard Hull, "is compatible with the aesthetic philosophy of many Tennessee postal patrons."[19] For his subject, New York artist Higgins interpreted the early settlement of the community, depicting both white families and black slaves. The artist claimed to have taken his subject from a frontier family story related to him by another artist, Suzanne Kenyon, whose family came from Mount Pleasant. Kenyon later complained that Higgins had gotten the locale wrong—her family had settled in Brentwood, in Williamson County, not in Maury County. Higgins's interpretation of the slaves followed the racial stereotypes of the 1930s; one male is even strumming a banjo in the back of a wagon. Higgins also portrays a black youth herding several sheep—appropriate for an area renowned in the antebellum era for its stock growing, especially cattle and sheep.

MONROE COUNTY
U.S. Post Office (1940), 701 North Main Street, Sweetwater

The Sweetwater Post Office, designed by the office of Louis A. Simon, is a restrained interpretation of Colonial Revival style, characterized by its red brick material, hipped roof, and recessed 8-over-12 windows. Thelma Martin's *Wild Boar Hunt* (1942), however, is a fascinating mural in its portrayal of hunting within the confines of an old, abandoned grist mill, combining both human forms and architectural forms. A hunter with rifle ready for the kill is the focal point; on the right side is the trapped, angry boar at her den, while in the left background are additional dogs and hunters. Martin chose the subject of boar hunting due to the popularity of the sport in Monroe County, where a large population of wild boars has been concentrated throughout the twentieth century.

OVERTON COUNTY
U.S. Post Office (1938), Town Square, Livingston

Overton County, where many residents were poor or unemployed loggers, miners, and farmers, was a focal point for New Deal relief efforts, receiving a state park, schools, courthouse renovations, and a Colonial Revival–style post office during the 1930s. The Livingston Post Office, located north of the courthouse, is one of the standardized Treasury Section designs found throughout Tennessee. Built by the WPA under the supervision of M. H. Hankins, it is a red-brick, symmetrical five-bay building with a central cupola and an American eagle perched over the central entrance. Plain brick pilasters separate the four 12-over-12 windows of the facade. When it opened, the building served as offices for both the postal service and the U.S. Department of Agriculture.

New York artist Margaret Covey's *The Newcomers* (1940) celebrates the county's settlement through a depiction of a group of neighbors welcoming a frontier family to the community. The family consists of a husband, wife, and their children, a boy and girl. The woman is working away, churning butter, while the man, with rifle in hand, greets the welcoming committee. It consists of two men, a woman, and a girl, who are carrying gifts of livestock, poultry, vegetables, and other staples. Covey's interpretation of the dynamics of settlement reflected a general consensus about the value of the frontier. "It is clear from these scenes," as Marlene Park and Gerald Markowitz argue, "that the pioneers built a strong foundation that would see people through the Great Depression if they would only heed the example of their forebears. By looking at the past, people get a sense of who they are and of the dignity that is theirs. In the face of uncertainty, people can see in the historical scenes a continuity with a meaningful past. And history as it appears in these works tells what people have in common—certain virtues and a heritage to enrich the present."[20]

As she attended the mural's installation in May 1940, the artist's mother noted that residents in general liked the painting, in particular praising her portrayal of the animals. The following month, the local newspaper printed a long article about the mural, praising its interpretation of a cabin raising in the early frontier days of Overton County.

RHEA COUNTY

U.S. Post Office (1936), 400 Main Street, Dayton

The Dayton Post Office is an unassuming Colonial Revival design from the office of Louis A. Simon. It features a square cupola and 12-over-12 windows flanking a central entrance that has two delicate fluted pilasters supporting a classical cornice on which rests an American eagle. The lobby mural is *View from Johnson's Bluff*, a 1939 landscape mural based on an actual spot on the east face of Walden Ridge in Rhea County. New York artist Bertram Hartman, who visited the area prior to selecting his subject, chose the spot (he claimed

Dayton Post Office, Rhea County.

in a later newspaper interview) because "the hills, the river and rocks—all make a wonderful setting for a study of nature's beauty."[21]

ROANE COUNTY
U.S. Post Office (1937), 340 West Rockwood Street, Rockwood

Located between the historic residential and business districts of this small East Tennessee industrial town, the Rockwood Post Office is a well-executed Colonial Revival design, with its projecting classical portico complementing its overall symmetry and fine craftsmanship. While the overall project design is attributed to the office of Louis A. Simon, the Atlanta and Knoxville firm of Good and Goodstein provided the actual architects of the building. It is listed in the National Register of Historic Places.

The lobby's ceramic sculpture, *Wild Life* (1939) by Christian Heinrich, is the only one of its kind in a Tennessee post office. Heinrich, a New York sculptor, depicted a family of deer at rest, yet attentive to their surroundings. The Freigang Ceramic Works of Long Island, New York, cast the work, which weighs over three hundred pounds.

SEVIER COUNTY
U.S. Post Office (1940), 167 Bruce Street, Sevierville

The Sevierville Post Office, now a local history museum, is a distinguished example of Louis A. Simon's standardized Colonial Revival designs for county seat post offices. It is listed in the National Register of Historic Places. Its square wooden cupola with weather vane is centered on a metal hipped roof. Marble lintels define the 12-over-12 windows; indeed, pink marble is used to trim the building throughout. The central entrance has a concrete American eagle set on a classical entablature, which is supported by two classical columns. The interior lobby has marble wainscoting and green terrazzo floors.

Although the standardized design is attributed to Louis A. Simon, the contractor for the project was local, the African American owned and operated J, F & N McMahan Construction Company, headed by brick mason and builder Fred McMahan. A graduate of Knoxville College, McMahan received a master's degree in engineering from the University of Illinois. Together with his brothers James and Newt, Fred McMahan operated the family construction company in the mid-1900s and left an important legacy of architectural landmarks throughout the town and county.

UNICOI COUNTY
U.S. Post Office (1935), 123 North Main Street, Erwin

Erwin was a nineteenth-century county seat, but most of its built environment dates to a period of planned industrial development in the early twentieth century. Its post office is an interesting variation on the standard New Deal design for Tennessee post offices. Most noticeable are the three Palladian-influenced central bays of the five-bay facade. Concrete belts accentuate the horizontal massing of the building while concrete keystones accent the 6-over-6 windows. Erwin received a new post office building in the late 1990s, and this older building is now a commercial business.

WEAKLEY COUNTY
U.S. Post Office (1936), Town Square, Dresden

North of the Weakley County Courthouse is the Dresden Post Office, an interesting Colonial Revival design from the office of Louis A. Simon, which was constructed by WPA crews. The Dresden Post Office differs from its West Tennessee counterparts in its slightly projecting center section, which has its own

Dresden Post Office, Weakley County.

pediment supported by brick pilasters. Flat concrete arches accent the 12-over-12 windows; an American eagle peers over the entrance door.

Minnetta Good's historical mural, *Retrospection* (1938), contrasts with other Treasury Section art in the region because it depicts several discrete scenes, from a log cabin to the county courthouse and to such famous people as Andrew Jackson and David Crockett, rather than a single landscape or event. Robert Weakley, for whom the county was named, is at the mural's center.

Good's overview of the county's early history met with strong local approval. The Dresden Garden Club, in fact, wrote Treasury Section officials: "we prize it for its exquisite beauty, the splendid workmanship, and for what it means to us. It is, indeed, a wonderful picture that Miss Good has given us."[22]

WEAKLEY COUNTY
U.S. Post Office (1940), 100 North Cedar Street, Gleason

The Gleason post office is the most modernist of all New Deal post offices in Tennessee's small towns. Its modernism is conveyed through the dominant single bay of the facade, which is composed of a central entrance flanked by tall bands of casement windows, and its use of multicolor brown brick. After agency reorganization and Simon's retirement in 1939, the Treasury Depart-

Gleason Post Office, Weakley County.

Gleason Agriculture by Anne Poor (1942), Gleason Post Office, Weakley County.

ment moved away from its tendency to favor standardized, in-house Colonial Revival designs, a fact reflected in the creativity of this building.

Anne Poor's *Gleason Agriculture* (1942) aggressively stated the importance of place and everyday activities in lives of rural Weakley County residents. Poor was the stepdaughter of American artist, and often Treasury Section juror, Henry Varnum Poor. Her mural celebrated Gleason's sweet potato industry, in particular W. R. Hawks, who was credited locally with introducing the plant as a cash crop. A representational likeness of Hawks is on the right side of the mural; when locals told Poor that the man did not look like Hawks, she replied that in murals "it was sometimes just as well to leave portraits more or less generalized."[23] The artist shows different people involved in the business—men, women, and children, all white—while the Gleason depot symbolized the importance of the railroad in moving the crop to larger national markets. Producing the crop defined life for many people in Gleason; by 1944 the county ranked fourteenth in the nation in sweet potato production. The most expressive part of the mural is Poor's use of a border composed of the sweet potato vines; such decorative borders were rare in Treasury Section public art.

WHITE COUNTY
U.S. Post Office (1936), 34 West Bockman Way, Sparta

Located a block west of the White County Courthouse, on the historic route of the Memphis-to-Bristol Highway, the former Sparta Post Office reflects restrained Classical Modern styling, using brick, stone, and aluminum to create a five-bay, symmetrical facade. The design, attributed to Louis A. Simon, is unique among the small county seat post offices in Tennessee. The building is now home to the local Sparta newspaper.

3

Community Buildings and Institutions

From 1933 to 1942 a broad spectrum of New Deal projects aimed at improving community life in order to lift depressed towns and neighborhoods from their economic and cultural doldrums. Many projects addressed basic needs and used existing buildings and facilities. To address the employment needs of working-class mothers and improve educational opportunities for their children, for example, the Tennessee Emergency Relief Administration and later the Works Progress Administration supported nursery schools in the major cities, typically locating these at existing public schools. At Murfreesboro, for example, a nursery school for African American children operated at Bradley Academy. In the countryside, these same two agencies sought to provide work to rural women by encouraging the development of canning projects, again often at local schools or gymnasiums, so rural communities could help feed themselves and start school lunch programs for their children. The program in Putnam County, for example, produced more than 250,000 cans of fruits and vegetables in its TERA-sponsored program. The WPA expanded the TERA programs significantly and sponsored community gardens to supply fresh fruits and vegetables to the needy and to schoolchildren. In Bradley County, for instance, the WPA planted twenty-two acres in community gardens and supplied almost one hundred thousand hot meals in 1939–40. Community gardens in Dickson, Marshall, and White Counties also supplemented a large effort of providing hot lunches at many county schools. These projects were not without their critics, both at the state and national levels. But "critics of the 'traditional' women's work done on many of the FERA-CWA-WPA service (women's) projects," historian Martha Swain has emphasized, "would do well to recognize that it broke tradition and long-established patterns for masses of uneducated, often illiterate women with no prior work history other than in the fields to be employed at nonagricultural tasks away from home."[1]

Other New Deal programs attempted to create an infrastructure for community gatherings through the construction of auditoriums, libraries, community halls, and scout lodges. These new venues, such as the combination gymnasium and auditorium in Paris, the seat of Henry County, created enhanced cultural and community activities for children and adults by means of performing arts, school plays, and adult education. Several buildings remain vital contributors to the community today, even as their function has changed. The former WPA-constructed gym and community center in White House, a small town in Robertson County, now serves as its city hall. In addition to the WPA, the NYA built a number of extant local libraries, community halls, and lodges, thus meeting a major goal of President Franklin D. Roosevelt when he established the agency in 1935. "Particular stress," Roosevelt asserted, "should be laid upon the building and the use of recreational and community centers which, depending upon local conditions and the energy, ability, and enthusiasm of local youth groups, can be anything from an old-fashioned swimming hole to a complete center, including all types of athletic facilities, community houses, library, classrooms, etc."[2]

Another new community building in Tennessee was the armory, built for both military and civilian purposes in the larger towns and cities during the late 1930s and early 1940s. The WPA usually provided federal money for the projects, under the assumption that three-fourths of the time the structure would be a community center; only one-fourth of the time would it be used for military functions. Tennessee built many armories (a total of fifteen by 1943), due to an intense interest in war preparation by Gov. Prentice Cooper as well as a federal threat to withdraw War Department funding unless units were housed in adequate facilities. In 1937 Cooper visited Europe, a trip that heightened his fears of another world war. Cooper began to preach war preparedness to almost anyone who would listen. Under his impetus, the state in 1939 launched an ambitious armory construction program, floating a $350,000 bond to pay its share, while local governments matched the state investment and the federal government picked up the rest of the tab.

Several of the new armories, such as the ones in Athens (1941–42) and Clarksville (1941–42), were striking Art Deco–styled public buildings. The largest complex—an armory and eleven units—was located at the transportation crossroads of Chattanooga. The Chattanooga armory was built in distinctive Crab Orchard stone and possessed the largest drill hall—110 feet by 180 feet—in the state. But the standard armory was typically plain in appearance and considerably smaller. The Nashville architectural firm of Warfield and Keeble received most of the commissions, and the firm implemented a rather standardized but vaguely Art Deco–style architectural plan, locating the structures on what were then the towns' primary highways. Although built for war, the armories were used for peaceful purposes almost weekly. Many buildings continued to play a dual role as a military and community center until a new program for building armories occurred in the 1970s and early 1980s.

Agencies also addressed the health needs of specific military veterans, whether by additions to the U.S. Marine Hospital in Memphis or by constructing the modern Veterans Administration psychiatric hospital complex outside of Murfreesboro. The largest transformation in public medical facilities took place in Memphis, where officials took advantage of PWA funding to add buildings and services at the University of Tennessee Medical College. Using a large amount of funds donated in memory of hotel owner John Gaston and some public funds to provide the necessary match, Memphis city officials also built the modern John Gaston Hospital to replace the inadequate Memphis General Hospital. In rural counties officials used New Deal funds to address public health needs, such as a small health clinic in Union City.

Many counties also participated in a state program to locate and record local historical records. Established in 1936, the Tennessee Historical Records Survey was part of the WPA's Division of Professional and Service Projects, sponsored by the Tennessee State Library. Six years later, the editor of the *Tennessee Historical Quarterly* praised the project for locating and making more accessible scores of local documents and government records. One such records project took place in Morristown, where Mayor T. D. Brooks had earlier opposed any proposal to commit local resources to federal projects. He believed that municipal indebtedness should not be increased until more prosperous times. But when it came to the county records program, Brooks voiced no known opposition to allowing his wife, Cora Davis Brooks, to work with the project, which published typescript copies of her "History of Morristown, 1787–1936" in 1940.

Across the country New Dealers also attempted to create worker communities by advocating labor organization with major new federal legislation. Interest in or sympathy for labor rights has a decidedly mixed record in Tennessee, depending on the individuals, unions, and industries under discussion. In Grundy County, one of the most economically depressed places in the state, pro-labor leaders at Highlander Folk School, near Monteagle, repeatedly clashed with local and state WPA officials over road projects and lower than average wages paid to WPA enrollees. WPA administrators within the county and state took a hard line with the protests, even at one point suspending a large county road project, which temporarily ended critically needed relief for an estimated seven hundred families. In Memphis, where "Boss" Crump was decidedly anti-labor, attempts to organize and help workers gained little in the New Deal.

The types of buildings constructed to house the wide-ranging community projects and newly established community groups varied in their building materials and architectural style. Some are magnificent examples of labor-intensive stone masonry, while others are grandiose and flamboyant examples of Colonial Revival or Classical Revival style. Still others are one-story, unadorned buildings designed simply to fulfill their function, and little more. Whatever their size, material, or styling, however, New Deal community buildings still speak of the reformers' hope to uplift rural and urban life, even in the harshest days of the Great Depression.

BEDFORD COUNTY
National Guard Armory (1941–42), Depot at Thompson Streets, Shelbyville

Now an industrial business, the National Guard Armory in Shelbyville, designed by Warfield and Keeble, still marks the historic route of the Dixie Highway south of town. The masonry building had a drill hall measuring seventy feet by one hundred feet. In addition to the armory, work crews constructed garages and a motor repair shop. Gov. Prentice Cooper, who spearheaded the state's armory building program, was a native of Bedford County and lived in Shelbyville.

BRADLEY COUNTY
National Guard Armory (1940–41), 29th Street, Cleveland

Cleveland's National Guard Armory, designed by Warfield and Keeble of Nashville, was located at the site of the former Central Grammar School, which the CWA had demolished in 1934. The project cost $53,074, shared by the city and county ($5,000 each), the state ($10,000), and the WPA ($33,074). Opened to the community in 1940, state and local officials in 1941 provided an additional $4,000 for the construction of a large stage, so the building could be used better for community events. The armory now is a YMCA recreational center and is open to the public.

In addition to the armory, the WPA did much to reshape the public landscape of Bradley County. Between 1935 and 1940, the agency built or repaired 141.4 miles of highways, roads, and streets, as well as 18 bridges and 426 culverts. It also renovated and expanded Bradley Central High School, Charleston High School, and the segregated African American College Hill School. The WPA constructed city sidewalks and Johnson Park. It also attempted to create communities of craft women in its Sewing Room Project, where local women knitted clothes for sale and for the needy. The agency even made a giant contribution to rural public health through its construction of 3,098 sanitary privies (see chapter 7).

CANNON COUNTY

Bluewing Community Garden (c. 1936), U.S. Highway 70S at Tennessee Highway 281

Until commercial development arrived in the late 1990s, this rural crossroads had changed little since the 1930s. Here a local road (now Tennessee 281), which provided access to several rural settlements, crossed the historic Memphis-to-Bristol Highway (U.S. Highway 70S). WPA officials thus chose the crossroads as a perfect location for a community garden, which stood at the southeast corner of the crossroads—still an open field in 1999. Residents from miles around came to the garden to acquire produce and vegetables for their families; it also provided food for the local school lunch program.

COCKE COUNTY

Town Library (1937), U.S. Highway 421 at Tennessee Highway 340, Parottsville

This small, rectangular-shaped stone building has served as the local library since 1937. Local NYA boys used stones of various sizes and colors in its construction, giving some distinction to its otherwise plain, symmetrical three-bay facade.

DAVIDSON COUNTY

City Market (1936–37), 100 James Robertson Parkway, Nashville

Nashville architect Henry C. Hibbs designed the City Market in an Adamesque Revival style, complete with a domed central entrance. This PWA project, which cost almost a half a million dollars, was part of the agency's effort to redesign and update the old town square of Nashville. The agency constructed several such market buildings throughout the South in an effort to provide rural residents and local entrepreneurs with enhanced opportunities to sell their products to city dwellers. The one in Nashville contained stalls, restaurants, and rest rooms with such interior finishes as glazed tile wainscoting and a terrazzo floor. "On the streets adjoining the

82   COMMUNITY BUILDINGS AND INSTITUTIONS

Parrotsville Library, Cocke County.

market house," noted the WPA guidebook to Tennessee, "farmers line up their wagons, loaded with fresh country produce, everything from wild fox grapes, persimmons, and sorghum molasses, to 'pyor' honey, split-bottom chairs, cut flowers, and fresh cider."[3] Today, however, only lines of police cars surround the market building since it has been extensively renovated into the Ben West police building of the Metropolitan Nashville government.

GIBSON COUNTY

Gibson County Central Library (1938), 303 North College Street, Trenton

In 1937–38 students employed by the National Youth Administration worked with officials of the county board of education to erect this plain brick building on the north outskirts of town, next to the county jail, on the federal highway heading toward Dyer. It may look unimportant today, but in 1938 it was recognized as one of the state's first central libraries in a rural area, holding both the collections of the school board and the city public library. The building is now part of the county jail and has been extensively renovated for that purpose.

Hancock County School Library and Shops, Sneedville.

HANCOCK COUNTY
Hancock County School Library and Shops (1939), Sneedville

Three years after the PWA funded the construction of an elementary school and high school, the NYA put local boys to work in building a new library and shops building. The designs of many NYA projects across the state had little architectural style, but in Sneedville, the popularity of the Colonial Revival style of the adjacent PWA school influenced the library's design. The library building has several restrained Colonial Revival features, such as a classical portico entrance, symmetrical five-bay facade, and central entrance with transom.

HICKMAN COUNTY
National Guard Armory (1941), Old Highway 100, Centerville

The vaguely Art Deco outline of this masonry armory, designed in 1941 by Warfield and Keeble of Nashville and built by the WPA, is visible from the Tennessee Highway 50 bridge that crosses the Duck River. The building is now home to the Hickman County Senior Citizens Center, a conversion that New Dealers may have found appropriate.

KNOX COUNTY
Moses Center (1933–42), 220 Carrick Street, Knoxville

Between 1933 and 1943, the historic Moses School, which has been renovated into the Moses Center, served as a "nursery school"—what we now call daycare—for working-class children so their mothers could have day jobs. The Moses School dates to 1916 and was named in honor of Col. John L. Moses, who in 1875 donated this land in the Mechanicsville neighborhood for the benefit of Knoxville's African Americans. As the depression worsened in the winter of 1931–32, the private City Federation of Women's Clubs of Knoxville worked with the local school board to establish the Opportunity Nursery School at the Pickle School near Brookside Mills. This was the first public nursery school for poor children in Tennessee and among the first in the South.

In February 1933, the operation moved to Moses School. With the coming of the New Deal later that spring, the partnership that funded and operated the nursery school expanded to include the school board, the Women's Clubs, the American Red Cross, and the federal government, represented by TSRA and TERA from 1933 to 1935 and the WPA from 1935 to 1943. The new federal funds expanded the program to fifteen nursery schools across Knoxville by the fall of 1933, with four facilities segregated for African-American children. That figure represented the height of the program; in 1934–35 the program only included seven schools, but each facility was adequately staffed with two teachers, two housekeepers, a nurse, and a dietitian.

LAKE COUNTY
Tiptonville Public Library (1940), 126 Tipton Street, Tiptonville

There was no public library in Tiptonville until 1928, when the local Woman's Club opened one in the home of Heloise Donaldson. This library closed in 1938. The Tiptonville Woman's Club then raised twenty-five hundred dollars—a sizable sum for a small town during the depression—and approached the local Young Men's Business Club for assistance in asking the National Youth Administration to build a new library. The result of combining the local money with NYA funds and labor was an attractive Colonial Revival building. Its gable-end, three-bay facade has paired classical pilasters to define the corners, while

Tiptonville Public Library, Lake County.

pilasters also flank the double-door entrance with fanlight. For the original library furniture, the NYA built tables while members of the Woman's Club donated chairs.

MARSHALL COUNTY

School Lunch Program Garden (1936), University of Tennessee Dairy Experiment Station, U.S. Highway 31A, Lewisburg

On a plot of land at the Dairy Experiment Station, WPA workers under the supervision of Emma D. Gillium planted and harvested a garden designed to provide fresh foods and canned goods for the county's first school lunch program. WPA women workers canned the garden's vegetables at the high school gymnasium (no longer extant) in Lewisburg.

MAURY COUNTY

National Guard Armory (1941-42), 503 Carter Street, Columbia

This well-preserved Warfield and Keeble–designed armory, located at the north end of town off of the old route of U.S. Highway 31, is now used by the Parks and Recreation Department of the City of Columbia. Its large

Columbia Armory, Maury County.

70-by-100-foot drill hall has been used for all sorts of community events. During World War II, the armory was the headquarters of the Tenth Machine Gun and Chemical Company.

MCMINN COUNTY
Lloyd Campbell Memorial Boy Scout Lodge (1938), Pennsylvania Avenue at Sixth Street, Etowah

Etowah in the early 1900s was a bustling industrial town, centered on the two-story Louisville and Nashville Railroad Depot and Offices and the extensive yards and machine shops maintained by the railroad. In the late 1920s, however, the railroad shifted much of its operations elsewhere, and Etowah entered a period of economic depression. In 1938, the NYA funded the construction of a small stone Boy Scout lodge, named in honor of Lloyd Campbell, who was scoutmaster from 1926 to 1931. Located within the town's National Register–listed residential district, the one-story, Bungalow-style lodge, with its stone craftsmanship, double-hung windows, and gable roof, remains little changed from when local boys constructed it over sixty years ago.

OBION COUNTY
National Guard Armory (1940–41), 415 West Main Street, Union City

Listed in the National Register of Historic Places, the Union City Armory was dedicated on January 31, 1941, at an elaborate public ceremony attended by the

Loyd Campbell Boy Scout Lodge, Etowah, McMinn County.

state American Legion commander, Bascom F. Jones, State Adj. Gen. T. A. Frazier and Gov. Prentice Cooper. Funded by the PWA, rather than the WPA, and designed by Nashville architects Marr and Holman, rather than Warfield and Keeble, the building has a restrained but unmistakable Art Deco influence in not only its overall contours but also in the streamlined styling of its entrance. The building was also constructed of brick and not masonry.

But like the others, the building served both military and community roles. During World War II, it was the base of Company K, 117th Infantry Regiment, of the National Guard. It also hosted various community events, dances, and war bond rallies. For instance, the Union City *Daily Messenger* of March 10, 1941, reported that 350 members from the county's Home Economics and Future Farms of America clubs met at the armory: "The boys and girls provided the entertainment through skits, singing, and musical performances." During a war bond drive at the armory in 1942, local politician Robert A. "Fats" Everett auctioned his clothing one piece at a time (until he reached his underwear)![4]

The Union City Armory became private property in about 1980 and is now home to a dance studio.

Union City Armory, Obion County. A rare example of a PWA-funded armory.

OBION COUNTY

Obion County Health Department Clinic (1940), Third Street and Church Street, Union City

For a decade prior to the New Deal, officials and physicians in Obion County sought outside assistance in providing better public health care. In the mid-1920s, Obion County looked for help from the Commonwealth Fund, a private foundation based in New York State, but the fund instead chose Rutherford County for its model program. Then in the mid-1930s, when it decided to fund a West Tennessee public health project, the Commonwealth Fund chose to support the construction of a public clinic in Trenton, the seat of Gibson County. Obion residents had better luck during the New Deal, when the Public Works Administration built this unadorned brick building for about ten thousand dollars in 1940. Health administrators launched initiatives in the 1930s to reduce the county's levels of tuberculosis, venereal disease, dental disease, and diphtheria. They also undertook various public education programs in the local public schools. Public health personnel even took their campaign directly to individual homes as they supervised the WPA's effort to build sanitary privies across the county. In 1938, for example, WPA workers installed 363 privies with the property owner incurring only the cost of materials. While no longer serving as the public health department, the building still serves a public role as offices for the county agricultural extension agent.

Obion County Public Health Building, Union City.

RUTHERFORD COUNTY

Boy and Girl Scouts Lodge (1939), 700 Ewing Boulevard, Murfreesboro

Scouting in Murfreesboro dates prior to World War I, but the local movement gathered momentum in the 1930s. In 1938 city officials announced plans to build a Scout lodge, for both boys and girls, on public land adjacent to the city water tower. Here would be "a civic center where boys and girls can find a cooperative spirit."[5] With local contributions in hand, they sought support from the National Youth Administration, which provided money and labor. Clarence E. Watson, president of the local Boy Scout council, designed the building. To prepare the actual construction materials, NYA workers reused 250 old electric poles, beams from old railroad cars, logs from abandoned log buildings, and an old limestone chimney. The end result was an impressive Government Rustic style building in which the first floor was of half-dovetailed logs and the second and third floors were frame, covered with staggered shingle cladding.

On October 19, 1939, the city council conveyed an easement to the local Scout Council so it could operate the facility as a lodge for white boys and girls scouts only. Although an African American Boy Scout troop had already organized in Murfreesboro, the new lodge was to be off limits to local blacks. Years later, the building had a second life as home to the Murfreesboro Little Theatre; it is used today for children theater productions.

RUTHERFORD COUNTY
National Guard Armory (1940–42), 1220 West College Street, Murfreesboro

The Murfreesboro armory is located on the historic route of the Dixie Highway (now West College Street) north of the town square. It is across the street from Redoubt Brannan, part of the Civil War–era Fortress Rosecrans, a historic site administered by the National Park Service. The city and county governments, along with the WPA, funded the armory project, which had a total cost of approximately seventy-five thousand dollars. Architect Edwin A. Keeble of Warfield and Keeble prepared the plans and specifications for the masonry armory. Construction began in April 1940 under the supervision of Capt. Hubert McCullough, who also was the city engineer.

Murfreesboro officials initially bragged that its armory would be the first constructed in the state, but completing the building on schedule proved difficult due to a lack of skilled labor in the city. In fact, local officials had to acquire special WPA approval to bring in additional labor from Nashville. At its formal dedication on April 24, 1942, Gov. Prentice Cooper proclaimed: "[T]his building has a great deal more significance that the general public realizes."[6] After the war, it continued to serve as a National Guard center, with its auditorium often being used for dances and other community events. The county government now uses the building for offices.

RUTHERFORD COUNTY
Veterans Administration Hospital (1936–40), 3400 Lebanon Road, Murfreesboro

At that same Armory dedication ceremony in 1942, Gov. Prentice Cooper praised Murfreesboro's Veterans Administration Hospital as "one of the great military hospitals" in the country.[7] Located on a 602-acre tract several miles north of town on U.S. Highway 231, the VA hospital was the major New Deal project in Rutherford County, combining funding from the PWA, WPA, and Veterans Administration.

President Roosevelt authorized the construction of a neuropsychiatric facility in November 1936, and the PWA allotted $674,000 for the project in the summer of 1938. Construction under the supervision of C. D. Franks began that fall at the former plantation of the prominent Rucker family. Contractors soon encountered a slave burial ground; they marked the site

Veterans Administration Hospital, Murfreesboro, circa 1950. Courtesy of Alvin C. York Veterans Administration Medical Center Archives.

on their maps and designed a road interchange in order to bypass (and therefore preserve) the cemetery.[8] Today, a monument and a grove of trees mark the cemetery's location.

The hospital officially opened January 1, 1940; at that time, it was the second-largest VA hospital in the nation with twenty-one separate buildings. Classical Revival and Colonial Revival architecture linked the buildings into a campuslike setting. At the center was the Administration Building, listed as Building One, which boasted a two-story portico modeled after the portico of The Hermitage, Andrew Jackson's home in Nashville. The buildings were placed into a designed landscape of trees, plants, and walks, with much of this work carried out by WPA crews. The goal was to create a bucolic, rural haven, outside of the busy modern world, one that would have a calming influence on patients. In fact, one WPA contractor went to his family farm in neighboring Cannon County and took saplings from a large variety of native trees to plant at the hospital. Another work crew built a stone-and-concrete dam at a spring to create a lake, while ball fields and a golf course provided additional recreational facilities for the recuperating war veterans. As part of their therapy and sustenance, the patients also worked the land, raising strawberries, fruits, vegetables, livestock, and broom corn from which they made brooms to sell. With its own electrical plant and a sewer and water system, the hospital was a self-contained facility as well as the primary federal employer for miles around. The hospital treated both black and white veterans but maintained segregated buildings and programs until the 1960s.

In the 1980s, federal officials formally associated the hospital with the Meharry Medical School in Nashville and broadened its services and mission beyond that of a psychiatric hospital. In 1985 they renamed the facility the Alvin C. York Veterans Administration Medical Center, a tribute to the famous World War I hero and a recognition of the facility's change in mission. The hospital is open to the public on a limited basis; due to privacy rights, visitors are requested not to take photographs without first securing official permission.

SEQUATCHIE COUNTY
Dunlap Community Hall (1938–42), Cherry Street at Rankin Street, Dunlap

NYA work crews constructed this large, two-story, cut limestone building between 1938 and 1942 as a relief program in the coal town of Dunlap, which had suffered from a severe economic depression since the closing of local mines and coke operations in the 1920s. The total cost was $18,384.72. The project employed a total of 96 youths, supervised by a local builder, Horace Reynolds. Other supervisory personnel included Jack Lockhart, Hershel Brock, and Grover Elliott, who taught the boys various construction techniques, so that by the time the project was complete, the boys ideally would know as many different aspects of the construction trade as possible. The demand for work was so high in Dunlap that officials created two work crews. A group of between ten and twenty boys would work on the building at a time for a two-week interval; then another similar size group would work. Both groups, however, received a full month's pay for the two weeks of work. The crews used hand-cut and hand-shaped limestone from nearby mountains in constructing the building. Willie Higdon, who worked on the building as a seventeen-year-old mortar mixer, became a local stonemason, and several local buildings, structures, and foundations are testimony to his craftsmanship.[9]

The Community Building served many audiences. It housed offices for local government, the public dental health program, the local Home Demonstration club, the local American Legion chapter, and after 1959 the county library. In 1991–92 the coordinator of the local adult education program,

Dunlap Community Building, Sequatchie County.

Susan Greer, led a movement to renovate the building in order to expand library services and improve the adult education center. When the community celebrated the renovated building in December 1992, ten of the original NYA workers—Wiley L. Harmon, Estel Seals, Ray Harmon, Nevan Carlton, Jack Hogue, Willie Higdon, James Ewton, Walter Spangler, Harley Martin, and Grady Kerley—attended the dedication. The building was listed in the National Register of Historic Places in 1994.

SHELBY COUNTY
National Guard Armory (1941-43), 2525 Central Avenue, Memphis

This large complex of buildings, located adjacent to the Mid-South Stadium, is now home to the Children's Museum of Memphis. Designed by Walk C. Jones and Walk C. Jones Jr., in association with Herbert M. Burnham and Lucian M. Dent, the former Memphis Armory is a forceful example of Art Deco–influenced WPA Modern design. Attention is focused on its central building, which has a large American eagle with an American flag banner in at its center. Flanking the central building are Assembly Hall and the Administration Building. The large WPA-constructed complex includes other structures and support buildings, which are unified as whole by the use of a particular New Deal manner of building with concrete. As architectural historians Eugene Johnson and Robert D. Russell Jr. point out, the buildings were "cast using horizontal wooden shuttering and allow the concrete to ooze out between the shuttering boards to create a strong surface texture. This is common enough nowadays, but almost no-one was doing it in the thirties and early forties, except the builders of TVA dams."[10]

In the flood of 1937, the armory and the adjacent Fairview Junior High School (1930) and Mid-South Fairgrounds became the center of local relief efforts for thousands of dispossessed farmers and tenants. As many as fifty to sixty thousand refugees received services at the fairgrounds. Fairview school was one of twelve schools across the city turned into a hospital for the refugees.

SHELBY COUNTY
Orange Mound Day Nursery (1941), Campus of Melrose High School, 2870 Deadrick Avenue, Memphis

In 1941 sociologist Shubael T. Beasley, of LeMoyne College, conducted a study of working-class women in the Orange Mound neighborhood. She concluded that a nursery school would help these women better their incomes and improve the educational development of their children. To support the school, Beasley contacted several civic groups, including the Orange Mound Civic Club, the board of education, the Memphis section of National Council of Jewish Women, and the WPA. Later that year, the nursery school opened in portable buildings on the Melrose High School campus, with thirty-five children in attendance.

The program survived the end of WPA and expanded during the war years. Today the Orange Mound Community Day Care Center (1971), at Grand Street and Saratoga Avenue, continues the original New Deal mission of daycare service to working families and their preschool children.

SHELBY COUNTY
U.S. Marine Hospital (1933-37), 374 Metal Museum Drive, Memphis

These Classical Revival buildings, resplendent with their two-story classical porticoes, possess a commanding view of the Mississippi River and are across the street from DeSoto Park in downtown Memphis. It is now home to the National Ornamental Metal Museum. The U.S. Public Health Service established the original facility in 1884 as the city's first modern hospital. Its services were open to government employees who held marine or waterways jobs. Construction of new additions to the hospital began in 1933, but the bulk of the buildings were completed with WPA work crews after 1935. Like the fairgrounds and National Guard Armory, the grounds and buildings of the Marine Hospital were in heavy use during the Flood of 1937. The hospital provided services to injured and sick refugees. Over eight thousand refugees required hospitalization in Memphis, taxing both public and private facilities.

Various architects are associated with the hospital buildings. Treasury architect Louis A. Simon, for example, designed the south wing, impressive for its Doric portico on its south facade. The north wing dates to 1933, designed by architects Regan and Weller. The hospital closed in 1966.

SULLIVAN COUNTY

Kingsport Civic Auditorium and Armory (1938–40), 1550 Fort Henry Drive, Kingsport

The first major Depression-era public works project in Kingsport was a community hospital, built with local donations and major financial support from the Commonwealth Fund of New York State. The first major PWA-funded building project was an Art Deco–styled Civic Auditorium and Armory, built with a PWA grant of $97,510 and $125,000 from the city in the late 1930s. Allen N. Dryden Sr. was the architect of this impressive buff brick and Indiana limestone structure. With a capacity of just over 2,000 people, the auditorium immediately became Kingsport's center for the arts and community events. The Duke Ellington Orchestra once played there at a white-only dance after World War II. In September 1955, Elvis Presley performed on its stage. The armory was headquarters for the 191st Field Artillery of the Tennessee National Guard.

Kingsport Civic Auditorium and Armory, Sullivan County.

4

Schools

From 1933 to 1942, New Deal agencies repaired, renovated, and built from the ground up hundreds of public schools across Tennessee. While the Tennessee Emergency Relief Administration and the Civil Works Administration undertook several schools projects in 1933–34, the vast majority of New Deal schools may be attributed to the Public Works Administration and the Works Progress Administration. Kenneth Markwell, state PWA director, reported that between 1933 and 1935 alone the PWA spent $7.4 million on public schools, providing new facilities for some 75,000 students. He claimed that it was "the largest single program of school building ever undertaken in Tennessee."[1] Tennessee communities, however, had undertaken their own efforts to build "modern," often consolidated, schools for white children in the 1920s. The Julius Rosenwald Fund also provided funding for the construction of over 300 new schools for African Americans from the late 1910s to the early 1930s.

PWA officials saw their agency picking up where these efforts had ended or slowed due to the worsening depression. From 1933 to late 1938, the agency provided grants for 5,406 schools nationwide. Another agency survey reported that in Tennessee, two-thirds of these grants were for the construction of new schools. And federal officials believed that these new schools were built to the highest possible standards. The PWA "left the schools free to plan their educational programs, but at the same time by giving them the money which made possible the type of building which every progressive school wants, it helped to spread knowledge of, and interest in, the modern type of school building."[2] The result, in PWA eyes, was better schools, with the best having both gymnasiums and auditoriums. In the town of Dyer, a small, rural trade center in northern Gibson County, the PWA in 1938 built a modern high school, complete with library, laboratories, gymnasium, cafeteria, and auditorium. It served as the high school until 1980 and became the middle school in 1986. The agency itself highlighted its Colonial Revival design for the all-black Hyde Park school in Memphis in its book *Public Buildings*. Monroe County, nestled against the Cherokee National Forest, received new high schools at Vonroe (1935–37), Tellico Plains (1938), and Madisonville (1938–39), in addition to two athletic fields. Hickman County, in Middle Tennessee, received almost thirty-six thousand dollars in grants and another forty thousand dollars in loans from the PWA for new school facilities.

The huge school program of the WPA began in 1935. Of all of the agency's public building efforts, constructing new schools received the highest priority. As W. Burr Cullom of the state WPA office explained, "[F]unds allocated for schools, which include the erection of new buildings, the remodeling and repairing of old ones, the beautifying of campuses and the improvement of athletic fields, amount to many times the combined estimates for similar work on other public buildings."[3] When Cullom looked back at his program in 1938, he expressed particular pride in the federal, state, and local partnership inherent in the successful funding and construction of the schools. "These coworkers," remarked Cullom, "know that from the fearful despondency that gripped a nation have come hope and cheer. They have seen great public works rise from broken lives, and like the lily of poesy whose head of beauty is lifted from the muck and slime of the marsh, they have seen the 'face' of the school system of the state 'lifted,' at least a little, from the ugliness and mire of the depression."[4]

As of June 30, 1938, the WPA had achieved much: 123 new schools and 480 renovated schools statewide. The agency's projects transformed the physical plant of public education in several counties. The WPA in Greene County, for example, added schools at Chuckey, Mount Carmel, Chestnut Ridge, and Hardin's View, while building a gym at Ottway.

Another important school-building agency not so often recognized was the National Youth Administration, a program launched specifically to keep teenage and college-age children in school. In Tennessee, the NYA provided deserving students with financial support, funded various school programs and teacher aides, and taught youths to build schools, libraries, mechanical arts shops, and other educational and community buildings. The program was especially active in plateau counties. For example, eleven buildings were attributed to the NYA in Jackson County, while in Scott County the agency in 1936 funded an agricultural building and began construction of a football stadium at Oneida. At the tiny county seat of Spencer, the NYA literally built the first public Van Buren County High School from the ground up between 1938 and 1939.

Typically constructed with brick and concrete, schools of the New Deal agencies included more than modern classroom space, but often came with gymnasiums and athletic fields to improve children's physical fitness, newly constructed lunch rooms and cafeterias to better children's nutrition, and auditoriums to improve cultural life in the community. Combination gymnasiums and auditoriums were built in such places as Linden in Perry County and Decaturville in Decatur County. Like a NYA project at Whitwell, in Marion County, school grounds and landscaping also were improved at both the new schools and at existing schools, which, in turn, were renovated or expanded. These efforts to improve the educational setting, according to a WPA official, often led "to an infectious movement in the neighborhood that brought like efforts to improve nearby homes. This, in itself, is a healthy, wholesome indication that 'sprucing up is catching,' and that it pays finer dividends than money alone offers."[5]

The federal programs also provided funds for new textbooks and increased library collections substantially at both existing schools and New Deal–built schools. Public schools across the state also became staging grounds for different federal cultural programs in music, theater, crafts, and fine arts as well as ambitious federal programs in adult education. New Deal reformers, like their counterparts of the Progressive Era documented by historian Mary S. Hoffschwelle, learned that schools were an effective entering wedge into the homes and lives of rural and urban Tennesseans.[6]

The architecture of the schools by New Deal agencies was functional and progressive, generally following the standardized plans developed in tandem by the Julius Rosenwald Fund, Peabody College professor Fletcher B. Dresslar, and the state Department of Education during the 1920s. Unilateral lighting provided by batteries of windows, closed foundations, sanitary privies, water fountains, and simple, functional design characterized most of the schools. Many were built of frame, while larger consolidated schools were built of brick. In several communities, however, agencies built in locally available stone, not only for the attractive appearance but also because by cutting and shaping the stone, more men were put to work on the projects. In their architectural style, the schools usually were of Colonial Revival, Classical Revival, or PWA Modern design.

Reflecting an inherent hope in the future, the new schools with their better equipment and facilities were places of community pride, especially in the state's small towns and rural areas. Large numbers of the schools remain in use today, meaning that this facet of the New Deal built environment has shaped the educational experiences of at least three generations of Tennesseans.

Caryville School, Campbell County.

CAMPBELL COUNTY
Caryville School (1938), U.S. Highway 441 at Interstate I-75, Caryville

The Public Works Administration featured this Colonial Revival–styled school in its book, *Public Buildings* (1940). Located near the Caryville Dam and Cove Lake State Park, the building replaced a two-story brick school of 1914 that was lost to the waters of Cove Lake in 1936. The PWA school still serves the community, its exterior having changed little in the last sixty years. It was initially a consolidated elementary and high school, with nine classrooms, a well-equipped science lab, a modern home economics room, a library, and a large combination gymnasium/auditorium. Its project cost was $76,930. In addition to Caryville school, the PWA built eight other schools and repaired four others in Campbell County.

CARTER COUNTY
Elizabethton High School (1939–41), West E Street, Elizabethon

Now the city middle school, the Elizabethton High School was a traditional yet progressive school building: traditional in its Colonial Revival style and symmetry; progressive in that its projecting end wings comprised an auditorium and a gymnasium. The school remained the city high school until 1971. TERA and WPA in Carter County also built rural masonry schools at Pierce and New Buffalo in 1934–35.

DAVIDSON COUNTY
Bailey Junior High and Elementary School Addition (1938–40), 2000 Greenwood Avenue, Nashville

In 1938 the city of Nashville and the Public Works Administration launched a major school building project, which took $2.894 million to build eight new schools, construct three additions to existing schools, and make improvements at thirty-two other facilities. The project's supervising architects were Hart, Freeland, and Roberts of Nashville, but other architects and/or firms designed most of the buildings. The different architects meant that the schools varied somewhat in architectural style, but all had "fire resistive construction, acoustical treatment, hardwood floors, radio and public address systems, and are fully equipped with the most up-to-date, comfortable, and useful types of equipment."[7]

The Bailey school was one of the three renovated buildings in the PWA project of 1938–40. It received a new gymnasium and elementary classroom wing, designed in a compatible Classical Revival style by Nashville architects Dougherty, Clemmons and Seale.

DAVIDSON COUNTY
Cameron Junior High and Elementary School (1939–1940), 1034 First Avenue South, Nashville

Designed by Nashville architect Henry C. Hibbs in a restrained interpretation of Gothic Revival style, Cameron was a PWA school for African Americans. It stands adjacent to the former south Nashville campus of the Meharry Medical College. In 1954 officials expanded the school to include a new senior high school for African Americans. The school gained a reputation for excellence in its choir, marching band, athletic teams, and student theater productions, all of which were encouraged and well served by the school's athletic fields and modern auditorium. Cameron was integrated in 1971.

DAVIDSON COUNTY
Eakin School (1935-36), 2400 Fairfax Avenue, Nashville

With its square Doric classical colonnade and courtyard creating an impressive entrance, the Eakin School is an excellent example of PWA Modern design from the Nashville firm of Tisdale and Pinson. This firm also designed a similarly styled PWA elementary school in faraway Union City, Tennessee. Eakin was one of Nashville's early New Deal projects; the PWA program constructed thirteen schools for approximately two million dollars from 1933 to 1935. The school was named in honor of Mrs. John Hill Eakin, the first woman member of the Nashville City School Board of Education and a founder of the Centennial Club.

DAVIDSON COUNTY
Fisk University (1935-39), 1000 Seventeenth Avenue North, Nashville

New Deal agencies rarely carried out building projects on private university campuses, but at Fisk University, New Deal programs benefited several departments. For example, in 1935, officials renovated the university's "Old Barracks," buildings left from the origins of Fisk in the aftermath of the Civil War, into a new university theater. Other federal monies went to the establishment of the Fisk University Social Settlement in 1937. This program, under the direction of notable sociologist Charles S. Johnson, provided educational and recreational programs to the surrounding African American residents. The Public Works Administration also funded Johnson's various survey projects of social, economic, and health conditions among rural blacks in the South while the Department of Interior financed Johnson's urban study on the training of white collar and skilled black labor in the region.

DAVIDSON COUNTY
Howard Junior and Senior High School (1938-40), 802 Second Avenue South, Nashville

Art Deco detailing and a sweeping horizontal mass along a busy city street highlight the modernist influences apparent in the design of Howard Junior and Senior High School, which was funded by the PWA. Hart, Freeland, and Roberts of Nashville were the architects. Located in the Rutledge Hill neighborhood, the school stands in front of the historic Literary Department building of the University of Nashville. Both buildings, however, no longer function as schools; rather they are offices for the Metropolitan Nashville government.

DAVIDSON COUNTY

Lockeland Elementary School (1939), South Seventeenth Street, Nashville

Another of the PWA projects from 1938 to 1940, the present Lockeland Middle School stands on the old Lockeland Springs estate of the Weakley family in east Nashville. C. K. Colley and Son of Nashville provided a graceful yet understated Tudor Revival design for the building, perhaps best expressed in the school entrance. Later additions of classrooms in the 1940s and 1961 give the building its present appearance.

DAVIDSON COUNTY

Pearl High School (1936–37), 613 Seventeenth Avenue North, Nashville

Now known as the Martin Luther King Magnet School, the historic Pearl High School was a cultural, educational, and athletic center for the large African American community of north Nashville from its PWA-funded construction in the late 1930s until the end of its days as a black-only school in 1971.

When it opened in 1937, Pearl High School was "considered one of the most modern, best constructed, and well-equipped buildings for Negroes in the South."[8] Designed by the African American firm of McKissack and McKissack, the school was certainly the most modernist in style of the city's New Deal schools, with the facade's stripped classicism highlighted by creative, abstract grillwork in an Art Deco manner above the central entrance. The new school contained modern laboratories, a library, and an auditorium, which was used often for school functions and public events. In 1945–46, city officials added a vocational education building to the complex. In 1964 came a new gymnasium, a belated recognition of the school's excellent basketball teams. The school is listed in the National Register of Historic Places.

DAVIDSON COUNTY
Tennessee State University (1935-37), 3500 John Merritt Boulevard, Nashville

In 1935 the WPA allocated over $143,000 for various construction and school supply projects at Tennessee State University, the officially segregated African American land grant institution in Tennessee. Another $75,000 in local funds were raised in support of the WPA projects. There was a major landscaping project, including the construction of a hand-laid stone fence of which parts remain. The WPA also built the university's initial football stadium and track field. In the years afterward, TSU became nationally renowned for its excellent football teams, with several star players having successful careers in the National Football League. The university became internationally renowned for its track-and-field program, especially the Tigerbelles Women's Track Club, coached by Ed Temple. Wilma Rudolph, Wyomia Tyus, and Barbara Jones were among the Olympic medal winners from TSU.

DAVIDSON COUNTY
Walter Stokes School (1935), 3701 Belmont Boulevard, Nashville

The Walter Stokes School is an attractive Colonial Revival design, with a central two-story portico entrance, set within the white middle-class suburbs of the Hillsboro-Belmont historic district. Originally the school had ten classrooms and a cafeteria; four additional classrooms and a "cafetorium" were completed in 1950-51. Built by the WPA, the school is named for Walter Stokes, a local resident who donated the original school lot in 1908.

DAVIDSON COUNTY
West End High School (1935-37), 3529 West End Avenue, Nashville

The West End High School is a superb example of Colonial Revival design by the notable Nashville architect Donald Southgate; the school's soaring 122-foot-high cupola is a west Nashville landmark. When the PWA-funded school was finished, some city officials wanted to name the school in honor of Mayor Hillary Howse, but that designation aroused controversy and the school's name instead acknowledges its location within the city.

The school's horizontal, three-story central block and cupola serve as the focus of a large landscaped city lot along busy West End Avenue, making the

West End High School, Nashville.

school an impressive statement of the place of public education in American culture. The traditionalism of the school's exterior, however, masked a progressive institution, stocked with the latest in technology and hardware. The school began with 35 classrooms, with 8 designated as science labs. It had a large library, cafeteria, gymnasium, and a modern auditorium, complete with a 63-by-28-foot stage. Thus, the school served that broader New Deal audience of children and their parents with various musical performances, theater plays, and public lectures.

DEKALB COUNTY

Liberty Elementary School (1939), Main at College Street, Liberty

Built with locally hand-cut and -shaped stone and located behind the town's earlier masonry high school, Liberty was one of three WPA schools built in DeKalb County during 1939. Projecting classroom wings on the east and west flanked a central section of administrative offices and an auditorium. Square stone posts supporting a pediment give the building a hint of Colonial Revival style. This type of H-plan was very popular in the state, having first gained acceptance by school boards in the 1920s. The school is part of the National Register–listed Liberty historic district.

FAYETTE COUNTY

Somerville Public School (1935–36), South Main Street, Somerville

From 1933 to 1935 the PWA spent over one hundred thousand dollars on new public schools in Fayette County, including this brick building located at the county seat of Somerville. Like many of the PWA designs for rural towns, the school reflects Colonial Revival style, with its symmetrical facade, classical portico entrance, and cupola. The school is an important twentieth-century contribution to Somerville's National Register–listed historic district.

FENTRESS COUNTY

Agricultural Building at York Institute (1935), U.S. Highway 127, Jamestown

Named in honor of a World War I hero, and later institute principal, the Alvin C. York Agricultural Institute is the only public school that is operated by the state. State funds combined with federal dollars and local support to raise the agricultural building for the school in 1935. Built from ashlar cut sandstone in a modified H-plan, the Agricultural Building was for the teaching of home economics and the latest in progressive farming techniques. It is part of the York Institute historic district, listed in the National Register of Historic Places.

GILES COUNTY

Puncheon School and Community Fruit House (1940–41), Puncheon Road, Minor Hill vicinity

The Giles County school board, with New Deal support, undertook a major program of school building and renovation in the late 1930s. New frame schools were built for such rural communities as Puncheon and Yokley. Modern brick consolidated schools were built in the county seat of Pulaski and at Beech Hill. Of the four schools, only the frame buildings remain, and both have been converted to new uses. The Yokley school is now a crossroads grocery store. The Pucheon school is a private residence west of the community of Minor Hill in southern Giles County. Behind the house is one of the state's unique WPA structures, a community "fruit house," which provided storage for the school's former school lunch program. In an article for the *Tennessee Teacher* in January 1942, Robert Townsend and Louise Binkley explained that the school needed cool storage for surplus government commodities as well as one thousand quarts of fruits and vegetables canned in the summer by a WPA worker, students, and parents. "We conceived the idea of building the needed cellar beneath a huge rock that jutted from a hillside near the school building," Townsend and Binkley remarked. Then an experienced stone mason taught the boys "how to mix mortar and how to point the walls. The boys then built rock steps leading to the doorway and a rock retaining wall. . . . The girls shared the work by labeling the cans of fruits and vegetables and arranging them on the shelves."[9] The resulting fruit house measured thirty feet by seven feet by six feet—certainly not large, but a functional building constructed by the students themselves. Binkley and Townsend noted that seventy-eight teachers from other Giles County schools had recently visited to see the fruit house and Puncheon's work for their school lunch program. The property now is privately owned and should not be entered without permission.

GRUNDY COUNTY
Grundy County High School (1935), U.S. Highway 41, Tracy City

Due to its overdependence on mining and the timber industry, Grundy County was particularly hard hit by the Great Depression. On a hillside northwest of town is the historic Grundy County High School, the primary section of which was built with over ninety thousand dollars in PWA funds after an earlier school building burned in 1935. Stone quoins and a dignified classical entrance on its west facade highlight the two-story brick building. The school's new auditorium and gymnasium quickly became popular community gathering places for plays, musical performances, dances, and athletic events.

HAMILTON COUNTY
Bachman Elementary School (1937), 2815 Anderson Pike, Signal Mountain

Located on the historic Anderson Pike, the Nathan L. Bachman Elementary School is a one-story Colonial Revival–style building, designed by the Chattanooga architectural firm R. H. Hunt and Company and built by Nashville contractor R. M. Condra for a total project cost of over fifty-six thousand dollars. The school features a large, approximately four-hundred-seat auditorium, which was designed to host both school and community events. The auditorium is also designed in a Colonial fashion with large classical pilasters flanking the stage. Other PWA-funded projects designed in a similar fashion in Hamilton County included the Bess T. Shepherd School and the New Ganns-Middle Valley Elementary School.

HAMILTON COUNTY
East Side Junior High School (1939 addition), 2200 East Main Street, Chattanooga

Acknowledged as the first junior high in the southern states, the National Register–listed East Side Junior High School dates to 1917. A generation later, school officials turned to the WPA to support the addition of a domestic arts and study hall wing in 1939.

HAMILTON COUNTY
Public and University Library Building (1938–39), University of Tennessee at Chattanooga, McCallie Avenue, Chattanooga

Facing the main thoroughfare of McCallie Avenue is this three-story red brick Collegiate Gothic library building, which exhibits high craftsmanship both in the exterior and interior. Originally funded in part with a PWA grant of $134,000, the library was initially a joint public and university library; the university wing opened in January 1940. This arrangement met well the goals of administrators, such as Alexander Guerry, who believed that the college needed to offer more public programs. The university's public affairs institute of 1934, for example, featured lectures by the three TVA directors—Arthur Morgan, Harcourt Morgan, and David Lilienthal—as well as Secretary of Labor Frances Perkins. Historian Gilbert E. Govan became library director in 1934 and served there until 1962. The PWA building remained the college's primary library until 1973–74, when the University of Tennessee at Chattanooga, established through a merger in 1969, opened a new facility, later named the Lupton Library.

HAMILTON COUNTY
James A. Henry Resource Center (1936–37), Grove Street, Chattanooga

Nestled by the PWA's College Hill Courts public housing project (see chapter 5) is this distinguished two-story Colonial Revival–style school building, a photograph of which is highlighted in the PWA's *Public Buildings* (1940). Originally named the "West Side Elementary School for Colored," the once segregated facility now houses the James A. Henry Resource Center, which serves as a community hub for local residents, and is a successful renovation project sponsored by the Westside Community Development Corporation. The original cupola of the school has been removed, but its impressive projecting central block, with the entrance defined by classical pilasters supporting a Palladian-influenced broken pediment, remains intact. Constructed between 1936 and 1937 for a total project cost of $118,053, the PWA viewed the school as a vast improvement in elementary education for African American children in Chattanooga. The new school consolidated thirteen previously existing schools and included individual rooms for a library, "handicraft" education, and a clinic.

HAMILTON COUNTY
Chattanooga School for the Arts and Sciences (1935 additions), 865 East Third Street, Chattanooga

Listed in the National Register, the former Chattanooga High School, built in 1920–21, is a handsome interpretation of Colonial Revival architecture, designed by the respected Chattanooga architect Reuben H. Hunt. In the mid-1930s, PWA undertook a major project to update and improve public education in Chattanooga and Hamilton County. Between 1933 and 1935, the PWA alone spent $1,231,071 on thirteen schools in Chattanooga and another $1,272,727 on thirteen additional schools in the county. Hunt received the commission to expand the original city high school with two compatible wings. The building remained in use as a city high school until 1983 and is now a magnet school.

HANCOCK COUNTY
Hancock County Consolidated Public School (1935–36), Sneedville

The Hancock County High and Elementary School was the primary PWA project in this rural Appalachian county. Designed by Knoxville architect Allen N. Dryden, who had designed the county courthouse in 1930, the attractive Colonial Revival–styled, one-story brick school overlooks the small town of Sneedville. A slightly projecting center section contains a pedimented entrance supported by Doric pilasters. A carefully crafted wooden cupola with weather vane tops the metal gable roof. The PWA put forth $85,455 for the school; the Fiske-Carter Construction Company was the builder.

HANCOCK COUNTY
Mathis Elementary School Lunchroom (c. 1937), Tennessee Highway 33, Sneedville vicinity

In the late 1930s the WPA built an unadorned, one-story frame gable-front lunchroom and kitchen for the Mathis school. Both the school and the lunchroom remain standing today, representing landmarks to public education in the rural countryside.

HOUSTON COUNTY

Stewart High School (1937 additions), Tennessee Highway 147, Stewart

In this small village along the boundary between Houston and Stewart counties is a large H-shaped frame school that is still used as a community center. The Stewart High School dates to 1928 and is the oldest school building in Houston County. The building was initially part of the state's effort to improve rural schools in the 1920s. In 1937 WPA work crews added the building's west wing and dug a basement under the school auditorium.

JOHNSON COUNTY

Johnson County High School Shop (1939), Old Johnson County High School, Mountain City

Behind the early-twentieth-century Johnson County High School, which now houses various county government offices, is a one-story concrete shop building, erected by NYA boys in 1939. The fluted pilasters of the entrance

Johnson County High School Shops, Mountain City.

have a vaguely Art Deco look; not all NYA projects exhibit the best available craftsmanship. Mechanical arts shops were favorite NYA projects because officials assumed that within the walls teenagers would learn an employable skill or a trade.

KNOX COUNTY
Corryton School (1936), Corryton

Located in north Knox County, this brick, one-story, rural school is a good representative example of the standardized school architecture built by the WPA. Although a later portico entrance takes away from the original design of architect Frank O. Barber, the surviving cupola and symmetrical fenestration of the building evokes Colonial Revival style. The construction supervisor was Fain V. Cluck.

KNOX COUNTY
Tyson Junior High School (1936–38), 2607 Kingston Pike, Knoxville

Designed by the well-respected Knoxville firm of Baumann and Baumann, with Albert B. Baumann Jr. as project architect, Tyson Junior High School is an

Corryton School, Knox County.

excellent example of PWA Modern style in its blending of Neoclassical forms with Art Deco elements. Between 1933 and 1935, the PWA began its Knoxville program of school construction with just over one million dollars for ten school projects; subsequent federal support helped the school board to upgrade its facilities significantly during the decade. At Tyson, officials took part of this money and built the first phase of the school in 1936, with a total project cost of approximately $180,000. The second phase was completed in 1938 at a cost of $106,000. Of the PWA–funded projects in Knoxville, Tyson, Eastport School, Maynard School, and Griffin School still stood in 1998.

Tyson Junior High is named for Gen. Lawrence D. Tyson, a veteran of the Spanish-American War and World War I who was chosen as U.S. senator. It served as a junior high, then a middle school, until it closed in 1986. At one time seemingly left for ruin, the National Register–listed building has recently been renovated with historic preservation tax credits into an office complex.

KNOX COUNTY

University of Tennessee campus (1933–37), South Cumberland Avenue, Knoxville

The University of Tennessee, which had just experienced a major expansion in facilities during the late 1920s and early 1930s, received additional buildings from different New Deal agencies. On "the Hill" surrounding Ayers Hall came the Austin Peay Building (remodeled later into offices for the psychology program) as well as the Hesler Biology building, designed in 1935 by the Knoxville firm of Barber and McMurry. The PWA put up over four hundred thousand dollars for the new buildings, which were designed in a restrained Collegiate Gothic style, as well as additional buildings at the university farm. There was little surprise that the agency turned to Barber and McMurry as the architects since the firm already had completed four major new buildings on the campus. Moreover, by 1935 the firm's Charles Barber was the chief architect of the Tennessee Valley Authority. In June 1936, the PWA also granted $166,909 for the construction of two new dormitories.

LINCOLN COUNTY

Petersburg Grammar School (1939), 400 College Street, Petersburg

After a 1938 fire destroyed Elizabeth College (established 1894), the PWA cleared the school lot and built a new grammar school. Compared with other PWA schools in rural towns, which often are either of Colonial Revival style or of PWA Modern style, this building is a little bit of both. The long horizontal block, symmetrical fenestration, and central cupola are all in keeping with the spirit of the Colonial Revival, yet the concrete medallion over the central entrance evokes modern style. The total project cost was $73,000, of which the PWA provided $32,000. The building in 1998 was no longer in use as a school.

MAURY COUNTY
Spring Hill School (1936-37), School and Duplex Streets, Spring Hill

For most of the twentieth century, Spring Hill was a small rural trade town located between the larger county seats of Columbia and Franklin. In the late 1980s, however, came the opening of the General Motors Saturn automobile factory, and life soon changed in Spring Hill. The town's consolidated school, built by the WPA, closed in 1992 and students moved to a new, larger and more modern facility.

The school is now used for private business, but it retains much of its architectural presence, especially in the four brick pilasters with Doric capitals that define its central entrance. Several residents remember the old school with respect, even reverence, for the days when Spring Hill was a country town with community life and events centered on the school and the adjacent football field.

MONROE COUNTY
Madisonville High School (1937-39), 175 Oak Grove Road, Madisonville

In this Appalachian county, the PWA-funded new high schools at Vonroe, Tellico Plains, and the county seat of Madisonville. The former Madisonville high school cost approximately $34,500, out of which the PWA gave the county a grant of $15,500. Now used as the city middle school, the red brick building reflects minimal Colonial Revival styling in its symmetrical facade.

MONTGOMERY COUNTY
Clarksville High School (c. 1935 addition), Greenwood Avenue, Clarksville

The historic Clarksville High School, which is listed in the National Register of Historic Places, was converted into apartments and condominiums in the 1980s. During the New Deal, the high school not only received $52,470 in PWA funds for additions and renovations, it also was a location for adult education programs for the city of Clarksville. CCC enrollees from a nearby camp, for instance, took night classes at the school. The biggest effort for adult education came under the auspices of the WPA as an important part of its efforts to reform and uplift the country. Agency officials especially wanted "to teach functional literacy to as many as possible before the 1940 census." The WPA hired classroom teachers, sponsored guest lecturers, and used motion pictures. Indeed, the innovative motion picture program, under the supervision of E. R. Lingerfelt, state director of the WPA division of education, used free films to capture a regular audience for the night classes. As Burr Cullom argued, such program creativity was a necessity to attack the problem of widespread illiteracy. "In their present condition," he asserted, illiterate Tennesseans were "at once a drag, a load, and a menace to the nation, and provide a fertile field for subversive 'isms.'"[10]

OBION COUNTY
Central Elementary School (1936), 512 East College Street, Union City

Designed by the Nashville firm of Tisdale and Pinson, the modernist blending of classicism and Art Deco at Central Elementary School placed the PWA landmark at odds with the more conservative public and commercial architecture of the town. The effect was intentional; local reformers took pride in stressing "how modern and convenient the building is."[11] Among its virtues, they counted its fireproof construction, circulation flow, ample light and air, structural insulation, sound proofing, sanitary floors, attractive furniture, drinking fountains, modern plumbing, and its auditorium. NYA work groups built most of the building's original furniture. In Union City a NYA training center taught approximately two hundred students in wood- and metalworking; student projects furnished local government offices and the schools. In 1976 school officials expanded the building with classroom wings on either end. Nominated for listing in the National Register of Historic Places, Central School continues to serve elementary children in Union City.

OBION COUNTY
Union City High School (1936–39), 1111 High School Drive, Union City

After demolishing the existing brick three-story high school as part of its Central Elementary School project, the PWA immediately began construction of a large high school complex on the southern outskirts of town. Now the city's middle school, the new city high school was a PWA Modern–styled, one-story brick building with outstanding recreational facilities for a small county seat, including a large auditorium and a football field.

These recreational buildings almost immediately became the staging grounds for a new federal project. In 1939 Obion County was selected as one of the four national demonstration centers for the "Home and Family Life" education program. The other communities were Box Elder County, Colorado, Wichita, Kansas, and Toledo, Ohio. A pilot program of the federal Office of Education, "Home and Family Life" had a simple but ambitious goal: "to demonstrate the fact that a community is capable of discovering its needs in family living and of setting up the means and procedures for meeting them."[12] The project involved not only the schools, but the health de-

Obion County High School Gymnasium, Union City.

partment, various state agencies, and community groups, such as the Farm Bureau, Parent-Teacher Associations, and a county youth council.

In Obion County, an early emphasis was placed on improved night recreational programs in order to improve family and community relations. Two county officials reported: "[T]he school grounds are being lighted for evening programs, and facilities for a wide variety of games and other activities provided for all age groups. About ten such programs have been held, attended by a large group with enthusiastic participation and interest." This federal initiative built upon earlier WPA adult education programs, but went a step further. As the county superintendent and director of education asserted, "[W]e believe parent education consists not alone in parent education classes, but in a wide program of parent activity designed to inform parents thoroughly in the whole of life, its responsibilities and activities."[13]

It is not clear how much of the federal program extended to the county's numerous African American schools, four of which had been constructed with support from the Julius Rosenwald Fund during the 1920s. The Miles School in Union City, for instance, received a new gymnasium in 1934, probably funded by the CWA and TERA. It was the likely location of night recreational programs in the black community.

OVERTON COUNTY
Alpine Institute School and Gym (1935–39), Tennessee Highway 52, Alpine

Alpine is a small rural community located east of Livingston, near the border of Fentress County. Alpine Institute was a settlement school, with its roots dating to missionary work by Dr. John L. Dillard in 1821. At first the Cumberland Presbyterian church supported the school, but it was destroyed during the Civil War, then rebuilt, but later burned by the Ku Klux Klan. It reopened in 1880, but the remains of the complex there today, however, belong to the twentieth century and the 1917 effort of Board of the National Missions of the Presbyterian Church U.S.A. to establish and maintain a settlement school for area children. *The WPA Guide to Tennessee* noted that "today (1938) classes meet in a gray stone building on a 100-acre farm. It is a self-help school, and students maintain the property. The boys farm; the girls cook and serve the meals, take care of the dormitory, and do the laundry work."[14]

The educators at Alpine Institute wanted to teach local children the modern, progressive ways of farming; reformers believed that meant the men produced the crops and the women produced the home. The strict division of labor

Alpine Gymnasium, Overton County.

described here, of course, was at odds with the reality of rural life in Overton and Fentress Counties, where typically families worked together in all aspects of producing farm products and crops. This difference between the goals of rural reformers and the realities of relationships between families, their communities, and their farms is one reason why settlement schools had a mixed record in rural Tennessee. In her research in the Upper Cumberland region indicates, for example, historian Jeanette Keith has found that the "school reformers hoped that education would be the first foundation stone of a whole series of reforms," but local residents usually accepted only those reforms that fit established ways.[15]

The WPA built an H-shaped Crab Orchard stone school at Alpine in 1935; the following year this school became a public school within the Overton County system. Three years later, the agency also built a Crab Orchard stone-veneer gymnasium, used by both elementary and high school students. The first basketball team at Alpine dates to 1922; the new gym finally gave the team a decent place to practice and play their games. The Presbyterians continued to operate the "grey stone" high school mentioned above until 1946, when it too became part of the Overton County public schools. Both schools are now closed, but the beautiful Gothic Revival–styled Alpine Presbyterian Church continues to serve the community and marks the Presbyterian commitment to the area.

Oak Grove School, Overton County.

OVERTON COUNTY
Oak Grove School (1935-36), Tennessee Highway 52, east of Livingston

At the same time that the WPA constructed the elementary school at Alpine, it also built this well-maintained Crab Orchard stone elementary school at Oak Grove, a rural community located about halfway between Livingston and Alpine. An excellent example of a Rosenwald school plan used for a rural white-only school, the building is now home to the Oak Grove Missionary Baptist Church.

PUTNAM COUNTY
Gentry School (1934), U.S. Highway 70N, Gentry

In 1934 TERA built two rural schools at Double Springs and Gentry in Putnam County for a total of ninety-five hundred dollars. The Gentry School is an attractive, one-story brick building still in use as the Gentry Community Center. "New Deal programs improved education in Putnam County," asserted historian Mary J. DeLozier. "The NYA trained approximately two thousand high school students in construction, carpentry, metalworking, secretarial skills, and home economics. Other agencies hired unemployed teachers to organize public

SCHOOLS 119

Gentry School, Putnam County.

school music and recreation programs, initiated night classes for CCC enlistees and other adults . . . , and paid workers to copy public records for preservation."[16] The WPA also operated a successful and popular school lunch program in the county.

African Americans in Cookeville also saw their schools benefit from New Deal efforts. The Julius Rosenwald Fund in 1927-28 supported the construction of Cookeville's West Side School. In the spring of 1935 TERA paid four workers to paint the school. The following year the school was expanded to a high school, serving grades one through twelve. At that time, the school was renamed Darwin School, after J. Claude Darwin, a white businessman who supported black high school education. Darwin had a large and positive impact on black education in the Upper Cumberland. It was the region's only African American high school, and students were bused in from White, Overton, and Clay Counties to attend classes. Darwin School, concluded historian Wali R. Kharif, "provided an outlet for participation in activities and organizations. It was also an important social center for fostered a sense of community among blacks in the Upper Cumberland region."[17]

PUTNAM COUNTY

Tennessee Technological University (1933-37), Cookeville

Three New Deal agencies—CWA, TERA, and WPA—combined monies and labor between 1933 and 1935 to build a modern football stadium for Tennessee Technological College (now University), and soon thereafter attending the Saturday games of the "Golden Eagles" became a ritual for students and local residents alike. Due to the poverty of the surrounding counties during the depression, the college almost closed its doors. In the late 1930s NYA funding to keep students in school helped to keep the school open. Statewide in 1936-37, for instance, the NYA provided funds for 3,899 undergraduate and graduate students.

ROBERTSON COUNTY

Springfield High School (1938-39), 715 Fifth Avenue West, Springfield

The Tennessee Education Association considered the opening of the Springfield High School, now the location of the city middle school, to be one of the most important events of the New Deal era. It featured the school in a well-illustrated feature article in its May 1939 issue of the *Tennessee Teacher*. The new facility was a model complex in several ways. The concrete, brick, and steel building, designed by Nashville architects Hart and Russell, was notable for its exemplary lighting, its centralized public address system, and its modern rest rooms. It also contained all of the specialized classrooms and public spaces viewed as necessary in a progressive high school. These included a clinic, cafeteria, library, two special rooms for secretarial training, auditorium, music rooms, home economics rooms, two manual arts rooms, science labs, two agricultural training rooms, and an art room. "The cream and green art room is an innovation that most of our high schools have not included in their buildings," admitted H. C. Headden, the director of Schoolhouse Planning and Transportation for the Tennessee Department of Education. "The time has come, however, in our revised curriculum to survey the field and make provisions for open and original expression among the pupils of our school."[18]

Modernist yet restrained in its architectural styling, Springfield High School was located on the outskirts of downtown on a landscaped and terraced twenty-two-acre lot, with plenty of room for various recreational facilities and buildings. The total project cost was almost $290,000; the PWA supplied $130,500 of this total, along with the services of supervising engineer James Condon. State schoolhouse planning director Headden concluded that the physical plant of this school expressed "a new relationship of administrator to teacher, of teacher to pupils, and of school to community." Indeed, "in serving the children of the community, the school will be thought of more and more as an adjunct of nature."[19]

RUTHERFORD COUNTY

Almaville School (c. 1938), Spanntown Road, Almaville vicinity

Located on a narrow paved road west of the community of Almaville is a two-room, concrete-block school, now in private ownership, built by the WPA for African American children. The school replaced a one-room frame school that dated to 1919. It served as the local black school until integration in the mid-1960s.

RUTHERFORD COUNTY

E. C. Cox Memorial Gymnasium (1940), 105 Olive Street, Murfreesboro

The E. C. Cox Memorial Gymnasium is an Art Deco–inspired building that increased classroom space for the adjacent Crichlow Grammar School and gave the community a fine recreational center that contained both an auditorium stage and modern basketball court. The building honors E. C. Cox, who was the first superintendent of schools for the City of Murfreesboro from circa 1891 to 1904. The WPA supported city officials' efforts to build the gym in order to have better public recreational facilities and to expand athletic and physical education programs at Crichlow school. George D. Waller of Nashville, who designed Crichlow school in 1927, also was the architect of this National Register–listed gymnasium.

RUTHERFORD COUNTY

Middle Tennessee State University (1935–40), 1301 East Main Street, Murfreesboro

In the depression decade, the present Middle Tennessee State University was named State Teachers' College, Murfreesboro. The college experienced significant growth from the mid-1920s to the early 1930s in the number of students and in the size and quality of its physical plant. The depression stopped this growth and the number of students dropped significantly. Thus, during the New Deal, there were few new buildings funded except for the WPA's work on the football stadium, landscaping projects (the Bell Street entrance is partially extant), and the construction of an Industrial Arts Building by the NYA. Financial support from NYA proved crucial. An undated photograph at MTSU's Gore Center archives shows eighty students, posed to spell out NYA, on the steps of the college's Old Main building.

SEQUATCHIE COUNTY

Cagle School (1939), Tennessee Highway 8, Cagle

Cagle School is the only one of three NYA schools constructed in Sequatchie County to remain in public use. Located adjacent to Tennessee Highway 8 in the hamlet of Cagle, the stone school building has been expanded into a community center and fire station.

SEQUATCHIE COUNTY

Liberty School (1939, NYA), Old State Highway 28, Cartwright

Located at the southern tip of Sequatchie County is this finely crafted stone schoolhouse, built in 1939 by the same group of NYA workers who constructed the Dunlap Community Building. The school is Colonial Revival in style, with a symmetrical three-bay facade, two dormers on its gable roof, and a simple portico, with the wooden posts containing the carved words "Built By NYA 1939." Liberty school replaced a frame building that had been destroyed in a fire. It is now privately owned and used for storage.

According to a September 1939 count, Liberty was one of seventy-five schools across Tennessee constructed by NYA. "Youths employed on these projects," according to Bruce Overton, state NYA director, "are able to live at home in most cases, to secure fair wages for their part time work and to receive a most valuable work experience and training under skilled supervision on the job."[20]

SHELBY COUNTY
Collierville High School (1933–37), 146 College, Collierville

The impressive Classical Revival architecture of the Collierville High School, complete with its ornate corner entrance porticoes, large auditorium, and sunken garden, is an anomaly among extant New Deal schools in rural Tennessee towns. The project began with $250,000 in CWA funding in the winter of 1933–34 and became a TERA project in the spring of 1935. WPA workers finished the school and grounds in 1935–36, and the school opened in 1937. This important public building is within the Collierville historic district listed in the National Register of Historic Places.

SMITH COUNTY
Smith County High School (1940), College Street at High Street, Carthage

Carthage was the Tennessee home of Secretary of State Cordell Hull and New Deal congressman Albert Gore Sr. Their connections helped the county secure federal support for the construction of an Art Deco–styled high school and gymnasium, which opened in 1940. Before the building of the high school, PWA funding had brought improved city streets and a modern sewer system to Carthage.

Bristol Tennessee High School, Sullivan County.

SULLIVAN COUNTY

Tennessee High School (1937–39) and Bristol Municipal Stadium (1934–37), 1112 Edgemont Avenue, Bristol

A magnificent example of Colonial Revival style set within a New South industrial townscape, the Bristol Tennessee High School has been an educational and cultural landmark since its construction. An imposing portico of a classical pediment supported by two-story-high classical columns dominates its long horizontal brick facade. A Colonial-inspired cupola tops its gable roof while fanlights with keystones distinguish the entrance doors. Tennessee High ranks with West End School in Nashville as the best extant examples of Colonial Revival school architecture produced by New Deal agencies in the state.

Efforts to build the modern facility date to the summer of 1937 when Sen. Kenneth D. McKellar announced his support for a PWA grant for new schools, including a high school for Bristol. Tennessee High was viewed as a significant improvement in both its design and its programs. According to the student annual of 1940, those who attended the new high school were "really proud of Tennessee High School. The intellectual education is rounded by both social and physical development." In the article "Mary Pupil Praises Her New School," readers were taken through an ideal day of instruction, from morning devotional to French and English classes, on to

The Stone Castle, Bristol Tennessee High School, Sullivan County.

mathematics, civics, manual arts ("though shop is open to girls, it is generally studied by boys"), science, music, commercial courses, and occupations courses. The day closed with physical education, home economics ("for tomorrow's wives"), and drama.[21]

For bringing the new school to fruition, the local PTA gave the lion's share of credit to Bristol mayor Fred V. Vance and the city commissioners. Mayor Vance and Commissioner Arthur Green had been instrumental in bringing earlier New Deal projects to their Depression-ravaged community. Next door to the high school was their most popular achievement, the Bristol Municipal Stadium, known locally as the Stone Castle. The stadium takes its nickname from two sources: its heavy stone construction, largely local limestone produced by the city's first CWA project of flood control on Beaver Creek in 1933–34, and from its architectural details of towers, battlements, arches, crenelated walls, and heavy wooden castle-like entrance doors. The stadium can seat approximately six thousand spectators and it contains a football field and a track. The architect was R. V. Arnold.

Construction of the stadium began in June 1934 as a TERA project. When that agency ended in 1935, approximately 50 percent of the stadium was complete. The WPA provided sixty thousand dollars, with an additional thirty thousand dollars from local sources and municipal bonds, to complete the stadium in 1936. The first game took place on October 8, 1936, between Tennessee High and Science Hill High School of Johnson

City. The Stone Castle was home to all local football games, from both Tennessee High School and the Bristol, Virginia, high school to the black high schools of Slater High (Tennessee) and Douglas High (Virginia). King College also used the field for its games. But for Bristol, the Stone Castle was more than a football field. Over the years it also has hosted horse shows, May Day dances, beauty pageants, 4-H Club events, fairs, and car shows. For its unique architecture and its association with community events, the stadium is listed in the National Register of Historic Places.

SULLIVAN COUNTY

Holston Valley School (1933-35), 1717 Bristol Caverns Highway, Bristol vicinity

Holston Valley School is another Colonial Revival landmark constructed by the Public Works Administration in Sullivan County. Funded in part with a $90,828 grant between 1933 and 1935, the school building features a two-story central block, with a central cupola and Georgian Revival entrance. Flanking the central block are wings with additional classrooms, the gymnasium, and the auditorium. Located near South Holston Dam, the school saw its enrollment increase as the TVA constructed that project during and after World War II.

WASHINGTON COUNTY

East Tennessee State University (1934-39), University Parkway, Johnson City

Several New Deal agencies affected campus life at East Tennessee State College. From 1933 to 1935, the CWA, TERA, and WPA combined monies and efforts to build a football stadium, initially named Roosevelt Stadium, where the college played its games. The first game, however, was between the University of Chattanooga and Emory and Henry College in 1935. In addition to providing funds to keep students in school, NYA built a woodwork shop on the campus in 1939.

The best-known legacy is the amphitheater, a WPA project of 1935, which provided seating for fifteen hundred people. With its stage highlighted by classical columns, the amphitheater reminded patrons of the ancient classics while, at the same time, it provided a venue for more modern programs in music and drama typical of those supported by New Deal arts agencies.

The university's D. P. Culp Center is also the location of a Section of Fine Arts mural, *Farmer Family*, by Wendell Jones. Originally installed in the city post office in 1940, the oil-on-canvas painting centers on a group of people admiring a new baby. But it also depicts two aspects of transportation: a family carrying cattle in a pickup truck and lumber being loaded onto a train owned by the local East Tennessee and Western North Carolina Railroad. Artist Wendell Jones painted four post office murals in New York, Ohio, Illinois, and Tennessee, and each embodied the conventions of the American Scene movement. He told the Johnson City postmaster: "I think Americans like these [people] in the picture, thoughtful, homeloving, industrious, independent shall never be destroyed."[22]

WASHINGTON COUNTY

Jonesboro Elementary School (1939), West College Street at Watauga Avenue, Jonesborough

This restrained interpretation of Colonial Revival style was one of the last PWA school projects in Washington County. Located within the Jonesborough historic district, the building now houses city school offices.

WILSON COUNTY

Wilson County Community House (1936–38), Cumberland University, South Greenwood Avenue, Lebanon

In theory, public funds were not to be used to build new buildings on private college campuses, but officials at Cumberland University worked with City of Lebanon officials to build the "Wilson County Community House" on the university's campus from 1936 to 1938. Funded in part with twenty-five thousand dollars from the WPA, the new brick-and-stone building, designed by the Nashville firm of Daugherty and Clements, included a gymnasium and stage. The dual function was designed to make the building "an excellent meeting place for political gatherings, club meetings, pageants, choruses, and other forms of entertainment" as well as country, district, and even state basketball tournaments. The other benefit for local citizens was the WPA's intention "to employ as many men on this project as can work without getting in one another's way."[23]

In World War II, training exercises and maneuvers of the U.S. Army took place throughout Wilson County. The U.S. Army Air Force and the Seventh Regiment of the Tennessee National Guard used the building as headquarters. The gymnasium was also the center of USO entertainment activities during the maneuvers. The building remained the primary university gym until the construction of the Dallas Floyd Recreation Center in the early 1990s.

5

Housing

In the chapter on "Architecture" in the *WPA Guide to Tennessee*, the authors asserted that "at the present time [1939], Tennessee is experiencing a more rapid development in construction than at any other time previous to the War between the States." The writers highlighted Cumberland Homesteads, one of the earliest New Deal experiments in housing and community building in the state; the PWA's demonstration projects of slum clearance and public housing in urban Tennessee; and TVA's Norris Village, described as "where a new standard for rural existence is being set."[1]

Housing, whether by means of entire demonstration towns or individual apartment projects, was an important part of the New Deal landscape in Tennessee. Many projects remain in use, while others have been forgotten over the years. For example, the Sardis Model Community was developed in and around a remote rural crossroads, which was near the county lines of Henderson, Hardin, Decatur, and Chester Counties. TVA, the University of Tennessee Extension Service, and the Sardis Farm School jointly administered the project. They instructed local farm families to terrace fields, instituted crop rotation at approximately 150 farms, remodeled farm homes and buildings, and improved yards and gardens as a demonstration of what a model progressive rural community could be.

Joint efforts like that at Sardis were the norm for most rural housing and community improvement projects, especially in rural areas. A number of New Deal agencies attempted, in one way or another, to address rural housing needs in the depression decade. In 1933, the National Industrial Recovery Act authorized the creation of a Division of Subsistence Homesteads, located within the Department of Interior. By the following year, FERA had launched its own Division of Rural Rehabilitation and Stranded Populations. Rural housing programs were then reorganized in 1935, when the earlier Department of Interior and FERA projects were placed under the supervision of the Resettlement Administration (except for the three largest villages that were given to the WPA).

The Resettlement Administration (RA) had two main divisions—one was for the development of suburban resettlement communities; the other was the Division of Rural Rehabilitation and Resettlement, which was the important division in Tennessee. Nationwide, the RA's Rural Rehabilitation Division from 1935 to 1937 supervised twenty-five original FERA communities and thirty-four original Subsistence Homesteads while establishing another thirty-four RA communities. The resettlement programs aimed to create modern, well-planned rural environments that would uplift and bring meaningful employment to poor, devastated rural communities. The projects were described as "subsistence homesteads" because reformers assumed that the best living environment for these depressed rural areas was one in which a family had enough land to produce a garden, raise some livestock and poultry, and then have good roads to provide access to nearby factories where cash wages could be earned. Landscape architect John Nolen, who had earlier participated in the design of Kingsport, Tennessee, best described the subsistence homestead ideal. "The subsistence homestead," Nolen remarked, "is a combination of several things which are usually separate, for example, in industry and gardening or farming; part-time industrial employment and desirable provision for food and shelter; work and better use of leisure time."[2]

In 1937 the Resettlement Administration's projects were turned over to the Farm Security Administration, which in the next two years worked to create a model rural community in the Douglass community of Haywood County. The Haywood County Farms Project was part of FSA's efforts, through the Bankhead-Jones Farm Tenant Act, to provide landless tenants and poor African American farmers with their own farms.

New Deal public housing efforts in urban Tennessee date to the spring of 1933 when a provision in the National Industrial Recovery Act created a Division of Housing within the Public Works Administration. The new agency developed programs for both slum clearance and low-income housing. The PWA's Housing Division, judging from recent studies by John F. Bauman, Gail Radford, and others, had both successes and failures in its projects across the country.

In 1935, the agency received one hundred million dollars to develop demonstration housing projects. To qualify the state for the program, the Tennessee General Assembly passed the Tennessee Housing Authorities Law, which allowed city governments to establish local housing authorities. Tennessee received four of the PWA demonstration projects, two each for whites and blacks:

Dixie Homes and Lauderdale Courts in Memphis; and Cheatham Place and Andrew Jackson Courts in Nashville.

Historian Gail Radford has recently commented that federal officials "hoped to create models for new kinds of residential neighborhoods that would prove widely appealing: more compact overall—but still with ample-sized and well designed units. Residences would be set in nicely landscaped grounds, with plenty of recreation facilities and one-site amenities, such as libraries, meeting rooms, and day care."[3] These patterns are found in the early PWA projects in Memphis and Nashville, especially at Dixie Homes, Lauderdale Courts, and Cheatham Place.

However, similar to the state's other New Deal building programs, public housing in Tennessee followed segregation codes, and typically the housing designed for whites, compared with that for the blacks, contained larger landscaped spaces, better parks, larger community buildings, and even more architectural style. In Jackson, for instance, officials organized the Jackson Housing Authority in 1939 and began construction of two projects. Located in the south end of the city, at the junction of South Highland Avenue (U.S. 45) and South Liberty Street, the eight-acre site of Merry Lane Courts was for blacks only. Its ninety-six four-room apartments are still in use today. The white-only Allenton Heights had only four more units, but it was located on a much larger urban lot of thirteen acres, meaning that the units were less compact and there was more open space. In Tennessee, at least, PWA idealism could not crack Jim Crow reality; public housing was separate but certainly not equal. In some cases, in fact, black public housing probably only existed because federal rules required it. Otherwise, it is difficult to explain the use of the name Dixie Homes for Memphis's first black housing project—unless it was someone's very odd sense of humor.

The PWA's public housing program, with the passage of the Wagner-Steagall Housing Act of 1937, was expanded into the U.S. Housing Authority (established November 1, 1937). Over the next two years the larger Tennessee cities established local housing authorities, and by 1940 New Deal agencies had built housing projects in Kingsport, Jackson, Chattanooga, Knoxville, Nashville, and Memphis. The projects often proved to be controversial; private housing groups brought lawsuits and encouraged local political opposition. Demands for labor, money, and resources during World War II brought an abrupt end to government housing projects in 1942.

In a review of Tennessee's New Deal housing projects written in 1948, William F. Larsen noted that the majority were "simple one- and two-story, semidetached, row type dwellings of what, for want of a better term, might be called a modified Georgian style." He found that the buildings were "generally set in relation to the contours of the site" and that they possessed the "essential utilities, and a construction standard which compares favorably with those in other parts of the United States." Larsen observed that since the residents "formerly used candles and kerosene lamps, burned wood in open grates, and obtained water from an outside faucet shared with others, public housing has a significance which goes far beyond the bare essentials of providing decent, safe, and sanitary homes."[4]

To grasp the rather mind-numbing count of the different agencies supervising housing is daunting enough. To appreciate the impact of the housing effort is even more difficult when one adds in the monies and/or labor supplied by the Civil Works Administration, the Civilian Conservation Corps, the Department of Agriculture, TERA, and WPA. Certainly there were failures and disappointments. Cumberland Homesteads never achieved the desired balance between industrial employment, small-plot farming, and rural uplift envisioned by its planners. Some housing projects in Memphis destroyed all or parts of existing African American neighborhoods to make way for new, modern, white-only housing. Statewide, too many housing projects became slums a generation later. The experiments at Sardis and Douglass never became models that other West Tennessee communities followed. Yet the reality also reflects that many of these buildings, from recently rehabilitated housing projects in Memphis to the Crab Orchard stone cottages of Cumberland Homesteads, are still in use. In the grand scheme of things, housing was a small part of the New Deal. But those places that remain of the effort to build a better tomorrow convey a personal, family story about the New Deal's legacy, a story different from any associated with the courthouses, post offices, schools, and parks of New Deal Tennessee.

CUMBERLAND COUNTY

Cumberland Homesteads (1933–41), U.S. Highway 27 and Tennessee Highway 68, Crossville vicinity

The majestic Crab Orchard stone water tower and administration building of Cumberland Homesteads, which stands at the junction of U.S. Highway 127 and Tennessee Highway 68, is one of Tennessee's most potent symbols of the New Deal era. The light on top of the tower literally was a beacon of change for the hundreds of displaced farmers, miners, and loggers who built a new home out of this rugged Cumberland Plateau land. The native stone not only rooted the project in the very soil of the countryside; it also connected the

Homesteads Tower, Cumberland Homesteads, Cumberland County.

administration building, as well as the project's other public buildings, to a local vernacular of building with the colorful sandstone. At the same time, the administration building and the surrounding structures of homesteads, schools, and factories were part and parcel of the latest modern thinking about rural sociology, revitalization, and economic diversification, what is sometimes called the "back-to-the-land" movement. "People living and working in small groups on their own land, growing the food they needed for survival and supplementing their labor with cooperative ventures in manufacturing," points out architectural historian Diane Ghirardo, "seemed vastly preferable to the reality that faced so many Americans during the 1930s: men traveling from one desolate spot to another, seeking work and living on handouts; families despondently living on relief checks with no work opportunities in sight; industries closed and huge quantities of surplus produce destroyed in order to prop up prices."[5]

The large complex of multipurpose buildings that stood at the rural crossroads of Cumberland Homesteads powerfully documented the intrusion of the federal government—and a myriad of reformers and social experts—into the landscape and lifeways of the Cumberland Plateau. As the *Knoxville News-Sentinel* proclaimed in February 4, 1934, front-page story, "a new kind of planning is in progress" at Cumberland Homesteads, "a pioneering project in social planning along the frontier of a 'stranded area.'"

At one time or another, almost every New Deal building agency played some role at Cumberland Homesteads. In January 1934, with funds from the Department of Interior, TVA purchased the initial ten thousand acres of the project from the Missouri Land Company. The CCC provided additional money and labor to clear thousands of acres, improve the roads, and begin construction of the Homesteads Park, later the Cumberland Mountain State Park. The Department of Interior provided designs and supervision; the first project engineer, H. E. Thomas, established a Crossville office in the second week of 1934. Project work then moved fast. By February 1, 1934, 375 men were at work and project architect William Macy Stanton had arrived. D. F. Folger, head of personnel, began the process of interviewing prospective homesteaders, assisted by Amy Cox, Marie Irvin, Clara White, and Kate Rigby. About the time when the project was half completed, the Resettlement Administration assumed its management; before the project was over, the Farm Security Administration was in charge.

At Cumberland Homesteads, even New Deal performing arts programs had their platform, as when the community put on the play *New Ground, A Pageant of Local Life (1838–1938)* at the park's Woodland Theatre to celebrate their achievements in late July 1938. *New Ground* used the same setting—the Cumberland Plateau on a July afternoon—as a backdrop to show the changes wrought in the land and in the residents over the past one hundred years. According to a copy of its program at the Homesteaders Museum, 150 residents participated in putting together the pageant. It began with the "transfer of land" between Native Americans and the initial frontier families. It next portrayed the "problem of squatter's rights," the "effects of the Civil War" (presented by the Linary community), and the "coming of the railroad" (by the citizens of Crossville). The last two parts of the pageant addressed more recent times on the Plateau. Part three addressed the theme of exploitation from two scenes. The first was dated 1910, titled "Neglect of the Farm for Ready Money." The second, dated 1928, was "Depreciation of Farm Life." The final section of the pageant addressed the theme of rediscovery through two scenes—the depression in 1934 and "Pioneering Today," representing the achievements of the homesteaders.

By July 1938 much had been achieved at Homesteads. A total of 251 homestead units, varying in size from 3 to 189 acres, were complete. The average homestead size was 35 acres. The residents lived first in their barns, with chicken houses sometimes serving as temporary kitchens and dining rooms. Early homesteader Edna Gossage-Blue recalled that her chicken house had "my stove, my table and two chairs, a bench and a cabinet."[6] Then the homesteaders built the stone cottages themselves, reflecting the "back to the land" philosophy favored by several leading reformers and a bit of the earlier Arts and Crafts philosophy that the handmade was infinitely superior to the machine-made.

The homes, based on different standardized designs from architect William Macy Stanton, ranged from four to seven rooms in size. In a report on January 25, 1934, the *Crossville Chronicle* praised the homes for representing "more beauty and comfort than ever assembled in like space in the United States." The dwellings were built with native Crab Orchard stone and reflected restrained interpretations of Tudor Revival and Colonial Revival domestic architecture. They contained running water and wiring for electricity. Electrical power would not reach the Homesteads until a rural electrification project was completed in 1939. This initial lack of power, however, meant that Stanton's quaint stone houses were cold in the fall and winter. Edna Gossage-Blue remembers the homes being colder than even living in the barns. Elizabeth Peaveyhouse has similar memories. But homesteader Pauline Pruitt concluded: "[W]e didn't mind doing without electricity because we had our own house and it even had running water."[7]

The planning for Cumberland Homesteads interjected standardization into the landscape where folk variation had existed before. For example, Stanton's stone dwellings were standardized plans, with standardized lot setbacks of between seventy-five and one hundred feet and uniform forty-foot frontages. Residents found that a seemingly endless stream of visitors, government experts, and inspectors compromised their privacy. Some resented the official bureaucracy and regulations of the project managers and regretted the loss of individual initiative.

Agriculture was the primary focus of life at Cumberland Homesteads. With a captive population, rural reformers took every opportunity, through night classes and special programs, to teach residents about the benefits of modern agriculture and home economics. The Department of Agriculture, TVA, and CCC provided expert advice on terracing, soil conservation and reclamation, crop rotation, home economics, and agricultural diversification. Agriculture Department and TVA staff, along with county extension agents, taught adult education classes at the Homesteads School. Residents learned new methods for producing potatoes, strawberries, and soybeans, along with raising goats for market and soil conservation and land-clearance techniques. Elizabeth Peaveyhouse remembers learning tips about gardening, sewing, cooking, and food preservation at regular Home Demonstration Club meetings. Marie Irvin established a local women's club and instituted an active demonstration program. Pauline Pruitt, for instance, received college instruction for a week through a club program, attended Farm Women's Week in Knoxville in 1938 through club support, and learned how to cook with a pressure cooker from club demonstrations. Pruitt concluded that through these activities, women homesteaders bonded together in a special way, "making the community more than just a place to live."[8]

Cumberland Homesteads never produced the miracle that reformers such as Eleanor Roosevelt had prophesied in her visit in 1934. The factories had difficulty staying in business; the homes were cold until electricity arrived; and workers complained about being shortchanged on their work credits toward purchasing their homes. But most homesteaders stuck it out. "Life was not easy but we were all working for the same goal and it was a good community," recalls Elizabeth Peaveyhouse. "We were young . . . it was a challenge and we didn't mind."[9] Today signs along the major highway entrances proudly mark the Cumberland Homesteads National Historic District. while an impressive stone monument, located adjacent to the Tower Museum, recognizes the homesteaders' many achievements.

DAVIDSON COUNTY
Andrew Jackson Courts (1935–38), 1457 Jackson, Nashville

The Public Works Administration located its two Nashville projects in the north part of the city. At first, such African American leaders as Charles S. Johnson, the eminent Fisk University sociologist, praised the proposed "negro" project. In 1934 Johnson called it "a rare opportunity to introduce enlightened social planning and guidance" into a neighborhood long handicapped by "poor physical surroundings."[10] But soon concerns arose about the project's proposed building site near Fisk University. A few African American realtors resented the competition and loss of income. A larger number of north Nashville residents, represented by their ministers, worried about the loss of treasured homes and churches, as well as the prospect of lower property values in a nearby middle-class neighborhood. These leaders argued that the community needed PWA money for sewers, streetlights, and paved streets rather than a massive apartment complex. When it heard that PWA director Harold Ickes was planning a Nashville visit, the Tennessee Conference of the African Methodist Episcopal Church told Ickes to go to Fisk and "look west and observe two square miles of Negro homes whose owners prayers for sewers and city improvements go unanswered, where the death rate exceed[s] the birth rate." The ministers asserted: "Might does not make right in the housing scheme of white promoters that cannot vote the endorsement of a single Negro organization."[11]

PWA officials acknowledged the complaints, conducted an investigation, and rejected the site these African Americans preferred for the project. Construction of Andrew Jackson Courts began in 1935 under the supervision of Nashville Allied Architects, a group of the city's leading white architects who joined together in order to receive the commission. Richard W. Clark led the architects, who also included Henry C. Hibbs, Emmons Woolwine, Francis B. Warfield, and Eli M. Tisdale. The buildings were ready for occupation in 1938.

The *WPA Guide to Tennessee* praised Jackson Courts: "[T]he houses are simple in design, carefully planned, and well built. There are individual yards and garden plots. The homes cover only about 20 percent of the entire site, the remainder of the land being used for yards, gardens, and play space."[12] Compared with Cheatham Place, the Jackson Courts had sparse landscaping, the apartments had a row-house appearance, and the buildings were generally clustered together. As an urban environment, it was clearly inferior to Cheatham Place.

There was a white face and a black face in New Deal public housing in Nashville. From 1938 to 1940 private developers began to exercise greater control over the Nashville Housing Authority and the New Deal's public housing program, which was redefined "as a mechanism for controlling property values," according to historian Don Doyle. Public housing was allowed to continue only as limited competition to existing private housing options. This agreement, Doyle concludes, "allowed existing slums to fester and perpetuated—even accentuated—the residential segregation of blacks and whites in Nashville."[13] For example, the James C. Napier Homes, built in the 1940s, were eventually bound on one side by the four-lane U.S. Highway 41 and on the other by Interstate Highway 40/65, isolating the neighborhood in a noisy, congested, and clearly segregated space.

DAVIDSON COUNTY
Cheatham Place (1935–38), 1564 Ninth Avenue North, Nashville

Construction began in 1935 on the white-only Cheatham Place, located in the Kalb Hollow district between Buena Vista School and the mammoth Werthan Bag Company factory. Designed by Nashville Allied Architects, the complex was centered on a large Colonial Revival–styled Community Building, where a clinic, offices, and social rooms were located. Its 352 apartments of two-,

Cheatham Place, Nashville.

three-, and four-room units were spaciously arranged on twenty-one landscaped acres. Due to its well-constructed "colonial" buildings and landscaped site, the *Nashville Tennessean* predicted that Cheatham Place would be a "new and clean little town within Nashville"; its ideal environment would encourage former slum dwellers to better themselves. "The spot will resemble a cozy English village," the newspaper predicted. "With green lawns, flower and vegetable gardens, parks, paved sidewalks, and an air of freshness and healthfulness," Cheatham Place would uplift its residents, thus reducing "crime, vice, immorality, disease, and all social evils."[14]

Today one would be hard-pressed to find anything much resembling a "cozy English village" at Cheatham Place. Yet many of its original features—the large mature trees, dispersed apartment units, and generally human scale of the buildings—remain to speak of the dreams of human and cultural transformation held by New Deal housing reformers.

HAMILTON COUNTY

College Hill Courts (1938–40), 1300 Grove Street, and East Lake Courts (1938–40), 2600 Fourth Avenue, Chattanooga

The Chattanooga Housing Authority dates to June 15, 1938. Its initial projects, funded by the U.S. Housing Authority, were the black-only College Hill Courts (497 units with 1,999 rooms, an average of four rooms per apartment) and the white-only East Lake Courts (437 units with 1,771 rooms, again averaging four rooms per apartment). The apartment size and the restrained Colonial Revival style of the two projects were similar, but a clear difference existed in the acreage and landscaping of the projects. As in Nashville, the African American project was placed on a much smaller urban lot (twenty acres compared with the thirty-five acres of the white project), with the white-only East Lake Courts having the added benefit of spacious landscaping, various plantings, and more ornate architectural details, such as tile roofs. The two projects cost $3.8 million.

Later interstate construction in the 1960s and 1970s affected both projects adversely. Yet the 1990s brought major renovations and both projects remain in use.

HOUSING 139

College Hill Courts, Chattanooga.

HAYWOOD COUNTY

Haywood County Farms Project (1938–40), Douglass Road, Stanton vicinity

The Farm Security Administration attempted through its Tenant Purchase Division and its Rural Rehabilitation Division to give promising poor southern farmers—both white and black—a new lease on life by establishing farms projects. An excellent Tennessee example is centered at the African American Douglass community of Haywood County. Residents have recently completed a history project about their community, and many of the original project dwellings still stand to document this little-known FSA effort.

Prior to the 1930s, a small group of African Americans had owned their own farms in the general area of the project. The FSA acquired the farm of Willis B. Douglass, a prominent white landowner, for the project. The agency wanted good land—not marginal property—so the new farms actually had a chance to succeed. Once federal officials divided the land into thirty-seven individual farms, they accepted applications and leased the farms to the residents, who paid rent with an option to purchase the farms outright. FSA improved the roads, built barns, smokehouses, privies, water pumps, and standardized but unadorned frame five-room dwellings for each farm. Federal agencies also brought electricity into the community long before other rural black communities received power.

Haywood Farms dwelling, Douglass community.

The agency also constructed the Douglass school for grades one through ten; young black males soon established a chapter of the New Farmers of America. The school and its grounds (still extant) became the community's heart, and the scene of many gatherings. On every August 8, for instance, it hosted a community celebration and homecoming. Older residents fondly remember the endless variety of food, featuring barbecue prepared by Jackson Sanderlin and others, and good music from the Fredonia Lodge Drum and Fife Ensemble. They also recall visits from FSA officials; a photograph belonging to Stanley Rice shows a group of white FSA officials, men and women, eagerly eating watermelon, thus reversing a long-standing stereotyped image of African Americans in the South. The federal administrators, according to original Farms resident Jesse Cannon Sr., "would lecture to us and after the meeting we would spread the food and sit down and eat like one big family. . . . We looked forward to that affair every year."[15]

Cannon's son, Jesse Jr., grew up at the Farms: "It was like we were in our own little world . . . we were sheltered from a lot of things that went on in the outside world. Because all of the houses looked alike, everybody farmed, everybody had a hundred- or hundred-fifty-acre farm for the most part."[16] The sense of pride and independence gained from their individual and collective successes led several Douglass community residents into leadership roles in the Civil Rights movement in Haywood County from 1940 to 1980. Jessie Cannon Jr. explained: "They did the legwork, and they organized the first massive groups to descend upon the courthouse . . . and they were the ones who stood there in lines for weeks to get registered. They could do this because they had their own farms. They weren't tenant farmers who, if they weren't out there in the fields, they were going to get kicked off the farms."[17]

KNOX COUNTY
Western Heights Homes (1938–40), 1701 Jourolman Avenue and Austin Homes (1938–41), 1225 Burge Avenue, Knoxville

A federal survey in 1934 ranked housing in Knoxville as "low" and noted that two out of five houses in the city lacked bathtubs or showers. New Deal agencies addressed these problems by designing and funding separate housing projects for blacks at College Homes and for whites at Western Heights. The Knoxville Housing Authority held its first meeting in June 1936, but due to legal challenges, actual construction of the city's New Deal housing projects did not take place until 1938 to 1941, when the two initial projects were joined by a segregated black-only project named Austin Homes.

The three New Deal projects in Knoxville were placed on urban lots ranging from six acres for the 200-unit Austin Homes to fifteen acres for Western Heights, which had 244 units. College Homes was the largest, with 320 units, and was located adjacent to Knoxville College. College Homes also was the most controversial, since, in the opinion of local African American leaders such as James Henry Presnell, the project would destroy a stable middle-class neighborhood that had developed outside the gates of Knoxville College. Similar complaints were directed at the Austin Homes project. In both cases, housing officials ignored the complaints and built the projects.

Two of three projects—Western Heights and Austin Homes—remain extant. (College Homes was demolished in 1997–98 as part of the Hope VI revitalization project in north Knoxville.) They exhibit the restrained Colonial Revival styling typical of New Deal public housing in Tennessee. Some of the units, however, were built with a reinforced-concrete, shell-type construction and had merely a brick veneer. As a concession to East Tennessee coal interests, the Knoxville units also had coal-fired ranges for cooking rather than the electrical and gas ranges found in other Tennessee projects.

SHELBY COUNTY

Dixie Homes (1935–38), 940–990 Poplar Avenue, Memphis

One of two pilot PWA public housing projects in Memphis, Dixie Homes—its name notwithstanding—was for African American residents only. J. Frazier Smith, the regional chief of the Historic American Building Survey, an important architectural historian, and a highly respected architect, was the project's lead architect, in alliance with some of the city's best designers: Walk C. Jones Sr., Edwin B. Phillips, Everett Woods, R. J. Regan, Anker F. Hansen, Dudley E. Jones, Louis Carlisle, and Herbert M. Burnham. The landscape architect was John F. Highberger. Architectural historians have lavished praise on the resulting International style–influenced project of 636 units on a large, landscaped 42-acre site of 28 one-story and 48 two-story buildings. "Dixie Homes are one of the high moments in the history of Memphis architecture," asserted Eugene Johnson and Robert Russell Jr. "Indeed, the high quality of the design is rarely matched in public housing in this country, or even in Europe," reflecting "the latest thinking in the field."[18] A photograph of Smith's achievement graced the architecture section of the *WPA Guide to Tennessee.*

The complex was also a laboratory for other progressive reforms. Dixie Homes had two Boy Scout troops; they met in the large community building, where there also was a clinic, social rooms, and a branch of the city library. Much of the dream for progressive reform died with the New Deal, however. Later urban-renewal schemes blighted Dixie Homes. By the late 1990s, many of the abandoned apartments had been vandalized, and the complex awaited renovation and a new life.

SHELBY COUNTY
Lauderdale Courts (1935-38), 234-274 North Lauderdale Street, Memphis

Since it replaced an African American neighborhood of poor and substandard housing with a segregated white housing project, Lauderdale Courts was the more controversial of the two PWA projects in Memphis. Slum clearance, in other words, did not lead to better housing for poor blacks—it meant that blacks were pushed farther away from downtown. J. Frazier Smith, with a slightly different alliance of Memphis architects including Edwin B. Phillips, Everett Woods, William J. Hanker, George Awsumb, Walk C. Jones, Jr., R. J. Regan, and W. C. Lester, designed the 26-acre complex in a restrained Colonial Revival style; its 66 buildings were divided into 449 units. It had a mix of two-, three-, four-, and five-room apartments. Its administration building contained a large and a small assembly room, a club room, offices, toilets, and a community kitchen. The site was attractively terraced and landscaped.

But maintaining the cozy village look of Lauderdale Courts proved to be a challenge. In 1940 the city employed two "'Women Visitors,'" educated experts "who understand the housewife's point of view" and who would "visit tenants, explaining the uses of various equipment and offering advice in housekeeping."[19] The visitors trained tenants how to use and maintain their gas stoves, gas space heaters, bathtubs, and toilets. They also held classes in good housekeeping and conducted apartment visits during which they graded individual housekeepers. In return for better housing, in other words, residents were expected to adopt new attitudes about living. We have no testimony about what the actual apartment residents thought of these intrusions—however well meaning—into their privacy. We do know that one Women Visitor was Jane Richardson, who recalled that Gladys Presley, the mother of the project's subsequently most famous resident, Elvis Presley, was a good housekeeper who kept her hardwood floors constantly waxed. Presley's biographer, Peter Guralnick, believes that the project had changed too much since the years when the Presleys lived there for visitors to "get a sense of what the Courts were like at that time: a humming, bustling little village, full of kids and ambition." Guralnick observes: "[F]or many of the residents it was 'like we'd come into the money.' For some it was the first time they had ever had indoor plumbing or taken a real bath." There was a "sense of social aspiration, and of pride," which became "the dominant tone of the Courts."[20] At one time in 1990s, officials considered demolishing Lauderdale Courts. However, a large coalition of residents, community activists, historians, and preservationists argued that renovation and modernization were better solutions. Their actions saved the project from the wrecking ball and renovations began in 1999.

SHELBY COUNTY

W. H. Foote Homes (1938–41), Vance at South Lauderdale Street, Memphis

To African Americans in Memphis, the placement of Foote Homes was even worse than that of Lauderdale Courts. Foote Homes, observed historian Roger Biles, was "a *cause celebre* in the black community" because white city officials wanted to destroy an emerging middle-class black neighborhood for public housing.[21] When the Memphis Housing Authority planned Foote Homes, it estimated that the project would displace 16 white families and 428 black families, many of whom had arrived in the 1930s.

Part of the targeted area was the partially integrated Vance-Pontotoc

Foote Homes, after 1998–99 renovations, Memphis.

neighborhood, dotted with large and impressive Victorian era dwellings. Soon members of both races protested the project. One of the loudest voices came from T. O. Fuller, who was a political ally of the Crump machine and pastor of First Baptist Church, Lauderdale, the city's oldest African American Baptist congregation. His church stood within the proposed project's boundaries, as did several buildings of other established black congregations and the campus of the historic Howe Institute. Reverend Fuller begged Mayor Walter Overton to move the project farther south and protect the neighborhood and its institutions. But Fuller's political connections made no difference; his pleas fell on deaf ears at city hall. The same chilly response awaited a group of African American property owners who predicted that the project would destroy neighborhood stability and one of the city's best streets for black commerce and community institutions. White protests were ignored as well, and soon the mansions and shotguns in the district came tumbling down. To add insult to the injury, the city even let its fire department burn down some of the properties in order to test new equipment.

In 1939, with much regret, First Baptist, Lauderdale, abandoned its older church on St. John Avenue to the wrecking ball after saving some furniture and stained glass windows. The congregation moved into a new Classical Revival–style building chosen by Fuller across from the Booker T. Washington school and within sight of the public housing project. Older members still talk about the loss of the church building and the neighborhood. "The callous disregard for the misfortunes of uprooted slum dwellers and the scrupulous selection of sites for black only projects confirmed what many black leaders had adduced," concluded Biles, "that the primary function of public housing was not only to maintain existing patterns of racial segregation, but also to further concentrate blacks in designated sections of the city increasingly being vacated by suburban-bound whites."[22]

J. Frazier Smith, Max Furbringer, and Dudley E. Jones were the architects of Foote Homes; the St. Louis firm of Harland Bartholomew and Associates was the landscape architect. It contained 900 units on 46 acres; the largest public-housing project built in Tennessee during the New Deal, it cost approximately $3.5 million. In the late 1990s, the Memphis Housing Authority spent more than 5 million dollars to modernize Foote Homes, adding new entrances to the buildings, improving the landscaping, building fences, and adding better playgrounds.

SHELBY COUNTY
Lamar Terrace (1938–41), Lamar Avenue and Camilla Street, Memphis

Built at the same time as the Foote Homes, Lamar Terrace demolished an African American neighborhood at "Roper's Alley" to make way for the city's second white housing project. The location was chosen, according to the *Memphis Commercial Appeal* of September 17, 1938, because the nearby black houses "have a tendency to blight the white residential property." The architect was J. Frazier Smith, in association with Everett Woods, Joe Wallace, and Anker F. Hansen. The complex rested on approximately 25 landscaped acres and had 478 units.

SHELBY COUNTY
LeMoyne Gardens (1941–43), Walker Avenue, Memphis

The third Memphis housing project for African Americans was LeMoyne Gardens, located in south Memphis near the historic LeMoyne-Owen College. The 25-acre project had 60 buildings, which contained 500 apartments. Housing Authority officials asserted that the project would not detract from LeMoyne, but instead it would allow residents to gain cultural, educational, and social benefits from the college.

The project architects were Walk C. Jones, Sr. and Jr., Herbert M. Burnham, and Howell B. Mulbry. Their design, like most in Tennessee, produced clusters of buildings in a restrained Colonial Revival style, with open, landscaped areas and a community building. The project opened on December 4, 1941, only three days before Pearl Harbor. In the spring of 1942, officials decided to build a Gardens addition of fifteen acres and 342 units to order to meet the segregated housing needs of African American workers flooding into the many wartime industries based in Memphis.

Three housing projects for blacks in just three years appear, on the surface, to be a laudable progressive gesture from the political machine of E. H. Crump. "Washington largess helped a good number of destitute blacks make ends meet, a considerable accomplishment given the tenor of the times," concludes Roger Biles, but the federal programs "did little to augment changes in the racial caste system."[23] During these same years, the Crump machine crushed the local Republican party and used slum clearance projects to push blacks into more segregated areas as civil rights violations increased in the Bluff City.

SHELBY COUNTY

Rosemary Lane Subdivision (1938), Rosemary Lane and Park Lane at Melrose Avenue, Memphis

The Federal Housing Authority, created by the National Housing Act of 1934, extended New Deal benefits to middle-class homebuyers in an attempt to help families acquire home loans and to help builders, contractors, and architects stay in business during the depression. Homebuyers could acquire a FHA loan through a participating local bank, if the local FHA administrator approved the loan. The federal government guaranteed the bank at least a partial recovery in case of default. Typically the loans were for 80 percent of the house's value, payable in twenty years with interest rates ranging between 5 and 6 percent. This financial arrangement was much better than earlier loan packages; thus, middle-class homebuyers, even in the depression decade, were encouraged to purchase their own homes at an earlier age. Unlike the New Deal's public housing projects, the FHA's support for private housing rarely generated much criticism.

Memphis is the best place in Tennessee to see the influence of FHA-backed loans on local domestic architecture, largely because of the work of local architect J. Frazier Smith. By 1936–37 the state FHA administrator became worried about federal guarantees on twenty-year loans for poorly built and designed homes. He approached Smith, a nationally recognized expert on middle-class housing, for assistance. In 1937 Smith established the Memphis Small House Construction Bureau, an association of local builders, contractors, and architects, which produced a series of house plans that ranged from two to eight thousand dollars. A similar bureau, established in Minneapolis in 1921, had been very influential in that Upper Midwest city and probably served as a model for Smith's program in Memphis.

The Memphis Small House Construction Bureau criticized the city's past preference for "carpenter" bungalows and favored Colonial Revival–styled houses, like those on Rosemary Lane. These are one-story, frame dwellings with gable roofs, dormer windows, symmetrical facades, and understated Colonial Revival entrances. FHA administrators liked architecturally conservative homes because their apparent resale value was much higher than more trendy, modernist styles.

SULLIVAN COUNTY
Riverview Apartments (1939–41), 1013 Douglas Street, Kingsport

Kingsport civil leaders took pride in the city's image as a model, progressive southern industrial city. A persistent reality, however, was the presence of deplorable slum housing, "among the worst he had seen," reported one USHA official.[24] In 1939 the Kingsport Housing Authority was established and that August, city officials approved two projects—the aptly named Robert E. Lee Homes for whites (128 units) and the Riverview Homes for blacks (48 units)—which cost a total of $607,000. The black housing project was located on approximately three acres, while the Robert E. Lee Homes stood on seven acres. In Kingsport, at least, the two housing projects were more equal than separate in the relative size of their facilities. Both contained brick buildings of a restrained Colonial Revival style. However, the African American project was located in an undesirable spot, south of the railroad and between two factories. Sixty years later, Riverview lies at the heart of the local black community. Its buildings and courtyard plan are largely intact, while its active community building still houses a branch of the city library.

Riverview Apartments, Kingsport.

6

Parks, Memorials, and Museums

In 1921 Tennessee had public parks in both large and small towns. The federal government administered several national military parks associated with the Civil War and parts of national forests in East Tennessee. But the state of Tennessee did not own or operate a single state park. The state established a State Park and Forestry Commission in 1925, but did little else to actually develop and promote parklands except for its still limited involvement to create a national park in the Great Smoky Mountains. Not until the 1930s would an effective and long-term movement to establish state parks occur. The history of the Tennessee state park system—widely viewed today as one of the true jewels of the state's public landscape—is intimately tied to the history of conservation and recreation efforts of New Deal agencies during the 1930s. Without the New Deal legacy, in fact, one wonders what type of parks would exist in Tennessee; seventeen parks in all were either established or substantially improved by federal agencies during the depression decade.

In his seminal 1962 study of the state parks, historian Bevley R. Coleman divided the state parks into four categories that reflected their New Deal origins: Tennessee Valley Authority Areas, Land-Use Areas, Recreation Demonstration Areas, and Miscellaneous Federal Projects.

Of the four, the TVA parks were the most important; indeed, Coleman observed that "had it not been for the aid and prodding of TVA, the state's development of parks would not have been as rapid. Nor would the state have achieved its parks system with as small an outlay of state funds."[1] After an internal agency debate on whether the development of parks fell within the its mission, TVA officials in 1934 began an aggressive campaign to work with various federal and state agencies to develop recreational areas. The TVA areas most commonly involved a partnership between TVA, NPS, CCC, sometimes the WPA, and the state parks division. These parks helped to ensure proper conservation along lake shores and promoted the overall well-being of citizens as well as economic development in the region. TVA had its own staff of architects, geographers, geologists, and landscape architects who worked with the park demonstration projects. In 1937, for instance, TVA architect Earle Draper wrote an influential article about the demonstration parks in *Architectural Record*. But TVA also relied on the expertise of the National Park Service on many issues of park design, and it called on the extensive labor available through the Civilian Conservation Corps to actually build the parks.

Land-Use Areas, established by the U.S. Department of Agriculture, had a more basic conservation and reclamation goal, targeting severely eroded submarginal land for reclamation through the relocation of original residents and the extensive replanting of forests and ground cover. One such plant was kudzu, an imported vine that planted deep roots and grew quickly—as it turned out, it bit too quickly and easily in some areas, as kudzu actually took over portions of the state's countryside. Land-Use Areas involved the U.S. Forest Service and National Park Service for supervision over the forests and park design, the CCC and WPA for construction, and the Division of Rural Rehabilitation and later the Resettlement Administration for the relocation of farm families and tenants. The areas were larger than the other New Deal parks, but that may be attributed to their dual missions as conservation areas (state forests) and recreation projects (state parks). Historians have directed attention to the process and problems of population removal in TVA projects. Unfortunately little attention has been given to the activities of the Division of Rural Rehabilitation and the Resettlement Administration at Tennessee state parks such as Cedars of Lebanon, Chickasaw, Standing Stone, and Natchez Trace.

National Recreation Demonstration Areas also involved a primary partnership between the NPS, CCC, and the Division of Rural Rehabilitation, later the Resettlement Administration. As the name implies, these parks were part of a national program that aimed at creating models for state and local park development. Montgomery Bell State Park, Fall Creek Falls State Park, Meeman-Shelby State Park, and Steele Creek Park in Bristol all began as recreation demonstrations. The projects mixed conservation, erosion control, reforestation, and planned recreational development.

Coleman's last category of "miscellaneous" combines several other federal initiatives. Cumberland Mountain State Park, for example, was established as a recreation center within the huge Cumberland Homesteads project. T. O. Fuller State Park was created as a segregated black-only state park for urban African Americans in Memphis. Pickett State Park began as a state forest project that in 1934 blossomed into a project similar to the Department of Agriculture's Land-Use Areas.

No matter the administrative roots of the park, however, the involvement of the National Park Service and the Civilian Conservation Corps were constants in the creation of park landscapes in Tennessee. Architectural historian Linda McClelland recently explored the importance of certain design aesthetics promoted by the National Park Service in the 1930s. In developing state parks, it was common for NPS personnel not only to provide guidance and suggestions, but also to create master plans and designs for individual structures, from cabins to swimming pools. Many of these plans are still on file at the individual parks or at the offices of Tennessee State Parks in Nashville. Moreover, "technical specialists employed by the park service, including landscape architects, architects, and engineers," McClelland emphasizes, "were assigned to each CCC camp and closely supervised the work of the CCC foremen and enrollees."[2] Later, to standardize park design, the NPS produced two influential architectural pattern books: *Park Structures and Facilities* (1935) and Albert H. Good's *Park and Recreation Structures* (1938). In Tennessee, the NPS supervision, expertise, and pattern books resulted in a remarkably consistent "parkitecture," one that architectural historians have classified as Government Rustic style. By utilizing locally available materials, such as stone and logs, and adopting one-story, horizontal forms, this style was meant to blend into the natural landscape as much as possible, allowing the beauty of the natural landscape to compensate for human intrusions. Ideas of simplicity, strength, and the exposed glory of craftsmanship from the earlier Arts and Crafts movement, along with grandiose Rustic style examples from the western national parks and resorts in the Adirondacks, clearly influenced Government Rustic style. But this park service aesthetic in Tennessee also embraced modern technology, especially the use of electricity provided by the power plants of TVA.

The Tennessee Valley Authority and the National Park Service may have provided the design expertise, but the amazing amount of work on state parks carried out by the Civilian Conservation Corps through the federal Emergency Conservation Work program, established in 1933, cannot be discounted. The CCC was literally everywhere in Tennessee, from the sixteen camps spread throughout the Great Smoky Mountains to the companies toiling away in the heat and humidity of Reelfoot Lake and T. O. Fuller State Park in West Tennessee. Most of the work focused on soil conservation and land reclamation, topics covered in the next chapter of this book, but CCC "boys," as these young men were popularly called, built roads, trails, and buildings still used by the millions of people who annually visit parks in Tennessee. As the editor of the *Columbia Herald* correctly observed and predicted on February 2, 1935: "The Civilian Conservation Corps, conceded on all sides to be among the New Deal projects most beneficial and least subject to criticism, has done some fine work to date in Tennessee, and according to present plans, will continue that work for some time to come." And while today the focus is on the actual landscape left behind by the CCC, the sense of work, discipline, and accomplishment associated with the agency also marked the thousands of Tennesseans who wore the CCC uniform. "I didn't think I could talk to people. I'd only come to third grade," recalled Arthur Jackson of Lebanon. "The C's gave me confidence that I was as good as anybody. It made me know I could do things, gave me some push."[3]

Recent literature across the country has focused on the relationship between federal agencies, especially the NPS and CCC, and nascent state park systems. In Tennessee, clearly, conservation and recreation were the dual goals of the massive effort to create state parks where there had been none. Comparatively little attention was given to the development of historic sites. Two Civil War–era forts in Knoxville and Nashville were restored, while a city park that was associated with the Battle of Memphis received some improvements by the CCC. Admittedly, the state already had several large national military parks, and the urban historic house museums, such as The Hermitage in Nashville and Blount Mansion in Knoxville, had their own means of support. The need, in the eyes of both state and federal planners, was for recreation areas, not commemorative landscapes. Yet, state and federal agencies did work together to address one glaring shortcoming in the state's historical landscape—the excavation and interpretation of Tennessee's rich prehistoric past. Although only one archaeological museum would result from the New Deal—the Chucalissa Village at T. O. Fuller State Park in Memphis—many important excavations took place and much valuable information was gathered, and eventually published.

Another forgotten side of the New Deal recreation effort involved local history and arts projects. Agencies such as the WPA and NYA undertook such projects as the simple landscaping and building of a gazebo at Kiwanis Park in Union City or raising a stone obelisk war memorial in Jacksboro. The WPA's art, theater, and music projects brought welcome programming and financial assistance to local museums, although in Tennessee most of these benefits accrued to the cities, since smaller towns lacked museums and historic sites.

But whatever the scope of project, the specter of Jim Crow haunted most New Deal programs for parks and museums. Of the many public parks, two were set aside for African Americans—the rest were basically off limits. Of the seventy-seven CCC companies in Tennessee at the height of the program, none were integrated and only a handful were reserved for African American young men. The Memphis WPA's Federal Music Project may have performed a concert honoring the music of W. C. Handy, but almost all other arts programs were unavailable to black audiences. Not until the Civil Rights movement of the 1960s would the public spaces of the New Deal finally become accessible to all Tennesseans.

ANDERSON COUNTY

Norris Dam State Park (1933-37), U.S. Highway 441, Norris

Norris Dam State Park has two separate units on either side of Norris Dam and Lake. The west unit is a modern facility developed in 1976; the east unit is one of the original TVA/CCC demonstration parks in Tennessee. This initial Norris park contained 3,887 acres, extending along three miles of the south shore of the reservoir to Norris Village. Although TVA was not legally authorized to develop public recreational facilities, it could address shoreline erosion and reservoir protection. The agency thus worked with the National Park Service, the U.S. Forest Service, and the Civilian Conservation Corps to develop the land as a public park. TVA contributed designs, some materials, some skilled labor, and supervised construction. The National Park Service also supervised design and provided funds for materials. The CCC did most of the actual work and supervised some design details. Like for other joint efforts in Tennessee, excellent records and historic photographs for the project are kept at the National Archives' regional archives in Atlanta. TVA officials hoped that this cooperative partnership "would serve as a guide to other agencies and

CCC cabin, Norris Lake State Park, Anderson County.

individuals in the design, development, and operation of similar facilities on other parts of Norris Lake and on other [TVA] lakes."[4]

From 1934 to 1937, three CCC companies worked on the park. The first group comprised New England boys, Company 4493, until local boys replaced them. Company 4495 arrived from Loyston, Tennessee, in November 1935. The final group was Company 494, also comprising Tennesseans. Thirty-six families were relocated from parkland; scattered archaeological remains and ornamental plantings mark the home sites. The CCC companies built a boat dock out of the dam quarry. They constructed picnic shelters and tables, a campground, an amphitheater large enough for five hundred people, twenty Government Rustic style cabins, riding stables, trails, and a Government Rustic–style lodge, which had a tearoom and a small store.

On the outskirts of the park, the CCC and NPS also relocated and restored the Rice grist mill (circa 1798) as both a historic site and a demonstration of what "machine power" was like along the Clinch River before the construction of Norris Dam. While TVA formally sold the park to the state of Tennessee in 1953, it retained the mill until the early 1970s when the agency deeded it to Norris Dam State Park.

Most of these original elements remain at the east unit today; historian Ruth Nichols concludes that "Norris Dam retains what may be the state's most intact collection of CCC buildings and structures, having undergone

Lodge and Tearoom, Norris Lake State Park, Anderson County.

very few alterations since initial construction."[5] The lodge, for example, is a long horizontal frame building resting on a cut stone foundation, with exquisite interior wood detailing and a large stone fireplace. It serves as the trailhead for three CCC-developed trails: Christmas Fern, Lakeside Loop, and Tall Timber. The trails provide access to the site of the CCC Camp—known as Camp Sam—where above ground archaeological remains exist.

The amphitheater is not used as much as it was during the park's earlier years. In part, this reflects continued budget cuts at state parks in the late twentieth century. But the diminished use of the amphitheater also reflects a more fundamental cultural change from the attitudes of the 1930s. New Deal–era educators and social reformers believed that society benefited from having "community centers" where the public could enjoy adult education programs, lectures, plays, and musicals. The amphitheater was to be such a place within the larger landscape of Norris Park. Today, however, most visitors have little interest in such gathering spots; they often entertain themselves by watching television in their cabins.

Initially, TVA personnel allowed African Americans to use certain areas and facilities of the park. It constructed separate rest rooms at the Norris powerhouse and at the information centers overlooking the project. Then in 1937, the authority and state officials studied the possibility of creating a "Negro park" at Norris. Although they admitted the necessity of such a segregated black-only park—if only for appearance's sake to African Americans across the country—officials also worried about negative white reactions. The "Negro section" at Norris was never built, with economic reasons given as the excuse.

Norris Dam State Park is also the location of the W. G. Lenoir Museum, which records and interprets the legacy of the thousands of Tennesseans displaced by the Norris Dam project. The museum exhibits an excellent set of photographs that document the construction of Norris Dam. Between the museum and the grist mill is a large threshing barn, another reminder of the agrarian lifestyles once common in this portion of the Clinch River Valley.

BENTON COUNTY

Nathan Bedford Forrest State Historical Area (1933–35), Pilot Knob Road, Eva vicinity

Located on the west bank of the Tennessee River, centered on Pilot Knob, the highest elevation in West Tennessee, is the Nathan Bedford Forrest State Historical Area. At first, the park was a local historical site, named the Nathan

Bedford Forrest Memorial Park. In 1929 Benton County citizens and state officials established the park to memorialize the Confederate victory, led by Forrest, in the battle of Johnsonville during the fall of 1864. Forrest had used his river bluff position on the west side of the Tennessee River to shell the Union supply base at Johnsonville and to sink several Union gunboats and ships. His daring attack was one of the few successes recorded by Tennessee Confederates in the fall of 1864, and the battle site had been one of considerable interest to local residents ever since. But due to the onset of the depression, local officials and groups carried out little formal park development, except for the construction of an obelisk monument in honor of Forrest.

From 1933 to 1941, however, three different CCC companies worked in Benton County and probably undertook various improvement projects at the park as part of their general effort to improve soil conservation and recreation in the county. Company 1470, known at Camp Gordon Browning, generally undertook soil conservation work, but it maintained a side camp at the park. CCC Company 497 may have worked at the park from 1935 to 1936, while Company 3468 was located in nearby Camden in 1940 and 1941.

The CCC boys are credited with the construction of a park residence, bathroom, picnic shelter, two log cabins, and a stone, two-story, Government Rustic–style observation building. In 1963 the county memorial park became an official state park. Today, the shelter, bathroom, and one log cabin remain from the original CCC projects. The observation tower, which provided a striking view of the Johnsonville battle site as well as the entire Tennessee River from the crest of Pilot Knob, was demolished in 1978 and replaced with the Tennessee River Folklife Interpretive Center. In building the folklife center, the contractors reused many of the stones used in the CCC structure; the center also contains a scaled model of the original observation building.

The construction of the new museum and visitor center signaled a shift in emphasis from the controversial Confederate cavalry officer and former Ku Klux Klan leader to disappearing folk traditions, such as musseling and crafts, along the river.

Nearby Forrest park, under the waters of Kentucky Lake, is the Eva site, another historic area of intense New Deal activity. In 1940 TVA archaeologists, supervised by Douglas Osborne, excavated the site before waters from Kentucky Lake inundated it. Over twenty years later, Thomas Lewis and Madeline Kneberg Lewis published their report, *Eva: An Archaic Site* (1961). Lewis and Kneberg Lewis concluded that the site provided significant insight into Archaic cultures in West Tennessee, underscoring their relatively healthy lives and general conservatism in adapting to outside change.

BLEDSOE COUNTY
Bledsoe State Forest (1934–36), Tennessee Highway 101, Pikeville vicinity

CCC Company 1466 was based at Camp Sam Houston near Pikeville from the fall of 1933 to the mid-1930s. During this period, the company worked with state forest personnel to improve Bledsoe State Forest, a tract of almost eleven thousand acres in the northwest corner of Bledsoe County. The company built roads and a fire tower along with bridle trails, hiking trails, picnic facilities, campgrounds, small fish-breeding pools, and various low dams on creeks to improve drainage and soil conservation. In Bledsoe County, the company carried out reforestation work and helped to finish the local high school gymnasium.

BLOUNT COUNTY
Cades Cove, Great Smoky Mountains National Park (1933–40), Tennessee Highway 73 and Laurel Creek Road, Townsend vicinity

In concluding its chapter on the Great Smoky Mountains National Park, the authors of the 1939 WPA *Guide to Tennessee* commented on the history and character of the people displaced by the park's development:

> The pioneer way of life is still to be found within its boundaries. During the great westward migration of the eighteenth century, when thousands of English and Scotch-Irish home seekers poured over the Appalachians, many families halted and took up land in the mountain valleys rather than undertake the hard journey westward. Stragglers coming into the mountains after the coves and bottoms were taken up were forced to settle on the ridges where the soil was thin and stony....
>
> Most of the cabins of the early settlers were built at 'log raisings.' Notched logs, cut at the right turn of the moon to insure proper seasoning, were assembled, and a house was often erected in two or three days with the assistance of neighbors. Chimneys were sometimes constructed of logs, laid in clay, and fired hard by chimney heat. Because large families prevailed, the loft provided sleeping quarters for youngsters when they graduated from trundle beds.
>
> The conversion of the heart of the Great Smokies into a national park ended the isolation of its people. The swift drastic changes, however, have affected chiefly the younger generation; older people still cling to traditions and customs practiced by their forefathers. In character, the highlander remains independent, unaffected, and sure of himself, and never seems hurried about his work or his play. His tastes are simple, and his tradition of open-handed hospitality has the force of a religious law. Much of his social life centers about the little 'church house.' Congregations are predominantly Baptist, with a sprinkling of Methodist and Presbyterian.

> Many of the old cabins were razed when the park land was purchased, and their owners were moved elsewhere. The homes that remained may be occupied through the lifetimes of present members of the family and will then become Government property. A few old log houses are maintained as typical examples of pioneer homes.[6]

Foremost among those "few old log houses" was the Cades Cove area of Blount County, a rural landscape that is the most popular historic site in the park.

Cades Cove purports to preserve and interpret a nineteenth-century rural landscape before industrialization and modernization forever changed life in the Appalachians. The assumptions found above in the *WPA Guide to Tennessee* characterized much intellectual understanding of southern rural peoples in the 1930s—they were "highlanders," stubborn, proud, independent, and backward. Being in touch with "real" Appalachian lives, traditions, landscapes, so thought many writers, historians, and sociologists, allowed modern Americans to somehow touch something basic, even primeval, in their culture. Evidence that mountain folk, however, had changed in modern times, adapting ideas, machines, and consumer goods to their traditional ways was at odds with this intellectual image of Appalachian life. Nor could evidence of farm tenancy—a reality in the cove during the early 1900s—square with the image of the independent highlander. Such doses of reality

Whitehead Family Dwelling, Cades Cove, Great Smoky Mountains National Park, Blount County.

within the landscape actually became viewed as intrusions into an ideal rural world. Thus, when federal officials acquired Cades Cove, they "restored" the area to an imagined world of the past, one that, as the WPA writer suggested, was dominated by logs, independent men, and draft animals.

Cades Cove is a landscape of mid-1930s assumptions about Appalachian architecture, history, culture, and historic preservation. The National Park Service sometimes moved and grouped buildings together, as at Cable Mill, the interpretive center of the Cove, that originally stood miles apart. It reconstructed others, including the often-photographed cantilever barn at Tipton Place, and tore down box-construction outbuildings and dwellings that did not reflect the log architecture theme that the Park Service considered worthy of preservation. NPS and CCC crews also removed later "non-historic" frame additions and weatherboard from the log buildings, leaving in some cases a shell of what had once been a larger dwelling. This type of "historic preservation" was common at the time, when historians and architects believed that a building must be "taken back" to a period of time when it "was most significant."

The deletion of outbuildings, frame additions, and the lack of furnishings at the dwellings enhanced another misleading image conveyed by Cades Cove—that only men mattered in the world of the southern highlands. Most of the farms are named solely for the "man of the house"—the Elijah Oliver Place, the Carter Shields Cabin, the Dan Lawson Place—as if the wives did not matter. Compounding this image was the type of farm buildings typically kept intact—they are stock barns, blacksmith shops, mills, and cribs. The buildings where farm women worked—chicken coops, gardens, dairies, and washhouses—are as absent as any sign of the domesticity they brought to the interior of the log homes. With the commendable exception of the Gregg-Cable House at Cable Mill, the interiors too are male domains; stripped of furniture, they emphasized the log craftsmanship that may be attributed, of course, to the men.

John Oliver was one Cades Cove resident who fought tenaciously to keep NPS from claiming his land. Oliver was like many residents; he wanted conservation and was not adverse to creating a national park, but he knew of no reason why the financial benefits of tourism and road development should not accrue to the actual residents. In late 1926 and 1927, park officials and boosters reassured Cades Cove residents that the national park would never condemn their homes, even though these leaders knew that legislation would allow them to do exactly that. The Tennessee park bill granted the park commission the power of eminent domain to seize the property of those unwilling to sell, as long as owners received fair market value in return. Frustrated by his inability to convince officials that place was something important and enduring to Cades

Cove residents, and unwilling to trust unofficial guarantees, John Oliver fought eminent domain through the courts, but three years of trials and appeals amounted to nothing except a settlement of $10,650 for his property.

In December 1935 only twenty-five families remained at Cades Cove and that month they received notice to leave in a month's time. NPS and CCC workers tore down unwanted dwellings, and carefully nurtured fields soon turned to wilderness. When the CCC removed the bell from the belfry of the Methodist Church, John Oliver appealed directly to President Franklin Roosevelt, who subsequently ordered the return of the bell to its rightful place. John Oliver was able to stay another year, until Christmas 1937. When he left, Cades Cove seemed an alien landscape in light of all the missing homes, outbuildings, fences, and people. "The single guiding principle" to the so-called preservation of Cades Cove, concluded historian Durwood Dunn, "was that anything which might remotely suggest progress or advancement beyond the most primitive stages should be destroyed. A sort of pioneer primitivism alone survived in the cove structures left standing."[7]

CAMPBELL COUNTY
Cove Lake State Park (1937–41), U.S. Highway 25E, Caryville

Cove Lake State Park was developed in the late 1930s as a third joint demonstration effort by TVA, CCC, and NPS. It centered along an arm of Norris Lake, created by the Caryville Dam, a subsidiary project to nearby Norris Dam,

Cove Lake State Park, Campbell County.

finished in 1936. TVA officials built the dam in order to diminish the impact of the Norris reservoir on the town of Caryville. As it was, TVA still condemned, demolished, or relocated more than seventy structures in the town, including the public school and First Baptist Church. It also relocated Tennessee Highway 63 and U.S. Highway 25E.

CCC Company 4493 began work on the 667-acre park in the summer of 1937. It is credited with the construction of the park's initial infrastructure and facilities. These included water lines, a parking lot, roads, fencing, boat dock, picnic tables and shelters, chipped stone curbs, water fountains, walls, sixteen stone cabins, restaurant, and a stone park office. The park was deeded to the state of Tennessee in 1950. The state has since expanded and modernized facilities; only a few original CCC structures remain, such as stone walls, a powder house, the park office, and portions of the original restaurant.

In creating the dam, lake, and park, TVA officials found that the park site contained evidence of Mississippian period occupation by Native American groups from about 1000 to 1200 A.D. University of Tennessee archaeologists excavated mounds and habitation sites in 1937. Remnants of one site are still visible at the park's "Duck Island."

CAMPBELL COUNTY

Campbell County War Memorial (1938), Campbell County Courthouse grounds, Jacksboro

This obelisk stone monument, topped by a metal sculpture of an American eagle, is a rarity among NYA construction projects in Tennessee. Typically, in its construction projects the agency employed young people to build schools, scout lodges, libraries, or recreational facilities. This memorial to soldiers in World War I, sponsored by local posts of the American Legion and Spanish-American War Veterans, rests on a raised platform of stone and soil, flanked by two period cannons.

CHEATHAM COUNTY

Mound Bottom archaeological site (1936-37), U.S. Highway 70, Ashland City vicinity

Mound Bottom is an extremely significant prehistoric site located along the Harpeth River; *Tennessee Anthropologist* editor Kevin Smith concluded that the site served "as the social, political, economic, and religious center for one of

162 PARKS, MEMORIALS, AND MUSEUMS

War Memorial, Campbell County Courthouse grounds, Jacksboro.

North America's most complex native civilizations."[8] The *WPA Guide to Tennessee* discussed the site, noting its stone grave burials, many mounds, and other extant features. In the winter of 1936–37, George K. Neumann and Stuart Neitzel, part of the University of Tennessee's program under the overall supervision of Thomas M. N. Lewis, directed a group of WPA-funded workers in limited excavations at the site. Neitzel found one small stone box cemetery of twenty graves while the excavation of Woodard Mound uncovered sixteen graves. More extensive work took place at the nearby Pack Mounds (which are privately owned). In 1974 Neitzel told Carl Kuttruff of the Tennessee Division of Archaeology: "mainly I froze living in tents with my booze buried in a pile of snow by the door. Luther Dobson used to bring his Walker dog and a jug of corn and sit on my doorstep running rabbits through the camp."[9]

Lewis was very interested in developing both the Pack Mounds and Mound Bottom sites into a highway wayside museum that would educate the public about archaeology as well as generate funds for his nascent Division of Anthropology at the University of Tennessee. Rarely, however, could Lewis devote time or money to the project due to the ever-increasing pressure to complete salvage archaeology projects in TVA reservoir areas.

In 1939 Lewis and William H. Hay submitted a report to Commissioner of Conservation Charles Poe and proposed the creation of the Mounds Bottom State Archeological Area. Lewis and Hay envisioned that the CCC would assist in the development of 640 acres and that museum buildings would be constructed over the excavations. However, not until 1972 would the state of Tennessee acquire the Mound Bottom site, which still awaits the resources and funds to become an archaeological museum and historic site.

CHESTER COUNTY
Chickasaw State Park and Forest (1934–41), Tennessee Highway 100, Henderson vicinity

The Chickasaw Land-Use Project, launched as a joint federal effort of the Resettlement Administration, the Civilian Conservation Corps, and the Works Progress Administration in 1934–35, initially called for the acquisition of some 35,000 acres of submarginal, eroded West Tennessee landscape. Project managers planned to relocate farm families through the Resettlement Administration; use the RA and CCC to reforest and reclaim devastated land; and use the CCC and WPA to establish a wildlife preserve, state forest, and public park. Due to budget cuts, however, the final project only included 11,215 acres, less than one-third of the original plan. Among the casualties of the budget cuts were plans to develop historic sites, such as James K. Polk's Hardeman County farmhouse, various Civil War earthworks, and the Pinson Mounds prehistoric site.

Chickasaw State Park contains two lakes. At the park headquarters is a fifty-four-acre lake named Lake Placid. On the western end of the park is Lac La Joie, developed initially by the Resettlement Administration. Here is the location of the park's group camp. The cabins there, according to the *WPA Guide to Tennessee* of 1939, "stand in a pine and hardwood grove at the approach to the lake; each contains a living room, bedroom, kitchenette, and bath, and is electrically light. A recreation building is on Honeymoon Hill, which is covered with white oak, dogwood, and redbud, and surrounded on three sides by the waters of Lac La Joie. The caretaker's home was designed to demonstrate to farmers of the area what can be done in planning a model farmhouse."[10] This model landscape, however, would not last long. In 1948–49, the state overhauled facilities at Lac La Joie, even draining then restocking the lake with new fish. Renovations continued from 1950 to 1954, when the group camp area was rebuilt and five more cabins along with a new superintendent's residence were constructed.

The park's headquarters and primary recreational area are centered around Lake Placid, where remaining New Deal–era structures include the picnic area, trails, and Piney Creek dam. Sagamore Lodge, built by the RA and WPA in 1936–37, is an impressive stone and brick building overlooking the lake. It was

Sagamore Lodge, Chickasaw State Park, Chester County.

the park's center for dances, lectures, dinners, and evening gatherings. Square dancing was especially popular. The lodge also served as the annual meeting place of the Southeastern Fox Hunters Association. The lodge interior is a splendid example of late Arts and Crafts styling as practiced by New Deal agencies such as the CCC, WPA, and PWA in the 1930s. Centered on the stone fireplace is a metal plaque with the words "Chickasaw Forest and RA," a reminder of the park's roots as a land-use reclamation project.

Chickasaw was the most popular of the New Deal era parks, recording over 170,000 visitors between 1939 and 1941. Unfortunately, the park was off-limits to the large rural African American population of West Tennessee. In 1938 planners had proposed that a segregated recreational unit be developed, but the proposal was ignored. The state continued to manage the property as a park-forest area until 1949, when the forests were placed under the state Division of Forestry while the two lakes came under the supervision of the state Game and Fish Commission. In 1955, all park and forest lands were deeded to the state.

CUMBERLAND COUNTY
Cumberland Mountain State Park (1935–41), U.S. Highway 127, Crossville vicinity

The 1,720 acres of Cumberland Mountain State Park once served as the outdoor recreational center for the massive Cumberland Homesteads project

Postcard of the CCC bridge, Cumberland Mountain State Park, Cumberland County.

of the Resettlement Administration (see chapter 5 for more on Cumberland Homesteads). From 1935 to 1938, Company 3464 of the Civilian Conservation Corps built a huge stone masonry bridge and dam out of local Crab Orchard stone to create Byrd's Lake as the park's central focus. The 347-foot-long dam proved to be the largest masonry structure constructed by the CCC in the entire nation. "It was amazing what the engineers could do with a bunch of ignorant kids," recalled Arthur Jackson, a Lebanon native who worked on the dam. "They were patient. They said we were going to do it right, and if you rebelled you got another job. They only wanted boys who were willing to learn."[11]

In 1938 the RA's successor, the Farm Security Administration, deeded 1,427 acres to the state, and Cumberland Mountain State Park was born. The park superintendent was Alvin C. York, the Tennessee hero of World War I. CCC Company 3464, assisted by Company 1471, continued to work at the park until 1941, building trails, picnic areas, cabins, boathouse, a bathhouse, and other structures. In addition to the dam, the bathhouse, various utility buildings, a stone water tank, pump house, drinking fountains, picnic areas, and a residence remain from the CCC work. The extant historic rustic cabins near the modern restaurant appear to have been a joint WPA and CCC effort. "I tried to find my camp at Crossville," reported Arthur Jackson in 1994, but "I couldn't locate a trace of it. But that's all right . . . what we did was lasting, and that's what matters."[12]

DAVIDSON COUNTY

Fort Negley (1936–37), Ridley Boulevard at Chestnut Street, Nashville

Fort Negley is the largest remnant of the various Federal fortifications built in Nashville during the Civil War. Designed by army engineer James St. Clair Morton, the fort was constructed by both Federal soldiers and African American "contraband" laborers. After its completion in 1862, soldiers of the U.S. Colored Troops often garrisoned the fort, and the fort was at the center of activity during the Battle of Nashville in late 1864. After the war, federal troops left the fort in 1867, and various materials were later used for new building projects in Nashville.

In 1928 the city's park board acquired the property. In 1936–37, the WPA decided to reconstruct the fort as part of its dual interest in creating public urban parks and in preserving significant historic sites. Engineer J. D.

Tyner supervised the restoration, and the fort opened as historic site. But with the end of the New Deal, city officials soon lost interest in a Civil War site that was located in the African American section of Nashville and was so closely associated with the Union cause and African American history during the Civil War. Fort Negley began to deteriorate due to neglect.

More recently, historians, African American leaders, and historic preservationists have joined forces to address another restoration of the site and the reopening of Fort Negley as the primary Civil War battlefield site in Nashville. Hopes are high that a combination of public and private sponsors can lead to the park's reopening.

DAVIDSON COUNTY

The Warner Parks (1936–38), Belle Meade Boulevard and Old Hickory Boulevard, Nashville

With 2,664 acres, the Warner Parks comprise one of the largest municipal parks in the nation. They honor Nashville businessmen Percy and Edwin Warner. The parks began with the donation of 868 acres by Luke Lea of the Belle Meade Land Company in 1927. Some development took place soon

WPA-constructed entrance gate, Old Hickory Boulevard, Percy Warner Park, Nashville.

thereafter, including the construction of the Beaux Arts–styled gateway at the Belle Meade Boulevard entrance. Nashville architect Edwin Dougherty designed the gate, while landscape architect Bryant Fleming designed a multitiered allee that climbs up 875 feet to the parks' first major hill.

The depression ended the parks' development. In 1936, the WPA spent $215,000 and hired 300 workers to significantly expand facilities. The men constructed a golf course, 37 picnic shelters, scout lodges, bridges, miles of limestone retaining walls, roads, bridle paths, trails, and seven limestone entrance gates, with the one on Old Hickory Boulevard being especially intact today.

The agency also worked with park officials, horse enthusiasts, and sportsman William I. DuPont Jr. to build a steeplechase course, which has been home to the annual Iroquois Steeplechase since 1941. The agency provided $45,000 to construct the course as well as $12,000 for a riding academy. The grants were controversial, since many saw them as unnecessary public benefits for the very rich who typically participated in the sport. The parks are listed in the National Register.

DAVIDSON COUNTY
Marrowbone Lake (1936), U.S. Highway 41A, Joelton vicinity

Located in the northwest corner of Davidson County, near its boundary with Cheatham County, is eighty-seven-acre Marrowbone Lake, a fishing and recreation spot developed by the WPA in 1936. State WPA Administrator Col. Harry Berry wanted Marrowbone to be a model for up to one hundred similar lakes across the state. Building earthen dams and clearing land cost little in materials but called for considerable labor, perfect for WPA projects. In November 1936, however, federal officials issued a new policy prohibiting the WPA from constructing lakes without steel-and-concrete dams. Berry's goal of one hundred lakes was never met. Historian James A. Burran in 1975 estimated that only ten to fifteen WPA lakes were built in Tennessee.

DICKSON COUNTY
Montgomery Bell State Park (1935–41), U.S. Highway 70, Dickson

The Montgomery Bell State Park, named in honor of early Tennessee ironmaster Montgomery Bell, combines both historical and recreational properties into one park unit.

The park began in 1935 as a national recreation demonstration area supervised by the National Park Service. The Resettlement Administration classified a large portion of the park's 3,782 acres as submarginal and eroded, due to decades of timber-cutting and iron-making activity in the area. The park, for example, contained the ruins and ore pits of Laurel Furnace, an early Tennessee manufacturing site. The RA acquired that property, along with several farms, and relocated the residents. Early development took place under the supervision of the RA and NPS. In March 1935, for instance, local civil engineer John B. Neblett supervised the construction of water lines and roads. At this time the PWA built cabins and lodges.

In 1937 construction of most of the park's structures began in earnest with the arrival of CCC Company 4485, composed of African Americans from East Tennessee. This company built two lakes—the fifty-three-acre Lake Woodhaven and the twenty-eight-acre Lake Acorn, where most of the initial recreational facilities would be constructed. After 1941, Company 3464 and Company 4497 finished the park. Unfortunately, there are no extant buildings of the original African American projects.

The National Park Service continued to administer the demonstration area until 1943 when it deeded the park and surrounding forest to the state of Tennessee. The state has significantly expanded the park with a new convention center and visitor facilities in 1998–99. Within park boundaries is the site of the Samuel McAdow house, where the Cumberland Presbyterian Church was established in 1810. Church groups have erected a reproduction of McAdow's log dwelling as well as a small memorial chapel for services.

GRUNDY COUNTY

Grundy Forest State Natural Area (1935–39), U.S. Highway 41, Tracy City

Northwest of Tracy City, near the fairgrounds, is the Grundy Forest State Natural Area, which is centered on Big Fiery Gizzard Creek. One-half mile from the trailhead is the original campsite of CCC Company 1475. The company arrived in June 1933 and began to carry out several reforestation projects in the county. Under the direction of project supervisors Herman E. Baggenstoss (1933–36) and William V. Lightfoot (1936–42), the company built seven fire towers, one of which stands near U.S. Highway 41 south of Tracy City, truck trails, and a telephone system. The CCC also fought fires, planted trees, and carried out erosion projects. For hikers, it carved the first section of Fiery Gizzard Trail, so named for an experimental blast furnace built there during the height of the coal industry in Grundy County. At that time, the trail was part of a tract of two hundred acres, which the Grundy County Forest Association had bought from the Tennessee Land Company for $440. The association donated the land to the state for conversion into a park. The scenic focus then was Sycamore Falls, which was at the bottom of a deep gorge surrounded by three tall "chimney rocks." In the late 1970s and early 1980s, state park personnel extended the park and trail to Foster Falls, which is the highest volume falls in the South Cumberland area.

GRUNDY COUNTY

Grundy Lakes Park (1938–40), U.S. Highway 41, Tracy City

Grundy County was ranked as one of the nation's most impoverished areas during the Great Depression. According to one count, seven out of ten workers were unemployed, largely due to the area's traditional reliance on mining and timbering. Grundy Lakes Park, now part of the state's South Cumberland State Recreation Area, was once a denuded mining landscape, punctuated by the ruins of over one hundred coke ovens operated by the Tennessee Coal, Iron, and Railroad Company. In the mid-1930s the company donated

Grundy Lakes State Park, Tracy City.

149 acres to the state, which, in turn, asked federal officials for assistance with the reclamation of the land. The effort to convert the land into a small state recreation area was designed to put men to work and to provide an outdoor respite for a community devastated by the depression.

Under project supervisor William V. Lightfoot, CCC Company 1475 carried out the park's development in 1938–39. The men reclaimed the land, built four lakes, planted new trees and foliage, and constructed recreational facilities. The park opened in 1940.

HAMILTON COUNTY

Booker T. Washington State Park (1937–40), Tennessee Highway 58, Chattanooga vicinity

In an attempt to provide segregated recreational opportunities for the sizable African American population of Chattanooga, the Tennessee Valley Authority, the CCC, and state park officials worked together to create Booker T. Washington State Park, named in honor of the famous Alabama educator and political leader. In light of the TVA's and state's decision to keep TVA parks segregated, TVA had been under pressure to provide a park for African Americans. The chosen site was along the future Chickamauga Lake; in 1937 CCC Company

Booker T. Washington State Park, Hamilton County.

3459 began clearing land. The following year, CCC Company 4497, a Junior African American outfit, replaced the first CCC unit. The original building plans called for the construction of a lodge, picnic areas, boating docks, cabins, and other structures, but necessary funding was slow to develop. While local, state, and federal officials could all agree that African Americans needed a state park, they did almost nothing more. By the time of World War II, little had been accomplished except for clearing the land, choosing final plans, and building roads. Most improvements to the park came after 1946; the park's dedication occurred in 1950.

Yet Booker T. Washington State Park has the distinction of being one of the first segregated state parks for African Americans in the South and one of the few constructed with the assistance of the CCC. That rather limited "distinction" in itself is a sad commentary on the raw deal most southern blacks got out of the New Deal.

HAMILTON COUNTY

Harrison Bay State Park (1938–42), Tennessee Highway 58, Chattanooga vicinity

North of Booker T. Washington State Park, and located as well on the east bank of the Chickamauga Lake, is Harrison Bay State Park. In 1938 TVA began development of what it named Harrison Island Park as a recreation demonstration area for whites. Later that year, the TVA leased 1,432 acres to the state for the development of a state park. State park officials found that TVA had done little to develop visitor facilities, but over the next four years, the state worked with CCC Company 4495 to build picnic areas, boat docks, swimming areas, maintenance buildings, and roads. In the middle of this construction, in 1940, TVA reclaimed a bit of its land and signed a new state lease for 1,235 acres. The park opened to the public in 1942, but like its segregated neighbor to the south, much work remained to be done and would not be completed until the 1950s.

HARDIN COUNTY

Pickwick Landing State Park (1935–38), Tennessee Highway 128, Counce vicinity

Construction of Pickwick Dam began in March 1935, and later that summer the TVA, NPS, and CCC began work on an adjacent recreation demonstration

PARKS, MEMORIALS, AND MUSEUMS 173

Picnic Shelter, Pickwick Landing State Park, Hardin County.

CCC-constructed trail, Pickwick Landing State Park, Hardin County.

area. CCC Company 3459, an African American company that named itself Company Paul Lawrence Dunbar in honor of the black poet, built park structures over a period of years. Although blacks built the park, it was a segregated white-only facility.

From 1935 to 38, the Dunbar company built trails, cabins, walls, rest rooms, and picnic shelters. One extant stone-and-timber shelter expresses well the rough-hewn appearance of Government Rustic style. From this vantage point are three different views of Pickwick Lake. Nearby the CCC-constructed rest room is the large Pickwick White Sulphur cemetery, a poignant reminder of the vibrant rural community that had existed here before the construction of the TVA complex. Hundreds of white and black farm families and tenants were relocated to make way for the dam, reservoir, and park.

The modern Pickwick Landing State Resort Park now dwarfs the initial park complex constructed during the New Deal. The resort has an inn and restaurant, ten cabins, a large campground, marina, golf course, three swimming beaches, and various picnic and recreational areas.

HARDIN COUNTY

Shiloh National Military Park (1933–34), Tennessee Highway 22, Crump vicinity

Within the boundaries of Shiloh National Military Park, which preserves the site of one of the important battles of the western theater during the Civil War, are Mississippian period mounds that received considerable archaeological attention during the New Deal. With support from the Smithsonian Institution, CWA money from December 21, 1933, to March 30, 1934, funded the excavation of six large mounds at Dill Branch. Bureau of American Ethnology archaeologist Frank H. H. Roberts Jr., assisted by Moreau B. Chambers, supervised the project. The archaeologists found important prehistoric evidence as well as items related to the Civil War. The site, concluded the archaeologists, "had served as a refuge for inhabitants of the numerous village sites nearby during floods and also had been the ceremonial center of the region."[13] The WPA *Guide to Tennessee*, however, identified the significance of the site as being an extensive prehistoric fortification.

HENDERSON COUNTY
Natchez Trace State Park and Forest (1934-39), Interstate Highway I-40, Wildersville vicinity

In November 1934 officials of the AAA's Land Policy Section of the U.S. Department of Agriculture established an office in the Henderson County Courthouse to plan a major reclamation and relocation project for the region. AAA officials, along with local county extension agents and later Resettlement Administration personnel, recognized that eroded land, often cut with deep gullies, characterized literally hundreds of thousands of acres in West Tennessee. They chose an area in Henderson, Carroll, and Benton Counties for a major federal demonstration project, one that would show families better ways to farm, to reclaim land, and, eventually, to provide recreational opportunities.

In April 1935 TERA purchased the project's initial ten thousand acres of submarginal land in Henderson County and its Division of Rural

Fairfield Gullies, Natchez Trace State Park, Henderson County.

Rehabilitation immediately began to move farm families off the land. Some families were moved to new farms in Henderson County; most were relocated elsewhere, with Gibson County receiving the largest number of new families. On April 5, 1935, the editor of the *Lexington Progress* applauded the project's beginnings. "Any government policy that tends to convert poor, worn-out land that never has afforded any standards of living into a worthwhile section," opined the editor, "and at the same time directs its efforts for the rehabilitation of the families in order that they might have a more satisfactory standard [of] living is worth any calculable sum to any town and county." At least seventeen federal and state officials, led by state project manager G. L. Cleland, administered the project from offices located in the second floor of the Ford dealership in Lexington.

In July 1935 a detachment from CCC Company 263, which had been working at Norris, was transferred to Lexington. That summer the company began the first reclamation work and established a local camp. On August 6, 1935, CCC Company 496 was formally organized, with Capt. Hoke S. O'Kelly as commanding officer. To control erosion, the State Division of Soil Erosion Control introduced kudzu, which soon grew abundantly throughout rural West Tennessee. To demonstrate the dangers of poorly maintained land, state and federal officials also "preserved" the Fairfield Gullies—a large area of eroded land near the park's present Interstate highway entrance—as a demonstration of what the landscape was like before the efforts of the CCC and soil conservation experts. Agricultural officials took many photographs in the 1930s of the poorly maintained and eroded land of the South; the work of Farm Security Administration photographers is particularly well known. But the photographs do little to prepare the visitor for the reality preserved at Fairfield Gullies. The steep, scarred land contained in Fairfield Gullies today remains an impressive demonstration of the devastation suffered throughout West Tennessee in the early twentieth century.

As part of its July Fourth celebration in 1936, the *Lexington Progress* published an optimistic report on the project's first full year of activity. By that date, the project encompassed over 20,000 acres and employed some 750 people. The Division of Forestry and the CCC had planted over two million seedlings of locusts, poplar, and pine on some 8,000 acres. The Division of Soil Erosion Control and the CCC had built check dams and planted kudzu on an estimated 10,000 acres. Fifteen miles of road had been graded and graveled, and a brick kiln for new construction had been built. A sawmill had produced 400,000 feet of lumber. In 1937 the CCC built a metal fire tower to keep a constant vigil over its newly planted and reclaimed forests.

Lodge, Natchez Trace State Park, Henderson County.

The Resettlement Administration by 1937 had completed its relocation of farm families and now looked in earnest at the recreational opportunities of the thousands of acres under its supervision. The CCC had built three lakes: Maple Creek Lake (93 acres); Brown's Creek Lake (151 acres), and Cub Creek Lake (58 acres). Officials tabbed Cub Creek Lake as the recreational hub of the park. WPA and RA labor built cabins and a beautiful red-brick recreational lodge, with a Colonial Revival–style exterior and a wood-paneled interior in Rustic style. This peaceful enclave has changed little since its construction in the late 1930s.

In 1939 the U.S. Department of Agriculture conveyed Natchez Trace Park and Forest to state authorities; at that time it contained facilities for boating, hunting, fishing, camping, lodging, hiking, and outdoor recreation. Due to its isolated location, few visitors came at first. Park facilities, however, have grown substantially, especially in the late 1990s, when the state developed a modern inn, restaurant, and cabins near Brown's Lake. Today, Tennessee State Parks operates Cub Lake and the Pin Oak Lake of 690 acres. The Tennessee Wildlife Resources Agency administers Maple Creek Lake and Brown's Creek Lake. Such dual administration is in keeping with the dual responsibility of Natchez Trace as a state park within a larger state forest of forty-three thousand acres. It is the largest state-owned recreational area in Tennessee.

HUMPHREYS COUNTY

Slayden and Link Archaeological Sites (1935–36), Old Highway 13, Hurricane Mills vicinity

WPA workers, under the supervision of Thomas M. N. Lewis, excavated the adjacent Slayden and Link sites in the winter of 1935–36. One of the major discoveries was a cemetery with at least sixty-four limestone and slate box graves. They also found a large ceremonial house and two rectangular houses that had wall trenches and post molds. The use of a rectangular shape for the houses was a surprise; most archaeologists had assumed that Mississippian period houses were circular. The work at Slayden, Link, and other Humphreys County sites taught Lewis, concluded archaeologist Ed Lyon, "much about Mississippian cultures in the county, including information on the burial complex, house patterns, architecture and artifacts."[14] Some of this new information was published in the WPA *Guide to Tennessee*, which included a description of the Slayden and Link sites.

KNOX COUNTY

Fort Dickerson (1936), Chapman Highway at Fort Dickerson Road, Knoxville

Like Fort Negley in Nashville, the restoration of Fort Dickerson in Knoxville was a WPA effort to preserve and interpret a Union fortification from the Civil War. Unlike Fort Negley, perhaps due to the fact that a large portion of East Tennessee was Unionist during the war, Fort Dickerson has survived the last six decades. It remains an intact and valuable artifact not only of Civil War Knoxville but also of the history and historic preservation efforts of the WPA during the New Deal.

Fort Dickerson, occupied by Federal troops under the command of Col. Daniel Cameron in November 1862, played a significant role in the Battle of Knoxville a year later. During Gen. James Longstreet's advance on Knoxville in November 1863, Cameron's troops repulsed a Confederate cavalry attack aimed at taking a commanding position over the city.

LAKE COUNTY

Reelfoot Lake State Park (1934–37), Tennessee Highways 21, 22, and 78, Tiptonville vicinity

Reelfoot Lake State Park preserves one of the state's most unique environments, a large lake with adjacent wetlands and forests created by the New Madrid

Check-In Station, Reelfoot Lake State Park, Lake County.

earthquakes of 1811–12. The state acquired the land in the early twentieth century, but no formal park development took place for some time. In November 1934, CCC Company 1453 moved from Tellico Plains, in the mountains of East Tennessee, to Tiptonville, the north gateway to the Tennessee Delta. The goal of the two hundred men was to build a public park around the lake. William B. Connelly was the project superintendent.

The company first cleared dead trees, foliage, and stumps from the banks of the lake so views of the its eerie landscape would be enhanced. Then the workers turned to building structures, from picnic areas to well-crafted Government Rustic–style check-in stations for the hunters and fishermen expected to use the park regularly. The CCC continued its work on the park until 1938, when it turned its attention to building two wildlife refuges. Lake Isom National Wildlife Refuge was established in 1938. It includes 1,850 acres and is located five miles south of Reelfoot. The project turned reclaimed land into a hunters' haven, especially for the Canada goose. Reelfoot National Wildlife Refuge contains 9,586 acres, representing the upper one-third of the lake area. Established in 1941, the Reelfoot refuge provides a winter home to a large number of waterfowl, such as coots, mallards, and Canada geese.

Despite the years of work by the CCC, Reelfoot Lake did not become a state park until 1956. Most of the facilities today date to the 1960s and 1970s, although the Blue Pond day-use area has a restored CCC check-in building and picnic shelter.

LEWIS COUNTY
Meriwether Lewis National Monument (1934-36), Natchez Trace Parkway, Hohenwald vicinity

In 1924 Tennessee state archaeologist P. E. Cox wrote the National Park Service about the gravesite of Meriwether Lewis (1774-1809), a Virginian who was one of the co-leaders of the Lewis and Clark Expedition (1804-6) and governor of Louisiana Territory (1806-9). Cox believed that he had found the grave as well as the location of Grinder's Inn, where Lewis allegedly either committed suicide or was murdered on October 11, 1809. Fearful of setting a precedent, the National Park Service was not interested in acquiring the gravesites of prominent Americans. Other officials in Washington, however, believed that Lewis should be honored for his prior services to the nation, and President Calvin Coolidge came out in support of a national monument. The NPS still demurred and passed the proposal to the War Department, which formally accepted the property on February 6, 1925, creating the Meriwether Lewis National Monument. Later that year, President Coolidge presided over the dedication of the monument.

Under War Department supervision, little development of the property took place. In the mid-1930s, CCC and WPA crews introduced several improvements. They built a new entrance road and loop road around the monument; raised the soil level around the Lewis monument (even covering its base) to create the memorial Pioneer Cemetery; and constructed a superintendent's dwelling and a public lodge with rest rooms. They further engaged in a limited historic reconstruction project, building a notched-log, two-room cabin to represent Grinder's Inn. The reconstruction was to be "typical of that period, but not intended to be a replica of the original."[15] Today, the Grinder's Inn reproduction remains as a small interpretive center, while the original New Deal-era landscaping of the site has changed little since the 1930s.

In 1938 federal officials began the construction of the huge Natchez Trace Parkway project, designed to link Natchez, Mississippi, and Nashville, Tennessee, by way of a paved, scenic highway of history. Lewis was traveling the Trace at the time of his death; large portions of the trail remained extant, and private groups, especially in Mississippi, wanted the road preserved. Plans for the parkway called for it to pass through the Tennessee counties of Wayne,

Lewis, Maury, Hickman, Williamson, and Davidson. Although some of the parkway was under construction in Mississippi during the New Deal, most of the project was finished in later decades. In 1961, the Lewis National Monument was annexed to the parkway. Most of the parkway in Tennessee was built in the 1960s, but the final portion in Williamson and Davidson counties did not open until 1996.

MONROE COUNTY

Fort Loudoun State Historical Area (1935–37), Tennessee Highway 360, Vonroe

Fort Loudoun (1756–60) was the first permanent fort built by English settlers within the boundaries of present-day Tennessee. Due to its significance in state and regional history, the Society of Colonial Wars in Tennessee began to push for its development as a historic site in the 1920s; the state in 1933 accepted a donation of the property and announced plans for its restoration. In 1935, it turned to the WPA for assistance. Under the supervision of historian Hobart S. Cooper, WPA workers cleared the site of trees and undergrowth, locating some extant remnants of the original breastworks. They next dug trenches to find what was beneath the ground. They found post molds and charred wood to suggest the location of palisades and fireplaces, in addition to locating the original fort well. The workers then began preliminary restoration of some of the features, including the well and powder magazine. The site was stabilized and work ended in 1937. Although important preliminary work was accomplished, the level of restoration and park development found today at Fort Loudoun dates to work completed after the original fort site was inundated by Tellico Reservoir in the 1970s. A replica of the fort, based on archaeological and historical research, was built on higher land overlooking the historic site.

MORGAN COUNTY

Frozen Head State Natural Area (1934–35), 964 Flat Fork Road, Wartburg vicinity

Established as the Morgan County State Forest, this wilderness preserve contains over 11,000 acres of beautiful, rugged land. Its history began in 1893, when the state acquired the land for the construction of a remote prison, named Brushy Mountain State Prison, where inmates would mine coal. Mining, in fact, took place on an approximately 3,000-acre tract at Brushy Mountain until 1966. The remaining 8,368 acres later became Morgan County State Forest. In the mid-1930s, the Civilian Conservation Corps made some improvements in the forest, building about 75 miles of fire trails, access roads, a bridge, and a 60-foot-high fire tower on top of Frozen Head Mountain (elevation 3,324 feet). The tower provided striking panoramic views of the Upper Cumberland. In 1938, after surveying the scenic resources at Morgan Forest, TVA officials concluded that "the quality of the views which may be obtained from the tower would seem to justify widening" the access road.[16]

State officials were slow to react to this recommendation. Finally, in 1971, the Division of State Parks improved and widened the old CCC roads and built visitor facilities. Three years later, the Tennessee General Assembly designed the state forest as a Class I Natural Area and renamed it Frozen Head State Natural Area.

OBION COUNTY
Kiwanis Park (1939), 100 Park Street, Union City

Park improvement projects of a much smaller scale also took place during the 1930s. A good representative example, which is listed in the National Register of Historic Places, is the work of WPA crews in improving facilities at Union City's Kiwanis Park, the historic railroad park across from the town's dual passenger stations. The park itself dates to the railroad beautification movement of the turn of the century. In the late 1930s, however, New Deal workers improved the park by moving a Civil War monument, erected by the local chapter of the United Daughters of the Confederacy, from the courthouse grounds to the park. The workers moved the obelisk monument due to the construction of a new Obion County Courthouse by the Public Works Administration. Next, WPA crews constructed a gazebo at the park for musical performances and other public events. Creating public venues for musical performances was important to New Deal reformers. The WPA's Federal Music Project, for example, wished to demonstrate that good music could be culturally invigorating during times of economic crisis.

OVERTON COUNTY
Standing Stone State Rustic Park (1934–39), Tennessee Highway 136, Timothy vicinity

Listed in the National Register of Historic Places, the Standing Stone State Rustic Park began as a Land-Use project of the U.S. Forestry Service, a division of Department of Agriculture. Its development involved a partnership of federal agencies, including TERA's Division of Rural Rehabilitation (later the Resettlement Administration), the Civilian Conservation Corps, the Works Progress Administration, and the National Park Service.

At the time of the Great Depression, this section of western Overton County contained severely eroded and denuded land, damaged primarily by extensive clear cutting of timber in the early twentieth century, some coal mining, and overgrazing by farm animals. Overton was one of the most economically depressed counties in the state, ranking ninety-third out of ninety-five in per capita income in 1934. Over half of Overton families received some level of federal relief in the first two years of the New Deal, compared with approximately one in eight Tennesseans in other counties.

To combat the problems, federal officials carried out a wide range of programs, many of which were announced in a WPA report titled *Local Rehabilitation Proposals for a Tennessee Rural County*, published in 1936. At the

Guest cabins, Standing Stone State Park, Overton County.

time of the report's release, reclamation and resettlement efforts at Standing Stone had already been underway for two years. In 1934–35, TERA and RA relocated farm families and purchased over eighty-seven-hundred acres for reclamation. CCC crews carried out most of the reforestation efforts while they also built trails, roads, and various check dams in the park. Due to the WPA's initial interest in the county, this agency took on the burden of constructing most of the park's structures from 1938 to 1939, with approximately fifty-three thousand dollars in federal funds. The WPA buildings and structures reflected the influence of NPS design standards and styles, and as a group, convey well the materials and aesthetics of Government Rustic style.

The WPA constructed the large three-hundred-foot stone-and-concrete Kelly Dam and the sixty-nine-acre Standing Stone Lake in 1938. The lake was the focal point of recreational development. The WPA then built Government Rustic–style cabins out of chestnut logs, a stone park headquarters, three group lodges, picnic shelters, two boathouses, and a large Group Camp that contained eight cabins for girls, eight cabins for boys, two bathhouses, a lodge, and three staff cabins. Its Group Lodge and the boathouses along Lake Trail are particularly impressive examples of Government Rustic style, while the intact amphitheater is one of the best-preserved stone and exposed timber structures in the state. It is really nothing more than a semi-

Amphitheater, Standing Stone State Park, Overton County.

circular arrangement of wooden and stone benches, with a stone platform, but that design met NPS guidelines. As the agency's *Park Structures and Facilities* (1935) stated, "the outdoor stage is often merely a platform, the distant view of a near-by stand of trees serving as a backdrop."[17] Even the stone camp stoves at the park reflected standardized NPS plans.

The federal government in 1939 leased the park to the State of Tennessee, and in 1955 federal officials conveyed full title to the state. Standing Stone State Rustic Park now contains almost eleven thousand acres. It is home to the National Rolley Hole Marble Competition, an important folk craft and recreational tradition in the Upper Cumberland.

PICKETT COUNTY

Pickett Civilian Conservation Corps Memorial State Park and State Forest (1934-41), Tennessee Highway 154, Jamestown vicinity

As the park's name suggests, Pickett State Park, next to the Great Smoky Mountains National Park, is Tennessee's most outstanding expression of the recreation and conservation landscape created by the Civilian Conservation Corps during the New Deal era. A large portion of the park is listed as a historic district in the National Register of Historic Places.

The history of the park and forest dates to the early twentieth century, when the Stearnes Coal and Lumber Company of Michigan in 1910 acquired thousands of acres in Pickett and Fentress County and began cutting extensive virgin stands of timber. By the Great Depression, the company had mined all of the land's valuable resources, leaving a wasteland behind. In 1933 the company donated much of its holdings to the state of Tennessee, which immediately began to plan for the land's reclamation. In February 1934, Gov. Hill McAlister designated the land as a state forest. James O. Hazard, the state forester, took a special interest in Pickett. He viewed it as "an area rich in a vegetative cover ranging from lichens to the big leafed magnolia having a leaf often more than three feet in length. The great variety of flowering shrubs provide continuous natural beauty effects from early spring until late fall when the great variety of hardwoods give autumnal effects of exceptional beauty. Many geological formations such as natural bridges, caverns, and cliffs are sources of unending interest."[18]

New Deal agencies became involved at the forest in 1934. CCC Company 1471 had begun various reclamation and soil conservation projects in

Trail shelter, Pickett CCC Memorial State Park, Pickett County.

Putnam County during the summer of 1933. In May 1934 CCC officials moved the company to Pickett State Forest, where a permanent camp was erected and reforestation work began immediately. This company stayed at Pickett until it closed camp in July 1941. Another CCC group at Pickett was Company 447 in 1934.

Initial CCC projects included cutting out fire trails and roads; planting hundreds of thousands of tree seedlings; and constructing forest roads, ranger stations, and fire towers. The company also built a dam and a twelve-acre lake as well as other check dams and drainage improvements.

Working with NPS personnel, the CCC from 1938 to 1941 carried out NPS plans for a recreational area within the forest. This project was first called the Pickett Forest Recreation Area. As architectural historian Claudette Stager has pointed out, "[T]he National Park Service designed park buildings and structures to utilize native materials and fit in with the local landscape, providing for functionally and aesthetically related components" throughout the park.[19] Such design consistency is certainly the case at Pickett. The handlaid rockwork of the Nature Center, Ranger Station, bathhouse, and boathouse are stunning achievements in CCC craftsmanship. The small scale of the Ranger Station, the park's initial administrative center, is a perfect example of the NPS philosophy that such buildings should

Nature Center, Pickett CCC Memorial State Park, Pickett County.

not "arrogantly imply special prerogative to compete with Nature as the 'feature' of the natural park."[20] While the Park Service provided architectural pattern books, its basic design philosophy was that the buildings must be adapted to the resources and landscape of each particular park. At Pickett, this idea is well expressed through the predominant use of rockwork and logs in such significant CCC structures as picnic shelters, various stone and log cabins, the swimming beach, stone culverts and bridges, and campgrounds.

CCC-constructed trails are a special resource within the park, allowing hikers an opportunity to connect this New Deal landscape with the adjacent Big South Fork National Recreation Area, which the National Park Service developed in the late twentieth century. Trail shelters, circa 1935, are extant along the Lake Bluff Trail and the Lake View Trail. Indian Rock House Trail takes hikers to a what was once a Native American habitation site. Other trails go to the Hazard Cave and a natural bridge over the park's human-made lake. The park's longest trail is the Hidden Passage Trail, which passes the location of the old CCC camp.

In 1949, the state forestry division transferred approximately one thousand acres to the Division of State Parks for the formal creation of the Pickett Forest State Park. Additional construction and park development took place in the 1950s and during the 1980s to meet increased visitor demand.

POLK COUNTY

Cherokee National Forest (1933–42), Tennessee Highways 30, 40, 68, 77, and 315, Benton vicinity

The Cherokee National Forest's southern section comprises most of the land in Polk County as well as a large chunk of neighboring Monroe County. There are several ways to explore its rich natural and cultural resources along state highways and U.S. Highway 64; the latter connects the forest with its headquarters at 2800 North Ocoee Street in Cleveland. District offices in the southern section of the forest—a total of approximately 299,000 acres—are at Parksville in Polk County, Etowah in McMinn County, and Tellico Plains in Monroe County.

The creation of Cherokee National Forest dates to 1911, when Congress passed a progressive conservation law allowing the federal government to purchase land for national forest. In 1920 President Woodrow Wilson decided to organize various scattered federal land holdings as an official national forest. The federal boundaries were redrawn in 1936 to place the entire Cherokee National Forest within the boundaries of Tennessee, with the Great Smoky Mountains National Park dividing the forest into northern and southern sections.

Cherokee National Forest, south unit.

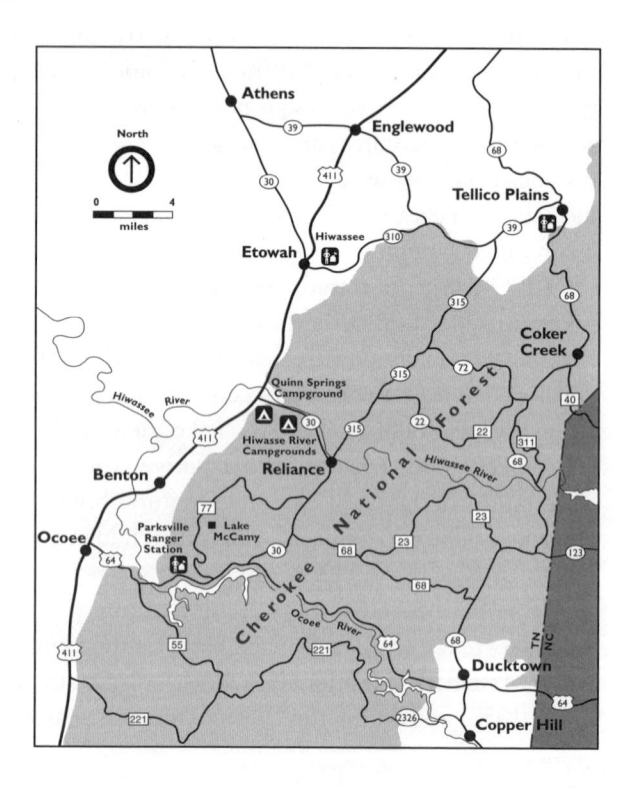

Throughout the 1930s, various CCC companies improved and built trails, roads, fire towers, and recreational facilities in the southern section. The CCC men planted hundreds of thousands of seedlings, improved drainage and soil conservation, built local roads and highways, and developed an extensive network of trails centered on the Appalachian Trail, which runs through both sections of the forest.

CCC Company 1451, known as Camp Old Hickory, was organized in Memphis, and in May 1933 the men set up their tents near Archville, on present-day Tennessee Highway 30, along Greasy Creek in the Cherokee National Forest. The company built and occupied a permanent camp of six frame buildings in October; by 1939 the number of buildings had expanded to twenty-five. While on duty, the company primarily built roads, replanted forests, raised fire towers, and removed underbrush and fire hazards from thousands of acres. The most lasting monument to their work is on Chilhowee Mountain near Parksville, where they constructed forest service road 77, which winds up the mountain to a dam, lake, and recreational center. The road itself is a marvel of landscape architecture, providing spectacular views of Parksville Lake and the Tennessee Valley. At one overlook, the company built an impressive stone gazebo that seemingly rises out of the rugged rocks of the mountain. The view of the Tennessee Valley from this spot is particularly inspiring. At Lake McCamy, the CCC workers constructed a twenty-foot-high dam, which was 225 feet in length, to create a small artificial lake, complete with a rock-walled beach. Today this area is known as the Chilhowee campground. Many of the original facilities have been modernized or replaced, but stone steps, the dam, the lake, picnic facilities, and trails from the CCC era remain extant. Also accessible by trail are the Rock Creek Gorge Scenic Area and Benton Falls.

Camp McCroy, on Tennessee Highway 30, is now the Polk County 4-H camp, but was the original campsite of CCC Company 1451. Company members recall April 3, 1937, as the camp's biggest day. To celebrate the fourth anniversary of the creation of the CCC, officials opened the camp to visitors from the surrounding counties and over one thousand people came to enjoy a free barbecue and to watch a competition of more than one hundred fox hounds. West of Reliance on Tennessee Highway 30 are two additional recreational areas—Hiwassee River and Quinn Springs—that contain extant CCC structures, such as water fountains and rock walls.

Company 1452, known as Camp Cleoga, was a second CCC unit assigned to the southern section of the Cherokee National Forest. Arriving in May 1933, this company set up camp on Baker's Creek Road, near the headwaters of Sylco Creek.

It too carried out various recreational projects, erecting campgrounds and picnic areas, but primarily the company built and improved roads, trails, and bridges. According to a 1939 count, the company constructed 15 bridges, with the longest being 140 feet, improved 26 miles of road, resurfaced another 28 miles, and built 36 miles of new roads. They also installed approximately 50 miles of telephone lines and constructed the Sheeds Creek Ranger Station.

CCC crews in 1941 also began the work of reclaiming an eerie moonscape of environmental destruction between the towns of Ducktown and Copperhill in Polk County. Years of cattle overgrazing, timber slashing, and especially the open roasting and reduction of copper ore in the area caused immense damage to the topsoil, leaving a few scraggly trees within a desertlike landscape. CCC and TVA officials began experiments, eventually successful, to find trees that would plant lasting roots into the soil. At one time, ironically, residents in Ducktown and Copperhill expressed pride in their different landscape of vivid colors and little vegetation. Today the red, moonlike hills largely have given way to new pine forests. As forest service official Quentin Bass recently observed, "[T]he Cherokee National Forest today is largely, and quite literally, a living testimony to the hard work of the Civilian Conservation Corps."[21]

SEVIER COUNTY

Great Smoky Mountains National Park (1933–40), U. S. Highway 441, Sugarlands Visitor Center, Gatlinburg

The development of the Great Smoky Mountains National Park was one of President Franklin D. Roosevelt's personal favorites among New Deal projects. When the park was formally dedicated in September 1940, Roosevelt himself presided over the festivities at Newfound Gap. The park's origins lay with business progressives, conservationists, and state and local government officials in both Tennessee and North Carolina. In 1923, a group of Knoxville boosters promoted the idea of a national park in the Appalachian Mountains. At the time, federal, state, and local governments owned pockets of land in the project area; timber companies owned the vast majority of the land. Conservative estimates placed the cost of land acquisition at ten million dollars, with approximately sixty-two hundred different property owners in Tennessee alone being involved.

Park boosters, led by the Great Smoky Mountains Conservation Association in Tennessee, began an aggressive public campaign to raise the nec-

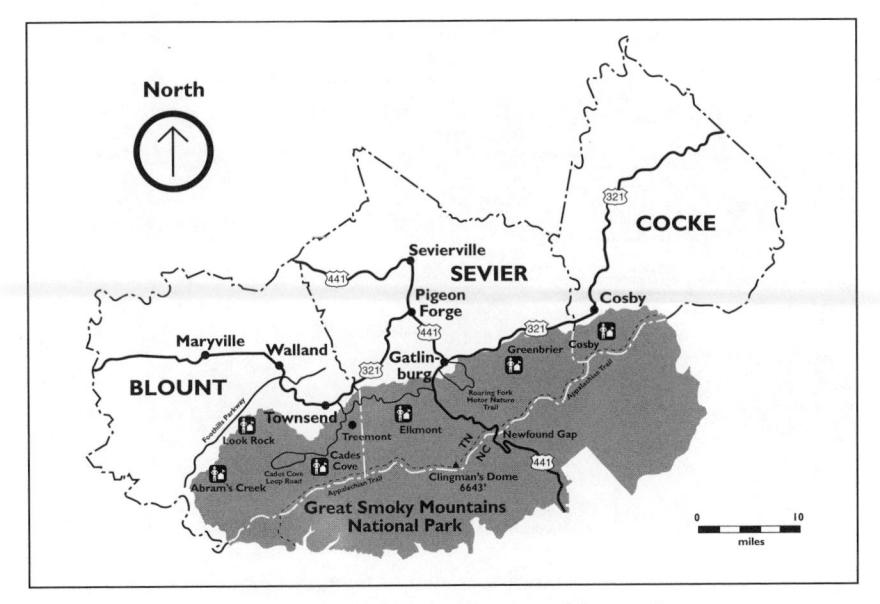

Great Smoky Mountains National Park, Blount and Sevier Counties.

essary money. When this private campaign proved popular and successful, politicians became interested. In 1926 President Calvin Coolidge signed a bill pledging federal support in administering the park once Tennessee and North Carolina donated 150,000 acres and in developing the park once the states donated a total of 423,000 acres. The federal legislation, however, also restricted the use of any federal funds for land purchases, and that restriction delayed quick development of the park. The following year, the two states approved two million dollars in bonds each for land acquisition.

The federal pledge galvanized private efforts to create a national park. In 1928 millionaire capitalist John D. Rockefeller Jr., who had donated money for the creation of the Grand Tetons National Park in Wyoming, offered five million dollars to the Great Smokies, a donation made in honor of his mother, Laura Spellman Rockefeller. With approximately ten million dollars available, officials began to purchase land and the actual development of the national park was underway.

The crash of 1929 dampened enthusiasm for the park—and money once pledged in good faith was not forthcoming in the early 1930s. The major landowners also fought the park with every available legal maneuver (with a few illegal ones thrown in as well). The beginning of the New Deal—and especially Roosevelt's interest in conservation and recreation—offered new opportunities for the groups supporting the Great Smoky Mountains National Park. Enter the

Postcard of the Laura Spellman Rockefeller Memorial, Great Smoky Mountains National Park, Sevier County.

Civilian Conservation Corps. In 1933, President Roosevelt issued an executive order spending over $1.5 million to complete land purchases; technically, he issued the order not to purchase land for a park but to ensure enough work for the Emergency Conservation Work program and its various CCC companies. Congress itself later reversed its 1926 law by approving the expenditure of another $743,000 for land purchases, finally allowing the park to meet the federal mandate of 423,000 acres for national park designation.

Certainly the CCC and NPS produced a conservation landscape unmatched in the southern highlands. In 1934 and 1935, according to historian Carlos C. Campbell, sixteen CCC camps employed some 4,350 men. Under the supervision of the National Park Service, the young CCC workers "busily engaged in building hiking and horseback trails, fire control roads, and a series of strategically located fire towers, and doing many other types of construction work" from culverts and bridges to drainage ditches and check dams. Without the CCC, concluded Campbell, "it would probably have taken a score or more years to get all of these fine trails and other needed projects through regular year-to-year appropriations."[22] Indeed, the rapid work in the park often reflected the adaptation of Park Service designs, many of which were published in the agency's *Park Structures and Facilities* (1935) and Albert H. Good's *Park and Recreation Structures* (1938).

In her 1937 account of the park, writer and conservation advocate Laura Thornborough agreed with Campbell that the NPS and CCC partnership worked wonders. A NPS engineer told Thornborough: "[I]n addition to telling members of the construction crews just what kind of trail we must have to be up to National Park standards, we show them. . . . The CCC boys soon got the spirit of the thing and co-operated beautifully in saving and preserving the natural beauties" of the park.[23] Over five hundred miles of trails may be credited to this massive CCC effort. The agency also built Adirondack Rustic–style trail shelters along the Appalachian Trail.

The NPS and CCC worked together to build more than trails. In the Sevier County portion of the park, for example, architectural historian Robbie Jones found that the CCC constructed a wide range of park structures. The county had four camps: Company 1460 at Greenbrier, Company 1212 at Elkmont, and Companies 1458 and 1459 at Sugarlands. Company 1458, known as Camp H. A. Morgan, was probably the first CCC camp in a national park and was among the first to begin work in Tennessee. The CCC workers constructed campgrounds at Greenbrier, Chimneys, Elkmont, LeConte, and Little Greenbrier. Of these five, Chimneys has the most extant examples of CCC craftsmanship. Other construction projects included "comfort stations," like the one at the Laura Spellman Rockefeller Memorial at Newfound Gap, water fountains, stone retaining walls, telephone lines, roads including the famous Loop Bridge on Newfound Gap Road, nurseries, and four fire towers.

The most impressive architectural legacies of the CCC in the Tennessee portion of the park are the Little River Stone Bridge at Elkmont, finished in 1937, and the Laura Spellman Rockefeller Memorial, completed in 1939. The Olmsted Brothers of Brookline, Massachusetts, a firm headed by renowned landscape architect Frederick Law Olmsted Jr., designed the two-tier stone memorial. This Newfound Gap landmark is one of the park's most visited historic structures and stands adjacent to the Appalachian Trail.

The CCC also worked with other New Deal agencies on various park projects in Tennessee. With the WPA, for example, the CCC built fish ponds for the raising of rainbow trout for the park. In 1939–40, PWA funding combined with CCC labor to produce the park's administration building at Sugarlands. Charles I. Barber of Knoxville designed this large hewn limestone building in a Colonial Revival style. "Modeled after the parlor of the revered Blount Mansion in Knoxville," notes Robbie Jones, the interior "paneled walls feature horizontal beaded boards and heavily molded wainscoting, door surrounds and window paneling" while "the lobby's fireplace is

Sugarlands Administration Building, Great Smoky Mountains National Park, Sevier County.

surrounded by a large Georgian-style mantel."[24] The Colonial Revival style was popular with PWA projects and with park patron John D. Rockefeller Jr., who had also funded the restoration of Colonial Williamsburg in Virginia. But within the overall Smokies landscape it was at odds with the dominant Government Rustic theme of most other park structures.

In building the national park, federal officials and personnel also demolished a large portion of the original historical landscape of the Great Smokies. Thousands of Tennesseans either sold their farms and homes to the project or later had their property condemned and taken by NPS officials. In the wake of this massive relocation were hundreds of buildings, some of which were log buildings that dated to the original settlement of the mountains, but most were frame or box-construction buildings from the early twentieth century. In general, NPS policy was to remove all buildings not in keeping with the rustic, naturalistic appearance of the park. CCC crews, for example, found themselves not only building new structures, but also razing what were determined to be "undesirable structures."

On the Tennessee side, there are three easily accessible areas where visitors may get a hint of the prior settlement history of the Smokies. One area, Cades Cove, was discussed earlier in the Blount County section of this chapter. Elkmont is in Sevier County. It is a former private resort, developed initially by various individuals and members of the Appalachian Club, an elite social club based in Knoxville from 1910–11 to the time of the park's development. The Elkmont historic district contains numerous Rustic-style cottages and hotels, such as the

Wonderland Hotel (1912). Part of the long history of southern elites building and maintaining summer resort homes, this district also shows the impact of early automobile tourism in the Smokies. Congress in 1932 approved legislation that allowed the property owners to have lifetime leases if they then agreed to sell their land for half its appraised value. These "life tenancy" arrangements left some family farmers with their land, but for the most part they benefited vacation homeowners like those at Elkmont. During the 1990s, however, federal officials invoked these various agreements and closed most of the Elkmont area to private development. The deteriorating buildings today mark the end of a significant chapter in the tourism history of the region, although a compromise reached in 1999 will lead to the preservation and renovation of some of the historic structures.

The Roaring Fork Motor Nature Trail, accessible from Gatlinburg, shows a rustic, log, nineteenth-century landscape similar to that preserved at Cades Cove in Blount County. What was once an agricultural landscape of fields, homes, fences, and animals has been allowed to grow into woodlands, occupied by a few farmsteads maintained as historic sites. There are especially good examples of log craftsmanship preserved in several of the buildings. One such farm includes the saddlebag type log dwelling, log barn, tub mill, and springhouse of Noah "Bud" Ogle. The Ogle family has played a prominent role in the history of Gatlinburg.

SHELBY COUNTY

Confederate Park (1937), North Front Street, Memphis

This small urban park facing the Mississippi River dates to the early twentieth century when Robert Galloway, then the chair of the city park commission, envisioned a park that would preserve a river view while commemorating the Battle of Memphis in 1862. In the mid-1930s, the CCC improved the park, constructing its stone rock wall, which separates the park from adjacent railroad tracks.

SHELBY COUNTY

Meeman-Shelby Forest State Park (1933–41), Tennessee Highway 388, Memphis vicinity

This 13,467-acre park was initially known as Shelby Forest State Park and was one of the National Park Service's recreation demonstration areas of the 1930s. Edward J. Meeman, an avid conservationist and editor of the *Memphis*

Memorial to Edward Meeman, Meeman-Shelby Forest State Park, Shelby County.

Press-Scimitar, had been impressed with forest reclamation projects when he had visited Germany; he believed that similarities existed between the German land and eroded southern land. In a series of newspaper editorials and private conversations with public officials, Meeman insisted that regional forests, largely clear-cut of valuable timber in the late nineteenth and early twentieth centuries, could be made to prosper once again. Meeman worked with State Forester James O. Hazard to identify a potential park area in Shelby County.

In 1933 the National Park Service gave the county money and CCC labor from Company 1442 for the park's initial development. Once again, relocation of residents took place under the supervision of the Division of Rural Rehabilitation (and later the Resettlement Administration) while CCC and WPA crews carried out reclamation work. The project also involved a partnership with the Tennessee Game and Fish Commission, which supervised wildlife control projects.

Land clearing came in 1935, and early objectives focused on establishing a wildlife reserve, planting the forests, reclaiming the land from erosion, and building recreational structures. The goal of the project was to reforest and conserve woodlands and wildlife; recreation was a secondary concern. The CCC planted some two hundred thousand Black Locust trees, dammed a lake, and built trails and an extant group camp area. The WPA built cabins and various recreational structures; the largest was the administration building, which included an auditorium, recreation hall, and cafeteria. The administration building has been replaced, but the semicircle of frame cabins still exists, although the buildings have been altered with new siding. By 1941, parks personnel had added picnic areas, playgrounds, and a swimming area. Park planners wanted to build another lake, swimming pool, and horse barn, but wartime demands for labor and material during World War II put those plans on hold.

The National Park Service transferred Shelby Forest to the state of Tennessee in 1944. The state began a new program of park development in 1949. In front of the park's nature center is a boulder monument and plaque in honor of Edward Meeman and his role as a Tennessee conservationist.

SHELBY COUNTY
Raoul Wallenberg Band Shell (1936), Overton Park, Memphis

Designed by Memphis architect Max Furbringer in association with M. G. Ehrman in an Art Deco style, the Raoul Wallenberg Band Shell was originally named the Overton Park Orchestra Shell. It was constructed as a joint city and WPA project for almost twelve thousand dollars, out of a total of seventy-five thousand spent on various improvements at Overton Park. The promotion of music and theater was important to many New Dealers. The WPA's Federal Music Project "wanted to bring its music to the American people, to give them every opportunity to hear cultivated music, so that they could participate and help unify a country fragmented because of the depression."[25]

As a part of a segregated white-only park, the shell proved immediately popular among white Memphis residents only. Six thousand attended the dedication concert of September 13, 1936, when the recently established all-white Memphis Symphony Orchestra, combining members of the Memphis Federation of Musicians and the city's WPA Band, performed a classical music concert. The WPA also provided financial aid to musicians of the Memphis Open Air Theatre, which began performances of light operas and operettas at the shell in the summer of 1938. Within three years, an estimated fifty thousand attended the theatre's summer programs at Overton Park.

From these beginnings, the shell became an established part of the city's music scene, hosting a wide range of programs and artists for the next fifty years. With public integration in the 1960s, the park and band shell also attracted African American artists and audiences. Over the years, prominent performers at the shell include the Allman Brothers, Ruth Welting, Beverly Sills, Rufus Thomas, Elvis Presley, Benny Goodman, B. B. King, Johnny Cash, Christopher Parkening, and Marguerite Piazza. In 1982, at the request of the National Council of Christians and Jews, the shell was renamed the Raoul Wallenberg Memorial Shell, in honor of the Swedish hero who saved thousands of European Jews from the gas chambers of Nazi Germany during World War II. Soon thereafter, city officials and civic leaders periodically announced plans to demolish the structure, and in 1985 no summer performances took place. But that year was an exception. A determined group of local citizens stepped forward to preserve this very important piece of New Deal musical history. "Music at the Shell" remains an important summer tradition in the Bluff City.

In 1936, another WPA program provided funds to the Brooks Memorial Art League, which operated from the adjacent Memphis Brooks Museum of Art, to establish the state's first systematized art library. This collection encouraged and improved art education and training in the city.

SHELBY COUNTY

Memphis Pink Palace Mansion (1933–34), 3050 Central Avenue, Memphis

As New Deal agencies built outdoor parks and historic sites across the state, they also provided assistance to several museums. A good representative example is the Memphis Pink Place Mansion. This historical and cultural institution began as the suburban estate of Clarence Saunders, who had made his first fortune developing the Piggly Wiggly grocery chain. In 1922–23, Memphis architect Hubert T. McGee designed a mammoth pink Georgia marble mansion for Saunders. Before Saunders could even move in, however, his business empire collapsed. In 1926 a land company donated the mansion to the city of Memphis for use as a museum, which opened in 1930 as the Memphis Museum of Natural History and Industrial Arts.

In the winter of 1933–34, as part of a Public Works of Art project, Memphis artist Burton Callicott produced a series of historical sketches as proposed murals for the new museum. The city park commission then appropriated five hundred dollars for materials and took Civil Works Administration funds to commission Callicott, along with his assistants Harry Dixon and Albert Hamilton, to paint murals depicting De Soto's arrival in Memphis in the museum's lobby.

SHELBY COUNTY
Memphis Zoological Garden (1935–38), Overton Park, Memphis

The Memphis Zoological Garden, now known as the Memphis Zoo, benefited significantly from WPA funds in the late 1930s. Established in 1905, the zoo was a centerpiece of Overton Park and was part of the parks and parkways movement in the Bluff City during the early twentieth century. The zoo's earliest buildings date to circa 1909. The WPA significantly enlarged the zoo in the mid-1930s. At the entrance, workers installed a pair of stone lions taken from the Van Fleet home. They also constructed a metal flight cage, a Monkey Island, a Sea Lion and Swan Pool, the Ibex Mountain, and stone cages for bears and other larger animals. Architectural historians Eugene Johnson and Robert D. Russell Jr. note: "All of these structures were in line with the most advanced ideas about zoo design, in which the animals were made to appear to be free and to occupy the same space as the humans who looked at them."[26]

SHELBY COUNTY
T. O. Fuller State Park (1938–41), 1500 Mitchell Road West, Memphis

T. O. Fuller State Park was initially known as Shelby County Negro State Park, designed to be the first segregated black-only state park in the south. Civilian Conservation Corps Company 1464 began park work in 1938 on a site near the Mississippi River, chosen not for its scenic qualities but because it was near the large African American population of south Memphis. CCC officials planned for recreational facilities similar to other state parks, but by the time of the agency's dissolution in 1942, few improvements occurred outside of a recreation lodge, trails, roads, picnic shelters, and cleared land for outdoor activities.

Race was one reason resources and manpower came slowly to this state park. An unexpected reason, however, was an accidental discovery made while crews were digging a swimming pool. The workers found extensive prehistoric remains; according to the *Memphis Press-Scimitar* of February 27, 1940, the site "was literally ankle-deep in crumbling bones, bricks and ancient pottery." Work immediately stopped while superiors in Washington and Nashville were told about the unexpected development. State Conservation Commissioner Charles Poe informed Dr. Thomas M. N. Lewis of the discovery, and Lewis, with a team of trained archaeologists, soon visited the

Reconstructed Chucalissa Village, T. O. Fuller State Park, Shelby County.

site. Lewis concluded that the site was of such importance that he quickly put a WPA crew, under the supervision of George Lidberg, to work in March 1940. Lidberg found a large Mississippian village, where ceremonial and burial mounds had been constructed from approximately A.D. 1000 to 1400.

Lewis envisioned that the property—now known as Chucalissa Village—could become a wayside museum, similar to his plans for the Mound Bottom site in Middle Tennessee. In 1940, Lewis presented a comprehensive plan for site development to the National Park Service. His plan had many strengths. The excavation project would be a partnership between the state department of conservation, the city of Memphis, and the University of Tennessee. The rich archaeological remains would be left in situ, but covered with suitable buildings so the public could visit the site. Lewis also envisioned a museum that would provide interpretive exhibits about the Mississippian period. Finally, Lewis also urged that Native Americans be encouraged to move from southern and western reservations to live at the site, where they could be employed in making pottery, handicrafts, and other items similar to those found in the excavations.

Lewis's plan found few supporters. In April 1940, Memphis WPA personnel ended project funding and excavation stopped. According to correspondence at Tennessee State Parks in Nashville, archaeologists George Lidberg and Charles Nash used thirty CCC workers to conduct further work in 1941. After that time, however, federal involvement at the site ended.

During the early 1950s, the Memphis Archaeological and Geological Society resumed the site's development. The Division of State Parks in 1955 employed Charles Nash, then an archaeologist at Memphis State University, to supervise the excavation and site development, closely following Lewis's plan of 1940. The state even recruited Choctaws to move from their Mississippi reservation to the Memphis area in order to serve as park interpreters and craftsmen. However, the state went beyond Lewis's recommendations to reconstruct various Mississippian buildings as part of the site's interpretation; it formally named the site Chucalissa Village in 1957. Five years later, 187.5 acres of Fuller Park associated with the Chucalissa site were formally transferred to the State Board of Education and the University of Memphis, which has since operated the site for research and education purposes. The reconstructed village portrays the site as it would have appeared circa A.D. 1400.

The state park was renamed the T. O. Fuller State Park sometime after Dr. Thomas Oscar Fuller's death in 1942. A respected theologian, educator, historian, and pastor of First Baptist Church, Lauderdale, in Memphis, Fuller had been a supporter of Edward "Boss" Crump during the early years of the New Deal. Fuller and Crump, however, parted ways over the development of the Foote Homes public housing project in 1938–39. Fuller was forced to abandon his church building and build a new sanctuary for his African American congregation in 1939.

SULLIVAN COUNTY
Steele Creek Park (1938–42), Tennessee Highway 126, Bristol

Although several of the parks projects initiated by New Deal agencies had their difficulties at one time or another, all of the projects—except for the Steele Creek Park in Sullivan County—eventually became part of the state park system. Steele Creek began as a twenty-five-hundred-acre federal recreation demonstration area, administered by the Resettlement Administration, the National Park Service, and the state of Tennessee. The Park Service in 1938 agreed to help develop a state park but stipulated that the state conservation department would supervise its administration, that the state would acquire necessary lands not classified as submarginal by the agriculture department, and that NPS would assist in building the park but that a major share of the responsibility would also lie with the Division of State Parks.

Construction of a property called Watauga State Park began in 1939, when the CCC arrived to build a dam and lake along with other shoreline public facilities. Then the problems started. The state failed to meet its funding promises; the lake water was so polluted that swimming was prohibited; the CCC camp disbanded before construction was completed; and necessary land purchases were not made before wartime demands made additional public funding impossible. In the face of all of these difficulties, the Division of State Parks concluded that the project was just not suitable for a state park. By 1945, officials had deleted Steele Creek from the list of state parks.

In 1953 the state leased a section of the park to the city of Bristol for its use as a municipal park. Six years later, the remaining state land also was transferred to the city, which still maintains and administers Steele Creek Park.

UNICOI COUNTY

Cherokee National Forest (1933), Tennessee Highways 107 and 395, Unicoi vicinity

The creation in 1911 of the Unaka National Forest, now part of the Unaka Division of Cherokee National Forest, meant that this unique scenic and natural resource was among the first southern forests designated under the new national forest legislation. However, when TVA personnel surveyed the forest in

Cherokee National Forest, Unicoi area.

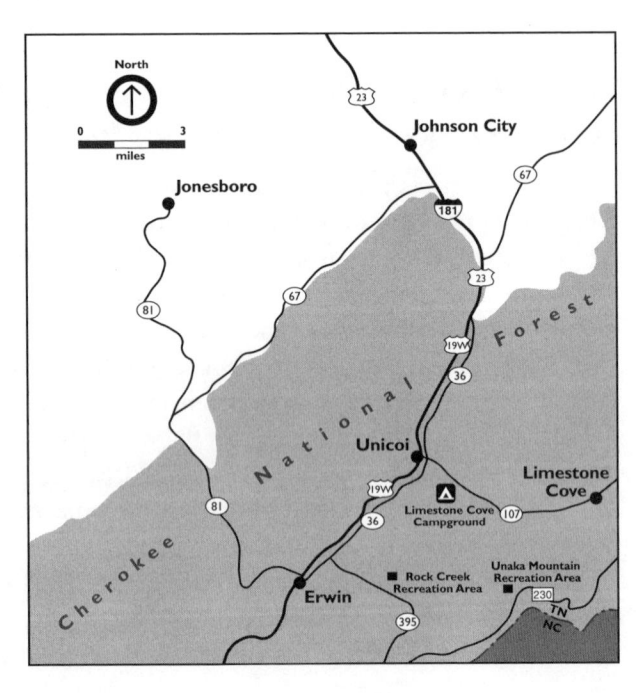

the mid-1930s, they concluded that the forests had suffered significantly from human hands. "The original forest stand of pines, oaks, hemlocks, and yellow poplar has been almost entirely cut; in some cases, notably the east slope of Unaka Mountain [in North Carolina], cutting and subsequent burning has been so destructive as to impair permanently future forest growth."[27] Although noting that little recreational development had occurred outside of efforts made by private interests, TVA officials observed that the U.S. Forest Service had recently begun to establish campgrounds in the forest.

Various companies of the Civilian Conservation Corps carried out the development of these campgrounds, trails, fire towers, and roads for the Forest Service in the mid-1930s. In fact, the first CCC camp in the state, Camp Cordell Hull, was located near Limestone Cove, off Tennessee Highway 107, in Unicoi County. A state highway historical marker stands at the camp's location. The CCC also planted hundreds of thousands of seedlings, constructed check dams, and completed other reforestation and land-reclamation projects. The agency undertook considerable work in improving the forest's sections of the Appalachian Trail. The trail crosses Tennessee Highway 91 and U.S. Highways 19E and 321 in Carter County and U.S. Highway 421 in Johnson County.

From the Watauga District's ranger headquarters at Unicoi, a loop drive of state highways and local roads provides an excellent overview of the forest's scenic resources as well as its cultural resources developed by federal agencies during the New Deal. The drive begins with Tennessee Highway 107 East along Indian Creek. This route passes the CCC-constructed Limestone Cove campground, Limestone Cove, and the Davis Springs picnic grounds. Then, taking Red Fork Road and Unaka Mountain Road to the southeast, the route begins to climb to the Unaka Mountain Wilderness.

After descending the mountain, the route follows the Tennessee–North Carolina state line, passing through Beauty Spot via the Beauty Spot Gap Road. Beauty Spot is a little-known scenic wonder. "The place is unspoiled and thoroughly charming," claimed TVA writers in 1938, "an intimate spot which affords breathless views in all directions." When the writers compared the east slope of Unaka Mountain with Beauty Spot, they found "an object lesson in wise and unwise land use, a lesson which carries an explicit moral in conservation methods to anyone who may happen to visit the two places."[28] Continuing on this road, visitors also encountered the white pine "plantation," a thick stand of white pine trees, which the CCC planted to reclaim an area damaged by forest fire in 1925.

The Beauty Spot Gap Road becomes Tennessee Highway 395 West, where the route returns to Erwin, the county seat of Unicoi County. Halfway to Erwin

Swimming beach, Rock Creek Recreation Area, Cherokee National Forest, Unicoi County.

is one of the best of the CCC resources, the Rock Creek Recreation Area. CCC Company 1455, "Camp Cordell Hull," began work in 1933 while Company 1472 finished the recreational center in 1934. Among the extant CCC structures is a rock-walled swimming area, complete with a beach and a Rustic-styled wooden bathhouse. CCC-constructed water fountains, trails, and picnic areas also are extant.

Today, the northern half of the Cherokee National Forest maintains two district headquarters. The Watauga District is at Unicoi, easily accessible from the interstate highway. The Nolichucky and Unaka Districts are headquartered on Austin Street in Greeneville.

UNION COUNTY
Big Ridge State Park (1934–36), Tennessee Highway 61, Maynardville vicinity

Big Ridge State Park, the second major recreational demonstration by TVA, CCC, and NPS along Norris Lake, contains an impressive array of New Deal structures. CCC Company 4495 began park construction in October 20, 1934. Under the administration of the National Park Service and the TVA Housing Division, the CCC built many recreational structures, including

"The Beach," Big Ridge State Park, Union County.

Government Rustic–style log cabins, a log recreation lodge, a swimming beach and bathhouse, trails, picnic shelters, a large group camp, and a blacksmith shop. It also restored the circa 1825 Norton grist mill to document the lifestyle of the rural people of Lone Mountain and Blue Mud, who lived there before the Norris project. The quality of craftsmanship, the use of log and stone in the buildings, and the successful land-reclamation and reforestation became distinguishing characteristics of the park. A 1961 description noted that "Big Ridge has been able to capture a rustic impression in its buildings and general area which cannot be found in any other park in the system."[29]

That observation holds true forty years later. Most of the park's historic buildings are extant, making Big Ridge an excellent example of the conservation and recreation landscape created by the TVA, NPS, and CCC during the New Deal. The buildings and structures follow the best principles of CCC and NPS design; in the words of architectural historian Linda McClelland, they exhibit "experimentation, innovation, refinement, and, above all, a steadfast search for sensible, simple, and pragmatic solutions that followed function on the one hand and nature on the other."[30]

The low pitch, gable-roof, log-and-stone Recreation Hall stands on a hill overlooking the lake and the surrounding park facilities. Immediately below this superb example of Government Rustic design is the park amphitheater, still used for nature programs and storytelling in the summer months. The most

CCC cabin, Big Ridge State Park, Union County.

popular gathering spot is the swimming beach, which features well-crafted stone walls that set off a grassy peninsula and a sandy beach. A beach situated in the southern highlands, on its surface, is a preposterous idea, as if the original landscape architects of the project had lost any sense of where they were. But the beach and bathhouse have been well maintained since their original construction, and the area is particularly popular with local youth in the summer months.

On the opposite side of the lodge are various examples of Government Rustic–style cabins located from the lakeshore to the forested hillside. The historic picnic areas are closer to the lodge and swimming beach. One log CCC shelter provides an excellent view of both the lake and the beach. The park's recreational facilities are rather compactly located—in keeping with TVA ideas that most of the park was best suited to be a wilderness area. The CCC and TVA restored hardwood forests and reclaimed hundreds of acres of eroded land within the park's 3,687 acres.

In addition to the restored Norton grist mill, which operated privately until 1930, extant historic cemeteries are compelling artifacts of the rural communities displaced by the Norris project during the 1930s. Six cemeteries are either extant in the park or now under water. The Loy cemetery, on a hill overlooking the modern visitor center, contains one headstone with a 1911 death date; most burials took place from the mid-1920s to 1933, although one

Loy Cemetery, Big Ridge State Park, Union County. Overlooking the park's administration building is this quiet, almost forgotten, artifact of the rural communities that once lived in the Clinch River Valley.

burial dates to 1948, when a wife was interred alongside her husband in the cemetery. The Dark Hollow cemetery is along the Big Ridge Trail in the park's interior forests. At other places along the trails there are stone walls and foundations of farms removed by the TVA and CCC as they developed the park.

The removal of original residents is the dark side of the many New Deal park projects of the 1930s. In their study, *TVA and the Dispossessed* (1982), historians Michael J. McDonald and John Muldowny point out that the Norris Basin project displaced almost three thousand families, more than any other TVA project. In an oral interview they conducted with two sisters, Ruby Hill Sampson and Evelyn Hill Longmire, the sisters commented: "[T]he thing that hurt so bad was that we just didn't want to be taken away from the place we loved. Even if we went away, we would like to come back and see the place again. Now it's a hundred feet under water. We can never go home again."[31] Familiar landmarks all along the Clinch River were gone—recorded today only in TVA documentary photography, such as Lewis Hine's image of the three-story Nicely Mill at the Goin community, taken in November 1933.

Besides the loss of landmarks, another major problem was the resettlement of displaced tenants, who of course received no monetary compensation for losing the homes they had occupied as they worked the land, sometimes the same home for years. Another problem was that Norris Basin property owners found it difficult to acquire roughly the same amount and quality of land with the "fair market price" they had received from the government. Beginning in 1935, the Resettlement Administration worked with TVA to establish special projects and settlements, such as the Clinch River Bridge Cooperative in Union County, to resolve the persistent problems of relocation.

The authority also had a large responsibility to relocate some five thousand graves in the Norris Basin. At first it considered establishing a TVA National Memorial Cemetery as a place to rebury the dead of Norris. Angry residents balked at such a scheme. The Campbell County Missionary Baptist Association proclaimed that to deny residents "the right of Christian burial near the church or in the communities of their faith is to outrage the sentiment of families in this section and will violate the spiritual background of the people."[32] As similar criticism mounted, TVA dropped the idea of a national cemetery and altered its building plans at several projects. When possible, historic cemeteries would be left in place; if that was not possible, the dead would be removed and reburied in locations chosen in consultation with local ministers, church groups, and residents. McDonald and Muldowny concluded that, considering the circumstances, TVA's cemetery program worked well, although the destruction of family and church cemeteries contributed much to the overall sense of loss—of place, history, and culture—among displaced Norris families.

VAN BUREN COUNTY

Fall Creek Falls State Park (1936–40), Tennessee Highway 284, vicinity of Spencer and Pikeville

One of the most popular state parks, the 19,684 acres of Fall Creek Falls State Park lie along the boundary between Van Buren and Bledsoe Counties in the Cumberland Plateau. Its rugged landscape includes four notable falls—the 256-foot Fall Creek Falls, the Cane Creek Falls of 85 feet, Rock House Falls of 110 feet, and the Piney Creek Falls of 40 feet. "Falls Creek Falls is potentially one of the outstanding scenic areas of the Eastern United States," concluded TVA planners in 1938, "potentially, because, like the rest of the plateau country, its scenic values have been impaired by the use of the surrounding land." The National Park Service, Resettlement Administration, and the Civilian Conservation Corps combined forces in the mid-1930s to reverse past overgrazing, land erosion, and clear cutting of timber in order to "restore the area's natural beauty more nearly to its natural state."[33] As the NPS stated in a 1938 plan, the land, once reclaimed, should be left in its natural state as much as possible.

Postcard of the Cane Creek Falls, Fall Creek Falls State Park, Van Buren County

The park began as the Fall Creek Falls Recreation Demonstration Area in 1935. Land acquisition was coordinated through the Resettlement Administration, which classified the land as submarginal, purchased the property, and relocated farm families and tenants. The forestry division of the Tennessee Department of Agriculture administered the park. The NPS supervised the development of park facilities, mostly constructed by the CCC and WPA from 1936 to 1938. These included roads, picnic areas, campgrounds, a group camp, a few cabins, trails, and scenic overlooks.

In 1944 the U.S. Department of Interior transferred the park to the state, restricting the land to conservation and recreation uses. State officials began to build additional recreational features in the 1950s and 1960s. The park then experienced a major overhaul of facilities in the 1970s, when a nature center, a large motel and restaurant, and other buildings were constructed. These modern structures either replaced or overwhelmed the scale of development from New Deal agencies. However, the New Deal roots of the park are clearly expressed through its trails, stone-walled scenic overlooks, and especially the reclaimed landscape. The CCC planted thousands of seedlings, restocked native wildlife, and built structures to control erosion. The stunning vistas that today attract thousands of tourists yearly are the most lasting legacy of the combined federal and state effort at Fall Creek Falls in the 1930s.

WILSON COUNTY

Cedars of Lebanon State Park (1933–40), U.S. Highway 231, Lebanon vicinity

About six miles south of Lebanon is a thick glade of cedar trees, one of the largest in the nation. In the early 1930s, however, this cedar glade was in poor condition. Its red cedar timber had been extensively cut in order to make buckets, pencils, and other items. "Because of this deforestation, and over-grazing of young timber growth by livestock, the glade-like (too rocky for cultivation) nature of the soil, and subsequent heavy erosion, the land had little agricultural or timber value," concluded historian Ginger Ramsey. It was "a major contributor to the poverty of the surrounding rural population."[34]

Once the U.S. Department of Agriculture announced in 1933 a new program to assist in reclaiming submarginal lands, officials proposed the cedars glade area of Wilson County as the first Tennessee project (Pickett State Park and Forest would be the first completed, however). In late 1934 Wilson County extension agent Louis Sawyers and forest service personnel proposed that the project—then called the Wilson Cedar Forest Project—be formally established. State forester James O. Hazard agreed with the recommendation. In September 1935, President Franklin D. Roosevelt announced the creation of the Lebanon Cedar Forest Project.

Cedar Forest Lodge, Cedars of Lebanon State Park, Wilson County.

Government officials began to acquire approximately eighty-three hundred acres to serve as the project area, with an average purchase price of six to eight dollars per acre, paid to some ninety-four owners. The proposed project largely displaced the rural community of Hurricane; older residents particularly resented the loss of home and place. According to the oral history research of historian Sean Reines, officials were not beyond tricking, or intimidating, residents into selling their land. While officials promised to relocate families to better land near the Cumberland River, most residents refused the offer and relocated themselves. Today, the Hurricane Baptist Church and Cemetery are lonely reminders of the families who once lived in this area.

This land-use project involved a partnership between state officials and those from the Resettlement Administration, the forestry division, CCC, NPS, and WPA. Its goals were ambitious: to build a recreation area, to create new jobs, to establish a wildlife refuge, to reclaim the cedar forest, and to serve as a conservation demonstration for surrounding farm families.

Project development began in the fall of 1935, with forestry personnel, along with RA and CCC workers, planting new seedlings of juniper cedar, black walnut, black locust, ash, yellow poplar, and mulberry trees. The crews introduced erosion controls and built roads and trails. Eventually over one million seedlings were grown at the project nursery and replanted. The WPA constructed recreational facilities, including picnic areas, overlook shelters on the Jackson Cave Trail, and the original park lodge. Lebanon Cedar Forest was officially opened in September 1937 when officials laid the cornerstone for the lodge, which is the focal point of the park's National Register–listed historic district. The building is of rough-cut, locally quarried limestone, and its style reflects a WPA interpretation of Government Rustic in its materials and cross-gabled roof. Some of the building's cedar logs came from the earlier dismantled residence of Susie Warren. Other New Deal–era buildings in the park include a stone storage building, the Dixon Merritt Nature Center (once a bathhouse for the swimming pool), and log cabins.

At their peak of activity, the various New Deal projects in the forest involved some one hundred workers. In March 1939, the Tennessee Department of Conservation leased the property, placed it within the Division of State Parks, and renamed it Cedars of Lebanon State Park. During World War II, troops of the Second Army used the park extensively during their training maneuvers in the area between 1942 and 1944. In 1955, the federal government deeded the park to the state, which has since divided its management between state parks (the recreational area) and state forestry (the large cedar forest).

7

Dams to Privies: A New Deal Foundation for Modern Tennessee

To hundreds of thousands of Tennesseans, the schools, courthouses, public art, community centers, and parks of the New Deal offered new and welcome opportunities and diversions during the depression decade. But to most residents, the most fundamental change came from the huge arena of public improvements—dams, roads, sidewalks, waterworks, electrical systems, soil conservation, even privies built across Tennessee from 1933 to 1942.

Certainly foremost among those creating and shaping public improvements was the Tennessee Valley Authority, that most unique New Deal experiment in regional development that is still viewed as a behemoth by today's Tennesseans. As President Franklin Roosevelt told the National Emergency Council on December 11, 1934, TVA was

> a social experiment that is the first of its kind in the world, as far I know, covering a convenient geographical area—in other words, the watershed of a great river. The work proceeds along two lines, both of which are intimately connected—the physical land and water and soil end of it, and the human side of it. It proceeds on the assumption that we are going to the highest mountain peak of the Tennessee Watershed and we are going to take an acre of land up there and say, "What should this land be used for, and is it being badly used at the present time?" And a few feet farther down we are going to come to a shack on the side of the mountain where there is a white man of about as fine stock as we have in this country, who, with his family of children, is completely uneducated—never had a chance, never sees twenty-five or fifty dollars in cash a year, but just keeps body and soul together—manages to do that—and is the progenitor of a large line of children for many generations to come. He certainly has been forgotten, not by the Administration, but by the American people. They are going to see that he and his children have a chance, and they are going to see that the farm he is using is classified, and if it is not proper for him to farm it, we are going to give him a chance on better land. If he should use it, we are going to try to bring him some of the things he needs, like schools, electric lights, and so on. We are going to try to prevent soil erosion, and grow trees, and try to bring in industries. It is a tremendous effort with a very great objective. As an incident to that it is necessary to build some

dams. And when you build a dam as an incident to this entire program, you get probably a certain amount of water power development out of it. We are going to try to use that water power to its best advantage.[1]

To Roosevelt and other New Dealers, TVA reflected what their entire program of change was all about. It might be just viewed as a generator of electrical power, but that was incidental to its real purpose: to bring that prototypical rural Tennessean "the things he needs"—better soil, better roads, better economic opportunities, and a better life for him and his children. The project represented coordinated planning by outsiders on a massive scale. As a vision, Roosevelt's words were both breathtaking, yet limited—that is, to whites. Historian Nancy Grant already has documented the rather checkered records of TVA and African Americans.[2] It also can be safely said that few of the other New Deal public improvements filtered down to black urban neighborhoods or rural communities where city lights, sanitation systems, sidewalks, better roads, and better land awaited a future era of change.

Tennessee in the 1930s was still overwhelmingly a rural state. Unemployment was widely viewed as the number-one problem, but right behind it was the future of the land itself. Poor land getting worse concerned a wide range of Tennesseans. Few were surprised when the U.S. Department of Agriculture in 1935 published a report that listed over 11 million acres as having lost between 75 to 100 percent of their topsoil, while a full 3 million acres were beyond hope, unfit for cultivation. Less than 4 million acres of the state's total of almost 27 million acres of farmland and forests were undamaged. "It does not take the report of experts, however, to convince any intelligent person in Tennessee that our fertile soil is fast disappearing," commented educator Dr. Robert H. White in 1936. "You may yourself ride or fly over Tennessee and view the results of soil erosion,—vast areas with yawning gullies and abandoned lands which were once fertile and productive."[3]

Better land was a basic TVA goal, which the agency pursued by enlisting hundreds of farm families in its popular and successful Demonstration Farm program, by producing new fertilizers at its operations in Muscle Shoals, Alabama, and by cooperating with federal and state agricultural officials on small and large soil-conservation projects. Between 1934 and 1936, for example, TVA worked with the CCC, extension agents, and approximately 1,700 private property owners to plant an estimated 18 million tree plantings on some 11,560 acres in the TVA region, and the authority's count of tree plantings reached 50 million by 1939.

A representative example of the impact of this work can be found in Bradley County, where CCC Company 3466 worked from a campsite on the grounds of the county poor farm. The first men arrived on May 19, 1935, and over the next two months they built the entire camp of fourteen buildings, with most being prefabricated structures from the Stivers Lumber Company in Cleveland. In the farm projects, CCC crews provided labor and expertise, while local farmers provided supplies and teams of animals. According to a tally published in the *Cleveland Weekly Herald* of April 3, 1936, the CCC culled 154 bushels of pine seeds and 3,874 pounds of walnut and poplar seeds; built 15 rock dams and another 147 log and rock dams; dug 1,590 linear feet of diversion ditches, and planted 398 acres in pine and locust trees between August 1935 and April 1936. In its two years of existence, Company 3466 undertook 60 erosion control projects, totaling 352 acres and 908,575 tree plantings on private lands. Another CCC unit, Company 2436, worked in Bradley County from 1937 to 1941. It too terraced fields, dug ponds, and reclaimed gullied land throughout the county.

Typically, the federal project supervisors worked closely with county agricultural extension agents. The U.S. Department of Agriculture was very concerned about reclaiming abused land, and from 1933 forward various agency divisions and programs implemented or administered several different soil conservation efforts, in addition to their work on the parks and forests detailed in chapter 6. As historian Timothy Lehman has emphasized in his study *Public Values, Private Lands: Farmland Preservation Policy, 1933–1985* (1995), soil conservation became a crusade for agricultural reformers. The initial Agricultural Adjustment Act of 1933 was a beginning, with county extension agents advocating its programs of voluntary crop reduction, benefit payments, and soil conservation. Three years later the Soil Conservation and Domestic Allotment Act helped immensely as it paid farmers for cultivating soil-conserving crops and implementing soil-building practices, such as terracing fields and planting windbreaks.

The law initially placed the Agricultural Adjustment Administration in charge of administering the new program, while in Tennessee each county had its own agricultural conservation association. Although some extension agents spurned the conservation associations, others embraced them. In Maury County, according to extension records, almost seventeen hundred acres had been terraced by 1937. After establishing special soil-conservation projects and demonstrations at local schools in 1940, conservation administrators gained additional converts by having sons teach their fathers. The following year found terrace demonstrators at work in the communities of Culleoka, Rally Hill, Kedron, and Fountain Heights. After World War II, many other counties established soil-conservation committees and programs.

A second federal law, the Agricultural Adjustment Act of 1938, also paid farmers for soil conservation on their private property as well as for cultivating a set acreage allotment for corn, wheat, cotton, tobacco, and rice. This act further established various farm price supports and subsidies. At the county level, three farmers, selected by delegates chosen throughout the county, served as the county AAA committee. All participating farmers were members of the county agricultural conservation associations. Over 150,000 Tennessee farmers, representing almost 8.5 million acres of land, participated in the program. In the program's first year, it netted farmers almost 11 million dollars.

Thousands of farmers terraced their fields, planted windbreaks, filled gullies, and used fertilizers as part of their conservation efforts. Labor from CCC companies, such as Camp Andrew Johnson in Greene County, Camp Joe E. Williams in McNairy County, Company 497 near Athens along the Lee Highway, and Company 3468 at Paris in Henry County, also carried out conservation work on private farms. According to the *Nashville Banner* of July 4, 1936, soil conservation efforts by the CCC already had resulted in thirty thousand gulley dams and eight million plantings of tree seedlings. The *WPA Guide to Tennessee* of 1939 notes several places in Tennessee where

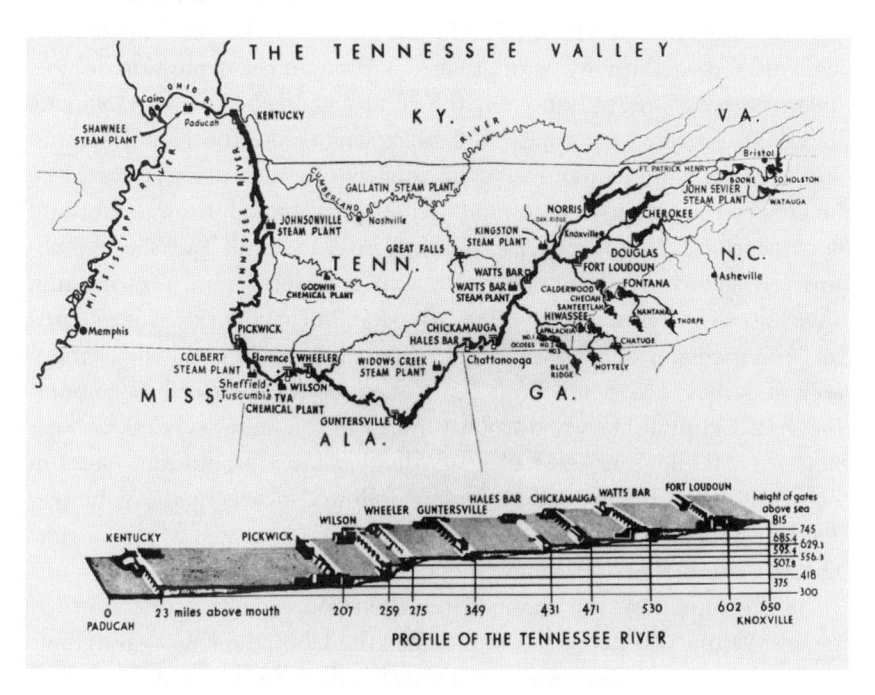

TVA system, c. 1960. Tennessee State Library and Archives.

the corps improved public land. Between Dandridge and Knoxville, for example, there "was a section in which many acres were so badly eroded that they were not suitable for cultivation until the CCC improved them."[4] In West Tennessee, a state forestry seedling farm operated south of Jackson on U.S. Highway 45; it provided hundreds of thousands of tree seedlings for regional conservation and reforestation efforts.

As President Roosevelt admitted to his emergency council in 1934, dams, reservoirs, and electricity would result from his programs to uplift the Tennessee Valley. In the New Deal years from 1933 to 1942, TVA constructed major eight dams in the state: Norris, Pickwick, Chickamauga, Douglas, Cherokee, Fort Loudon, Watts Bar, and Ocoee No. 3. These huge concrete-and-steel engineering marvels impounded hundreds of thousands of acres of Tennessee farmland—some counties lost their best "bottomland" and thousands of Tennessee families had to find new homes. But the federal effort to implement regional planning attracted the attention of reformers from across the country, even internationally. Economist Stuart Chase admitted: "[T]o see the authority in operation is a spiritually refreshing experience.... Here, struggling in embryo, is perhaps the promise of what all America will someday be."[5] TVA became the best-known institution in the state's history.

The huge dams and their powerhouses symbolize the transformation in public utilities and infrastructure that took place in the depression decade. Private corporations, most notably the Tennessee Electric Power Company (TEPCO), provided electricity to many towns before the New Deal, but rarely did their lines extend into the countryside. Electricity produced by the new dams made its way to rural Tennesseans through the federal Rural Electrification Administration, established in 1935. Until TVA's legal problems were solved and more powerhouses were completed, rural electrification moved slowly in Tennessee. By 1938 only a handful of counties had benefited from the program, but those that participated received hundreds of thousands of dollars. The South West Tennessee Electric Membership Corporation, based in rural Haywood County, received the most—$522,000. Next came the Middle Tennessee Electric Membership Corporation, based in Murfreesboro, with $334,000 in funding, followed closely by the Volunteer Electric Membership Corporation, based in Meigs County, at $311,600. The Lincoln County Electric Membership Corporation got $200,000.

Just as important was the modernization and expansion of city utility systems. While WPA crews often provided the labor, the PWA gave grants and loans for the construction of modern transformer stations and electrical utility systems in several county seats, small towns, and large cities across the state. Chattanooga was awarded $3.1 million in PWA loans and grants for

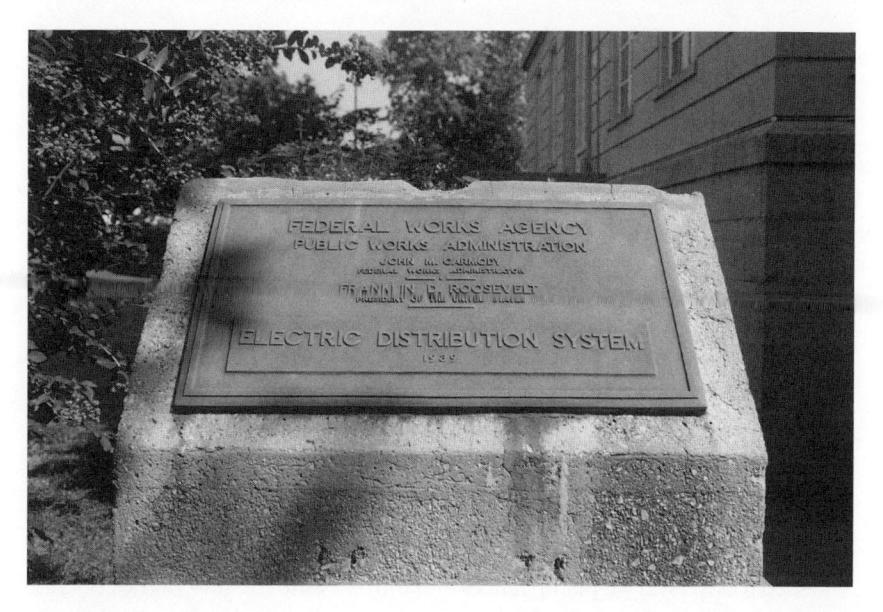

PWA Public Utility Marker, Marshall County Courthouse grounds, Lewisburg.

its electrical systems, while Newbern in Dyer County got $59,000 in loans and grants, and Paris in Henry County received $32,000 in grants. In Lewisburg, a simple bronze plaque on a concrete block, located on the courthouse square, memorializes the installation of a modern electrical system by the Public Works Administration in 1939.

Electricity was the high-tech reform brought to such small towns; others gained almost as much from having New Deal work crews install municipal water and sewer systems, as was done in Camden, the seat of Benton County and Ashland City, the seat of Cheatham County. PWA grants and loans funded both projects. Where the population was not large enough for a municipal water system, WPA crews would built a modern sanitary privy on any private home or farm, as long as the owner would provide a small amount of money (usually between three and five dollars) for materials. Thousands of privies were constructed, beginning with a CWA program in the winter of 1933–34 that constructed statewide some fourteen thousand privies. Two historians in Cumberland County remarked in 1956 that the WPA project that would be appreciated the longest would be the construction of thousands of privies. Each county school received two privies—some had never had one. Other towns improved their appearance; WPA workers installed Woodbury's first concrete sidewalks during the late 1930s.

CCC crews also were involved in this transformation of public utilities as their companies strung nearly thousand miles of state-owned telephone lines, built hundreds of bridges, and graded a thousand miles of roads. The company that improved the road (now U.S. 64/41a) up Sewanee Mountain from Cowan, in Franklin County, proudly marked its name along a stone retaining wall; this is a rare artifact of CCC road building outside of the national and state parks.

Building new roads and improving existing routes was a major preoccupation of New Deal agencies in Tennessee. A political dispute in 1931 had almost totally eliminated the state highway department, leading to the layoff of four thousand workers. Federal monies soon came to the rescue, and road construction continued in the depression decade. Agricultural groups wanted better farm-to-market roads; new bridges were needed everywhere. The WPA alone employed twenty-seven thousand workers for farm-to-market roads and bridge construction. In a 1984 interview with Dr. Samuel H. Shannon of Tennessee State University, H. B. Cathey of Maury County proudly recalled: "I worked all over the county. I ran a rock crusher and built—we just built roads—[and we] widened roads. And we put up fences . . . [and] we were the start of the concrete culverts in Maury County." According to Cathey, "[L]ots of farmers would come visit with us and watch us when we were building those roads. We done a big thing for them."[6] Memphis streets were paved with PWA grants to a total of $493,000, while another $203,000 went for concrete culverts in the Bluff City.

In addition to hundreds of miles of roads, New Deal agencies took on many bridge projects. In Knoxville, the PWA provided almost $120,000 in grants for new bridges. The V. L. Nicholson Company used WPA labor to build the concrete Hill Avenue Viaduct (1936), designed by Luten Bridge Company, while WPA crews assisted the state in the construction of the 483-foot-long Pate Memorial Bridge over Little River south of downtown Knoxville from 1937 to 1938. By 1939, the WPA statewide had built 225 steel-and-concrete bridges and had another 149 bridges under construction. According to a recent Tennessee Department of Transportation survey of historic bridges, conducted by Martha Carver, many New Deal–era bridges remain in use. One of the most striking is the 605-foot-long Cordell Hull Bridge (1934–36), which spans the Cumberland River at Carthage in Smith County.

The WPA also addressed the needs of the state's nascent airport system by continuing improvement programs began by the CWA. The WPA undertook seventeen projects, constructing runaways, control towers, hangars, and landing fields.

In West Tennessee, transportation was also related to the construction of high roads that could serve as dikes in times of flooding. The great Mississippi flood of 1927 had demonstrated the need for better ways to contain the waters of raging rivers. The terrible flood of 1936–37 led state and federal officials to spend millions on improving the levees around Memphis as well as in the northern Tennessee Delta counties of Dyer and Lake, which had been hard hit in 1927 and 1937. In 1933, the PWA provided Memphis with thirty-two thousand dollars in grants and loans to improve its dikes. Then the Flood Control Bill of 1937 produced a new series of flood-control works around Memphis, costing approximately thirteen million dollars but protecting the city from waters as high as fifty-five feet. The flood-control system is perhaps the Crump machine's most positive legacy provided to the Bluff city during the New Deal.

The legacy of the mammoth TVA facilities, complete with visitor centers, has always been easy to grasp for resident and visitor alike. It is more difficult to "see" the impact today of the other New Deal public improvement projects in Tennessee because they are located underground, on private property, or have been replaced by later waves of public improvements and utility upgrades. But the amounts spent on New Deal public improvements indicate the transformation wrought by these efforts. According to a count by the Tennessee State Planning Commission in 1940, a full 47 percent of the money spent on public works in Tennessee between 1935 and 1938—a total of almost 38 million dollars—was devoted to highways, roads, and urban streets. Another 7.4 percent—almost 6 million dollars—went to waterworks and sewers while over 16 percent—some 13 million dollars—was spent on electrical utilities. Airports and other transportation improvements received almost 2 percent of the total, or 1.4 million dollars. In other words, between 1935 and 1938, over 70 percent of the money spent on public works in Tennessee was devoted to public improvements: roads, airports, electrical systems, sewers, waterworks, and other infrastructure projects. The public landscape of the New Deal cannot be properly understood without a representative overview of these improvement projects, from the largest of the TVA dams and reservoirs to the lonely WPA privy on a Dickson County farm.

ANDERSON COUNTY

Norris Dam, Lake, and Freeway (1933–36), U.S. Highway 441, Norris

Norris Dam, almost from its inception, was TVA's model project of what the authority stood for and what it would bring to the people and landscape of the Tennessee Valley. It began in the 1920s as a proposed dam of the Bureau of Reclamation, designed to complement and support the more important

Norris Dam, Anderson County.

Rice Grist Mill, Norris Lake State Park, Anderson County.

project at Muscle Shoals, Alabama. TVA officials changed all of that quite rapidly in the summer and fall of 1933. Through redesign, new engineering, and comprehensive planning—all accomplished with breathtaking speed—TVA made Norris its signature project, the ultimate "yardstick" of all future TVA endeavors. All of its major components and design elements—Norris Freeway, Norris Village, the Norris parks, Norris Lake, and the Norris overlooks—remain much as they were sixty years ago, making Norris a powerful metaphor of hopes, image, and reality of the Tennessee Valley Authority.

The Norris project was conceived on a large scale, much as if landscape architects had been given tens of thousands of acres to redesign as a nature reserve, as long as they placed a huge modern machine in the middle of it. The Agrarian writer Donald Davidson almost perfectly described the overall effect of this combination of nature, man, and machine as he took a hypothetical tourist on a visit to Norris in the second volume of his *The Tennessee* (1948). Visitors first drove onto the Norris Freeway where they observed "neatly fostered illustrations of the forest conservation and proper land use which the authority was committed to sponsor." The closer they got to the actual dam, the roadside "took on the appearance of an amiable wild park," which said, "without words, how Tennessee ought to look if it were benevolently protected." Next came Norris Village, with its homes, school, stores, and church "as ideally spick-and-span" as those in the recently completed Colonial Williamsburg. Davidson admitted that the village was a commendable effort by TVA engineers to produce something better than the shotgun shacks of typical construction sites, something more in line with the model rural settlements under development by the Resettlement Administration. Yet he wondered if Norris was "a little too fine" because "country folks could not live in a park, away from means of subsistence." He correctly recognized that the village was ideal for Norris professionals, a type of rural suburb for modern technocrats of TVA. Again making a comparison with Colonial Williamsburg, Davidson concluded that the quiet streets, quaint houses, and open spaces of Norris Village told the visitor that "modern America on the whole had done rather poorly with its resources, and it reminded him what might have been."[7]

Before arriving at the dam, visitors still encountered one important lesson—the restored Rice grist mill. The difference between the old mill, mill race, and slowly turning water wheel and the TVA dam and powerhouse "was the difference between the land of the pioneers and the planned society of the New Deal." TVA planned to change the old world yet still maintain a healthy respect for the old traditions and individualism of the past. The dam and lake, with its overlooks and commanding view, brought visitors the full realization that Norris "represented the proper modern thing and you had to accept it because it was modern."[8] After spending the night at a park cabin, visitors left to spread the gospel of Norris and TVA to their friends and neighbors.

As Davidson conceded, Norris Dam, especially from its west overlook, is a powerful statement of modernism. When architecture critic Kenneth Frampton compiled his international survey of *Modern Architecture* (1980), the only example from Tennessee—and one of the few from the United States not designed by Frank Lloyd Wright—was Norris Dam. The Bureau of Reclamation developed the dam's initial design and construction plans, but scholars today credit Roland Wank (1898–1970), the authority's chief architect, with the structure's style, landscaping, and overall appearance. Wank wanted "a sculptural recasting of the dam's elements, pulling the powerhouse and spillway face into a coherent composition," observes architectural historian Marian Moffett. "Wank tried to make the dam look as functional as the engineers had designed it to be."[9] Ironically, TVA engineers did not like Wank's design, and the authority brought in the respected industrial architect Albert Kahn, famous for his automobile plants for the Ford Motor Company, to settle the dispute. Kahn strongly endorsed Wank's plans, and from that point on, all TVA dams in the New Deal era would be designed in a modernist style. This legacy to American architecture is significant. As Walter Creese has argued, Norris Dam's "outstanding achievement was in establishing a bold beginning for future cooperation among architecture, engineering, and landscape architecture. The dam materialized itself, represented democracy in a noble way, and engaged the attention of many of the best thinkers of the time."[10]

Norris Dam is a concrete-and-steel gravity-type, measuring 1,860 feet in length and 265 feet in height. On top of the dam, U.S. Highway 441—the Norris Freeway—is 22 feet in width. Norris Lake affects land in Anderson, Campbell, Claiborne, Grainger, and Union Counties, with TVA owning 58,147 acres and holding easements on another 5,458 acres. The powerhouse has the generating capacity of 100,800 kilowatts of electricity, produced by two hydraulic turbines manufactured by the Newport News Shipbuilding & Dry Dock Company and Westinghouse-constructed generators. The powerhouse also contains a reception center where tours may be arranged.

Norris Dam State Park is discussed in chapter 6. Norris Freeway connects the dam, its west and east overlooks, and the park to Norris Village. It was a demonstration project showing how new highway and bridge construction should respect, even enhance, the rural countryside even as the highway functioned as a practical, construction road. The freeway was originally twenty-one miles long and cost approximately $1.5 million. It was the first limited-access highway in Tennessee and is considered the world's first limited-access road that was built for utilitarian—or construction project—purposes.

Like the freeway, Norris Village was more than a practical construction camp for the project; it too was to be an architectural and planning model. The authors of the "Architecture" chapter of the *WPA Guide to Tennessee* asserted: "[T]he future architecture of the Tennessee Valley is indicated by the city of Norris, where a new standard for rural existence is being set" in the village's design, its stress on comfort and economy, and its variety in house plans, building materials, and domestic architectural styles.[11] Recent architectural historians agree that Norris Village represented a new beginning. In *The Public Landscape of the New Deal* (1985), Phoebe Cutler calls Norris Village "the best representative of thirties planning ideology" of all New Deal planned communities.[12]

The town site, designed by TVA landscape architect Tracy B. Auger and his staff under the supervision of Earle Draper, embraced some forty-two hundred acres, and only about one-fourth of that amount was used for homes and related community buildings. TVA strove to maintain a rustic setting for its modern village by maintaining reserved greenbelt areas to the north and south, thus becoming one of the first towns in the nation to implement the progressive greenbelt principles developed by British reformer Ebenezer

Howard. TVA also directed construction crews to keep as many original trees on individual lots as possible.

Central to the village plan was a two-story Colonial Revival–style school, staffed by TVA personnel, which proved to be one of the project's lasting institutions. The school too was to be a model project, promoting the latest ideas in progressive education and utilizing the latest in classroom technology. The authority also established other demonstration projects, such as dairy and poultry farms, a ceramics lab, and the Norris Creamery, considered to be the world's first all-electric milk plant. The town was the first in Tennessee to have a complete telephone system.

The initial houses at Norris Village expressed the contradiction of introducing modernity into the agrarian world of the Clinch River valley. TVA director Arthur E. Morgan wanted the model village to reflect the local vernacular and for the houses to fit into, and not dominate, the landscape. Thus, the houses were placed along natural contours; most were on small lots. The dwellings were small and had central-hall floor plans, like the common dogtrot house, but they were fully electrified and had modern appliances. Some cottages were covered in shingles or native stone to convey a rustic quality, while another 130 dwellings were built from cinderblocks, which spoke to the technological experiment embodied in the Norris project.

Stone dwelling, Norris Village, Anderson County.

Upon its completion in the spring of 1935, architects and planners proclaimed the many virtues of Norris Village: its quaint dwellings with electricity, its varied community buildings, and its natural rural setting that evoked the best ideas of Garden City planning. But the village had cost twice what TVA had originally estimated. Worse, it pandered to southern racism by not allowing African Americans to reside there, even though the races often lived side by side in this region. Eventually, as Davidson noted above, it evolved into little more than a pricey TVA suburb for its employees. By 1948, with the Republican party in control of Congress, the federal government finally balked at the annual subsidy given to Norris Village. TVA had little choice but to get out of the model town business, and on June 15, 1948, it sold the village to a private company, which, in turn, sold the homes to private owners. The authority thus surrendered, concluded historians Michael McDonald and John Muldowny,

Postcard of Norris Dam—Before and After, 1937.

"another opportunity to formulate, coordinate, and execute a workable grassroots policy which would have truly benefited residents of the Norris Basin."[13]

The Norris project represented a composite of what was perceived as America's best in architecture, engineering, and landscape architecture. But it proved to be a model that few other TVA projects ever came close to matching, perhaps because the idealism and hope of the initial New Deal years quickly dissolved into a bureaucratic mind-set that emphasized efficient power production over the ideas of reform and renewal that had initially propelled the authority into action.

To many people in the Clinch River valley, the Norris project was more an agent of destruction than an accepted prophet of modernism. As TVA condemned their land and demolished their towns, churches, and farms, it stripped away the physical environment that gave residents their very identity. It even crushed earlier stabs at modernization, such as three concrete arch bridges constructed in the 1920s over the Clinch River in Union County. At Norris's Lenoir Museum, a powerful display of period photographs shows not only the amazing engineering of the dam construction but also what was lost when the floodgates closed. Exhibits at the museum also feature artifacts of rural life in the Clinch River valley before the coming of TVA—a theme also portrayed at the nearby Museum of Appalachia between Norris and Interstate I-75.

In 1933 many farmers fought the arrival of TVA the best way they could. The most famous act of defiance came from William H. Hawkins, who owned property at the dam site. When TVA personnel came to talk with him, he lit a circle of brush around his house and burned it to the ground. As discussed at Big Ridge State Park in chapter 6, TVA dams did more than destroy home places; it destroyed the fabric of community by demolishing or relocating local churches, cemeteries, and community landmarks. Those dispossessed of their land, especially older residents, often had difficulty sustaining a sense of family and community in their new homes, no matter how modern and improved the dwellings appeared to outsiders. The power and importance of a sense of place and belonging to the people of the Clinch River was rarely understood by New Deal planners, engineers, or social experts.

BLOUNT COUNTY

McGhee Tyson Airport (1935–37), Alcoa Highway (U.S. Highway 129), Knoxville vicinity

In its brief existence during the winter of 1933–34, the CWA began planning for the development of a major airport between Knoxville and the company town of Alcoa in Blount County. Officials in both Knoxville and Blount

County wanted a rural location so the airport could easily expand in the future; the Alcoa Highway (U.S. Highway 129) was constructed, in part, to diminish the time it took a Knoxville resident to reach the airport. Between 1935 and 1937, the land was acquired and WPA labor constructed the airport, which had two runways, one which was 4,200 feet in length and a second 3,200 feet in length. According to the *Knoxville News-Sentinel* of October 15, 1937, the airport cost a total of $726,000, of which Knoxville provided $100,000 while Maryville and Alcoa each contributed $5,000.

The local governments worked well together, until it came time to name the facility. Knoxville officials in the past had committed to name the city airport after McGhee Tyson, a U.S. Navy Air Corps lieutenant who had died in World War I and the son of the socially and politically prominent Lawrence D. Tyson and Bettie McGhee Tyson. Blount County officials, however, wanted the airport's name to attract tourists; their preference was the Great Smoky Mountain Airport. In 1937 the Tennessee General Assembly sided with the Blount countians and officially named the facility the Great Smoky Mountain Airport. Yet when dedication ceremonies took place in October 1937, the name used was McGhee Tyson—and it stuck. And despite its distance from the city center, approximately fourteen miles according to the count in the *WPA Guide to Tennessee*, the airport proved successful. In fact, the airport's first major expansion came in 1943, when the U.S. Navy took over its operation during World War II. The main airport building maintained its WPA appearance until the 1960s.

CANNON COUNTY
City Waterworks, Sewers, and Improvements (1935-37), Water Street and McCrary Park, Woodbury

Woodbury, the seat of Cannon County, modernized town services with the installation of waterworks and sewers in 1935-37. The plant, although modernized and expanded, still stands on Water Street, a block north of U.S. Highway 70S. The PWA provided a grant of $100,000 for 40 percent of the cost, combined with a federal loan for the remainder. A steel water tower was located on a small hill overlooking the town. It too remains standing in the city's McCrary Park. Construction of the PWA-funded sewer system began in 1937. WPA crews provided labor for both projects.

Local WPA workers, under the supervision of William New, also leveled and landscaped the rocky area around the public square. A more visible project was the construction of a new county high school in Woodbury in 1935, which

WPA crew installing sidewalks in Woodbury, 1937, Cannon County.

served residents until its demolition in 1980. The WPA also funded the construction of the town's first sidewalks, a project supervised by Hoyte Roach, as well as filling in an open gully that existed on College Street. The sidewalks were five feet in width, and property owners paid twenty-five cents for each linear foot. Most owners paid their bills by putting down 20 percent of the total cost, then paying 20 percent interest-free each year until the bill was paid off. "In those Depression years," concluded county historian Robert L. Mason, "Woodbury made more progress than it had made in the last hundred years."[14]

CUMBERLAND COUNTY

Meadow Park Lake and Waterworks (1937–39), Tennessee Highway 101, Crossville vicinity

Southwest of Crossville, city officials worked with the PWA and WPA to fund and construct a waterworks plant at Meadow Creek Falls. The result was a dam, a five-hundred-acre lake named Meadow Park Lake, and a modern filtration plant, which opened in late November 1939. From the plant fresh water was piped to Crossville municipal water users. County historians point to the ample supply of water from the new facility as a primary reason, along with the town's general isolation from major population centers, that Cumberland County became the location of a large German POW camp in World War II.

DAVIDSON COUNTY
Berry Field (1935–37), Beverly Briley Parkway, Nashville

For most of the twentieth century, Berry Field was the center of aviation in Nashville. Named in 1939 for Col. Harry S. Berry, a World War I veteran who just happened to also be the state WPA administrator, the airport was one of the region's first major WPA projects. The initial 340-acre airport, which opened in late 1937, had a three-story terminal, a control tower, and paved runway. "Rumors of boondoggles among contractors and politicians marred the opening celebration," notes historian Don H. Doyle. "The original cost estimate of $385,000 had vaulted to $1.2 million by this time."[15] During World War II, the U.S. Army enlarged the field to over fifteen hundred acres as it served as home base for the 4th Ferry Command, a key clearing station for military aircraft. In September 1987, the Metropolitan Nashville Airport Authority opened the new International Terminal, marking an end to Berry Field's aviation prominence.

Nashville's city streets also benefited from New Deal work programs as a $2.5-million WPA program paved and expanded the city's street system during the late 1930s while another $119,000 in PWA grants went to street improvements and a new viaduct.

Postcard of Berry Field, Nashville.

DICKSON COUNTY
Leech-Larkins Farm Privy (c. 1939), 4199 Highway 47, Charlotte vicinity

The Leech-Larkins Farm is both a Tennessee Century Farm and listed in the National Register of Historic Places. It is private property, and there is no trespassing. However, from the roadside of Tennessee Highway 47, just north of the farmhouse, is a WPA-constructed privy. Its board-and-batten construction and metal shed roof are typical of the structures built by the agency throughout Tennessee in the late 1930s.

DICKSON COUNTY
Public Utilities Projects (1937-38), Tennessee Highway 46 and U.S. Highway 70, Dickson

Dickson was one of the first city governments to contract for TVA power in 1935. The next year the city received a PWA grant of $61,000 and a grant of $49,000 to fund and supervise the construction of a modern waterworks facility. The city issued $61,000 in municipal bonds to pay the loan. Two years later, at the urging of TVA personnel, the city applied for and then received, in March 1938, a grant of $67,000 from the Rural Electrification Administration to extend the city power lines to rural customers in the Yellow Creek area west of Dickson. Lines were first extended along Yellow Creek Road (present-day Tennessee Highway 46) and eventually some 68 miles of electrical lines served 294 new customers.

The new public-utility infrastructure constructed between 1935 and 1938 paid additional dividends in the fall of 1940, when NYA administrators told city officials that Dickson could receive a NYA Resident Industrial Project, if it provided land, city water, and electricity to the site. The Dickson Industrial Trust borrowed $7,500 to purchase thirty acres on the western outskirts of Dickson. The project only operated for a few months but Robert S. Clement recalled that it was "one of the best projects offered by the Government."[16] The location then served as the city's industrial park. Several of the project buildings remain extant on the private property of Valley West Furniture Company and may be easily viewed from U.S. Highway 70.

GIBSON COUNTY
Camp Coie Foster (1933-39), Old Dyer-Trenton Road, Dyer vicinity

CCC Company 490, named Camp Coie Foster in honor of a Gibson County soldier who died in World War I, was located on the original U.S. Highway 45W (now the Old Dyer-Trenton Road) between the county seat of Trenton and the rural railroad town of Dyer. The camp was located 2.5 miles south of Dyer on the farm of Carl Holt, and the original stone gate post still survived in the 1990s to mark the camp site.

The company operated from June 1933 to 1939 and engaged in a wide range of reclamation and conservation projects in the middle counties of West Tennessee. The company planted four hundred thousand tree seedlings in its first year. It terraced many local farm fields, built concrete check dams to improve drainage, improved local roads, and began reclamation work on the areas now known as the Tigrett and Gooch Wildlife Management Areas. When farmers provided the materials, the company also constructed fences on farms. After the terrible flood of 1937, the company shifted its work to helping homeless families, rebuilding the Obion Levee (part of which is now Tennessee Highway 181 in Lake and Dyer Counties), and restoring damaged farmland.

GRAINGER COUNTY
Buffalo Springs Wildlife Management Area (1939), Buffalo Springs Road at Indian Ridge Road, Rutledge vicinity

South of Rutledge is the location of one of the more interesting projects carried out by the Civilian Conservation Corps. In 1939, at the urging of Lynn Wood Hoskins and members of the Knox County chapter of the Tennessee Wildlife Federation, the CCC, the National Park Service, and the Tennessee Department of Conservation established the Buffalo Springs Game Farm and Reserve. The CCC built a stone bridge, developed roads (Game Farm Road), and cleared land for buildings and facilities. On this 375-acre property, state conservation officials raised quail, wild turkeys, and partridges to replenish deleted wildlife populations. The quail incubator and brooder produced approximately one hundred thousand birds annually, allegedly the largest such facility in the nation in 1939. Today Buffalo Springs is best known for its trout hatchery, added in the 1970s. The property has been renamed as the Buffalo Springs Wildlife Management Area and is administered by the Tennessee Wildlife Resources Agency.

GREENE COUNTY
Soil Conservation Projects (1933-42), UT Tobacco Experiment Station, 2255 East Allen's Bridge Road, Greeneville

New Deal agencies such as the CCC, TVA, and WPA carried out a wide variety of projects in Greene County. At the Tobacco Experiment Station of the University of Tennessee Agricultural Extension Service, TVA administrators worked closely with extension service staff to develop programs and designate model demonstration farms. WPA crews improved roads not only to the experiment station but throughout the county as farm-to-market roads. CCC Company 4492 set up headquarters east of downtown, at the present location of a funeral home. Known locally as Camp Andrew Johnson, in honor of the former President and Greeneville resident, the company carried out soil-conservation projects as well as building or improving several farm-to-market roads in the county. One of the county's agricultural demonstration farms during those years was Elmwood Farm, located along the banks of the Nolichucky River south of the town of Chuckey. Listed in the National Register of Historic Places, Elmwood Farm also is the oldest Tennessee Century Farm.

HAMILTON COUNTY
Chickamauga Dam and Lake (1938-40), Tennessee Highway 153, Chattanooga

Chattanooga was headquarters for the Tennessee Electric Power Company (TEPCO), which was the largest supplier of electricity in Tennessee at the time of the Great Depression. The city also was home to about half of the company's stockholders, with many of these people counted among the social, economic, and political leadership of the city. Chattanooga thus became a political battlefield between the advocates of public power (the Tennessee Valley Authority and its municipal allies) and the advocates of private enterprise (represented by TEPCO and its industrial and political allies). The creation of TVA in the spring of 1933, and the transfer of authority for river navigation from the U.S. Army Corps of Engineers to the authority, also directly affected Chattanooga. Since 1867 the corps had maintained a district office in the city and undertaken various navigation projects in the greater Chattanooga area. After August 1933, the corps only administered dam locks. TVA now controlled the Tennessee and assumed responsibility for its future development.

While the Corps of Engineers was not in a position to impede TVA, private power fought the authority with a vengeance in state and federal courts as well as the court of public opinion. In Chattanooga its most effective spokesman was Jo Conn Guild Jr., president of TEPCO. Regionally and nationally, the champion of private power was Wendell Wilkie, a TEPCO director and president of the Commonwealth and Southern Company, a holding company that controlled TEPCO.

To counteract the torrent of criticism from private power, citizen and civic groups prodded TVA to begin planning and construction for Chickamauga Dam immediately and to locate important offices in the city. Hamilton County Judge Will Cummings was a powerful proponent of public power and called on the support of U.S. Sen. Kenneth McKellar and local congressman Sam McReynolds. The authority responded promptly by placing such key offices as the General Engineering and Geology Department and the Electric Division in downtown Chattanooga.

Building the dam, however, proved another matter. The Chickamauga project did not have high priority among TVA engineers because they first wanted to direct the authority's energy toward the construction of tributary storage dams for flood control. But political pressure mounted in 1934–35, especially during a heated campaign to approve some eight million dollars in public bonds to finance the creation of a municipal electrical system powered by TVA energy. At a critical point in the campaign, TVA surveyors began their work along the dam site. In March 1935, Chattanooga voters overwhelmingly approved the bond issue.

Although the vote seemingly ensured the future of public power, TEPCO announced that it would not sell out to the city or to TVA. It would fight to the finish, and it took its case to the courts. TVA began construction of Chickamauga on January 13, 1936, while its attorneys defended the authority in federal court. Thomas K. McCraw's *TVA and the Power Fight, 1933–39* (1971) details the legal maneuvering and the authority's eventual victory. On August 15, 1939, at an elaborate public ceremony, TVA director David Lilienthal handed Wendell Wilkie a check for $78,425,095—all of TEPCO's various holdings were now part of TVA.

Once construction at Chickamauga began in the winter of 1936, the authority moved quickly to purchase approximately 69,000 acres and to remove some 900 families, along with 425 burials from 24 cemeteries in the project area. The plight of families taken from their historic homes was later dramatized in the movie *Wild River* (1960).

Another significant loss was the destruction of the Dallas and Hiwassee Island prehistoric sites, long recognized by historians and archaeologists as among the most important prehistoric properties in the Tennessee Valley.

The WPA provided workers and funds for extensive, but quick, archaeological investigations of the project area. It was the first project to be administered wholly through the University of Tennessee program of Dr. Thomas M. N. Lewis. As his staff, Lewis hired several of the best young experts in the nation, who went on to secure well-respected reputations in American archaeology. These staffers included Jesse Jennings, Stuart Neitzel, Charles Fairbanks, Charles Nash, John Alden, Paul Maynard, George Lidberg, Earl Loyster, and Madeline Kneberg. Lewis and his staff identified over seventy sites of archaeological significance; time and funding constraints meant that only thirteen were excavated. Despite these constraints, the project "produced the first comprehensive, detailed descriptions of prehistoric cultures in the Upper Tennessee Valley in a sequential framework," concludes Lynne Sullivan. "The project also recovered a wealth of basic information from and about the archaeological sites in the basin."[17]

The Chickamauga project made three important contributions to Tennessee archaeology. First, project artifacts are in the collections of the Frank B. McClung Museum at the University of Tennessee, Knoxville. The museum was established to curate and store the hundreds of thousands of artifacts uncovered in the various TVA and WPA excavation projects. In addition, two significant archaeologist reports by Lewis and Kneberg were eventually published: *Hiwassee Island: An Archaeological Account of Four*

Postcard of "Florida Sunbeam Crossing Tennessee River Bridge, Chickamauga Dam," Hamilton County.

Tennessee Indian Peoples (1946) and *The Prehistory of the Chickamauga Basin in Tennessee*, compiled and edited by Lynne P. Sullivan (1995).

With the archaeology excavations completed, the families removed, and their properties demolished, TVA cleared the land for the Chickamauga reservoir. The first water impounding took place on January 15, 1940, almost exactly four years after construction began. The project had the highest percentage of African American workers (approximately 25 percent) of any TVA dam project in Tennessee. African Americans workers, from electricians to quarry workers, were employed in many tasks, but faced harassment and discrimination. TVA investigated the tense race relations at Chickamauga in 1938, but failed to reinstate African Americans who had been dismissed unfairly. Most black workers thus kept their mouths shut rather than lose their jobs.

When finished Chickamauga Dam was 5,800 feet long, 129 feet high, and held some 506,400 cubic yards of concrete. The dimensions of Chickamauga Lake were just as impressive. Almost 59 miles in length, the lake contained some 35,400 acres and some 800 miles of shoreline. The CCC and TVA eventually developed two segregated parks, Booker T. Washington for African Americans and Harrison Bay for whites, on the east shore of the lake (see chapter 6).

At the dam's dedication on Labor Day, 1940, President Franklin Roosevelt presided over ceremonies attended by an estimated 80,000 people. Chickamauga Dam was a "monument to a productive partnership between management and labor, between citizens of all kinds working in the public weal," asserted Roosevelt. "The only note of sorrow that can properly be sounded on a great day like this is in the misplaced emphasis which so many people have put on the objectives of the government in building up this great Tennessee Valley project."[18] The political battle had been long and difficult, but TVA celebrated its victory, marking a new era in the history of Chattanooga.

HAMILTON COUNTY
Lovell Field (1936–37), Airport Road, Chattanooga

Lovell Field at the Chattanooga Municipal Airport traces its roots to the late 1920s when John E. Lovell, head of the local chamber of commerce's aeronautics committee, led the push for a local bond issue to build a new city airport. Voters approved the bond issue, the city purchased 130 acres, and the airfield opened in 1930. Commercial passenger flights from Eastern Air Lines began in 1934.

From 1936 to 1937, the WPA funded and constructed several major improvements at Lovell Field. In addition to enlarging the field, the WPA project involved "elevating the dikes around the field to exclude back water, installing a pumping system, installing hard-surface runways, lowering a knoll on the edge of the field, and the constructing of a new hangar."[19]

HARDIN COUNTY

Pickwick Landing Dam and Lake (1934–38), Tennessee Highway 128, Counce vicinity

As the second completed TVA dam, Pickwick Landing Dam was designed to complement the operations of Wilson Dam at Muscle Shoals, Alabama. The roots of the Alabama project can be traced to the early 1920s and Henry Ford's interest in the Muscle Shoals nitrate factories left over from World War I. Ford and his engineers envisioned a large nitrate fertilizer plant powered by Wilson's generators. By placing dams upriver (the later Wheeler Dam) and downriver (the later Pickwick Landing Dam), Ford engineers would be able to provide the Wilson Dam operations with a constant waterpower source, thus increasing its efficiency and expanding its production. In 1922, the U.S. Army Corps of Engineers recommended a dam at the present site of Pickwick Landing. Nothing happened until, in the mid-1930s, the Tennessee Valley Authority carried out the basic plan of three related dam projects along the long bend of the Tennessee River in northern Alabama and south-

Postcard of Pickwick Dam, Hardin County.

ern Middle Tennessee. Construction at Pickwick began on March 8, 1935, and lake formation began less than three years later, on February 8, 1938. The first electrical power was produced on June 29, 1938. TVA placed the total project cost at $45.88 million.

Pickwick Landing differed from the Norris project in several aspects. Unlike the mammoth 265-foot-high concrete wall at Norris, Pickwick Landing Dam rose a mere 113 feet. But Pickwick was considerably longer—7,715 feet compared with Norris's 1,860 feet of length. Pickwick's construction also combined concrete and steel at midstream with earth-fill construction on either side. Its lake was huge—covering an area of approximately sixty-four square miles with a capacity of 1.09 million acre-feet. Its six turbines were also capable of producing three to four times the amount of electricity that Norris could produce. Kentucky Dam was the only larger TVA dam on the Tennessee River.

Like Norris, Pickwick had an associated permanent village, but it was tiny, consisting of a mere fifteen houses. At least seventy-five of its frame cottages for construction workers were later shipped down the river to the construction camp for Kentucky Dam. Demonstration parks and recreational areas were not considered important at Pickwick; the CCC built only a few structures, and no major park development took place until decades later. Yet, like Norris, the project affected the lives of five hundred families in Tennessee and northern Alabama and Mississippi, displacing property owners and a large number of tenants, many of whom were African Americans.

Underneath Pickwick Lake are the remains of several significant archaeological sites, only a few of which received salvage excavations from a team of archaeologists and workers, funded by TVA and the WPA and sponsored by the Alabama Museum of Natural History. The project's twenty excavations uncovered important new information about most periods of southern prehistory, especially from five mound and two village sites associated with the Copena focus of the Hopewell phase.

HUMPHREYS COUNTY
Waterworks and Dairy Plant (1934–35), U.S. Highway 70, McEwen

McEwen is a small railroad town in eastern Humphreys County. In an effort to diversify its agricultural base and raise farm incomes, the Public Works Administration partnered with local officials in McEwen to build a modern waterworks, the presence of which soon attracted the Kraft Cheese Company to build a dairy plant next to the water tower. Although the dairy later closed, its factory building is extant, as is the water tower.

JEFFERSON COUNTY

Cherokee Dam and Lake (1940–41), Tennessee Highway 92, Jefferson City vicinity

Located on the Holston River, on the boundary between Jefferson and Hamblen Counties, is Cherokee Dam. As part of the authority's wartime readiness program, the dam was built in a mere two years, with much of the work taking place around the clock. The speed of the project was one reason that Cherokee lacked some of the facilities found at earlier TVA projects. There were no model villages for workers or administrators. Most workers were housed in flimsy, wooden barracks shipped in for construction, and then taken elsewhere for the next agency project. Due to wartime concerns and budgetary restraints, few voices called for recreational facilities along the lake. During the 1960s, however, local, state, and TVA officials looked at recreation and tourism along Cherokee Lake as new incentives for economic growth. This interest eventually led to the creation of Panther Creek State Park on the east side of the lake.

The design of Cherokee Dam is attributed to Roland Wank. The concrete structure is 175 feet high and 2,060 feet long, easily the largest TVA

Cherokee Dam, Jefferson County.

facility on the river. Its powerhouse is capable of generating 126 megawatts of electricity, similar to the output produced at Chickamauga Dam. By 1942, much of its electricity was funneled to the military's secret operations at the Clinton Engineering Works at Oak Ridge.

Once the dam closed off the waters of the Holston River in 1941, it created a 59-mile long lake, displacing hundreds of valley families in Jefferson, Grainger, Hamblen, and Hawkins Counties. The dislocation proved difficult for many residents, as some families divided over where to relocate, and almost all reported a deep sense of loss, both personally and financially. Town and business leaders in nearby Jefferson City and Morristown, however, welcomed the dam and powerhouse as a way of encouraging new industrial and commercial investments.

LAKE COUNTY
Tiptonville–Obion Levee (1937–38), Tennessee Highway 181 and Levee Road, Wynnburg vicinity

After the disastrous flood of 1937, state and federal agencies combined to build the Lake County Levee (since then expanded and now known as the Tiptonville–Obion Levee), to protect the rich farmland of southern Lake County from future ravages of the Mississippi River. Officials from the U.S. Army Corps of Engineers provided advice and supervision, while WPA work crews and CCC companies provided labor. To drive the high levee today, which is southwest of Tiptonville, and to look down upon local farms protected by the high banks of soil is a unique way to experience the impact of federal projects on the landscape of the Tennessee Delta.

LINCOLN COUNTY
Rural Electrification Projects (1935–38), Fayetteville

Lincoln County was among the first in Tennessee to take advantage of the Rural Electrification Administration. Dixie L. Conger was owner of the Beech Lawn Stockfarm, which is a Tennessee Century Farm and is listed in the National Register of Historic Places. Conger was also a progressive farmer, who was president of the county's Farm Bureau, chair of the county school board, and one of the original directors of the Lincoln County Electric Membership Co-operative. In September 1935 Frank Rambo and B. M. Stewart from the local chamber of commerce asked Conger to accompany them on a business trip to Knoxville, where they hoped to convince TVA to provide electricity to the city of Fayetteville. Conger agreed and set up the meeting through his friendship with TVA director Harcourt Morgan. Between 1935 and 1938, the Lincoln County electric co-op received $200,000 in REA funding to extend lines from the city of Fayetteville to such rural communities as Boonhill, Taft, and Mimosa, near where Conger lived. In 1938–39, the city of Fayetteville used a $67,000 PWA grant to help fund the modernization and expansion of its electrical system while in those same two years the PWA and WPA combined money and labor to improve city streets.

LINCOLN COUNTY

Petersburg Pike (1937–38), College Street and Public Square, Petersburg

The Petersburg Pike, now known as U.S. Highway 431, was one of several road improvement projects conducted by WPA crews in Lincoln County. Local citizens impatiently awaited the completion of the project throughout 1937. In the *Lincoln County News* of April 29, 1937, the editor whined:

> We can't quite see the reasoning behind the delay in the construction of the grade of the new road from Fayetteville to Petersburg. While we wait for the construction of the road we are subjecting ourselves to the risk of breaking our collective neck every time we drive over the present road between here and Petersburg at a speed of more than twenty miles per hour. We know there are lots of reasons for automobile accidents, but seldom have we seen a better reason than the Petersburg Pike. If it isn't a first-class, super-refined, A-1, death-trap then we never saw one. S-curves, hairpin curves, loose gravel, one-way bridges, and all the other trimmings that go towards helping us to meet St. Peter at the earliest possible moment.

The editor's complaints failed to get the WPA to speed up completion of the road—it was not finished until 1938. But, when finished, the new road entered town on College Street at the Morgan preparatory school, went around the Public Square, and headed out College Street, passing a new school then under construction by the PWA. It then continued to Lewisburg. The new road significantly cut driving time between Petersburg and the neighboring county seats of Fayetteville and Lewisburg.

LOUDON COUNTY

Fort Loudon Dam and Lake (1940–43), U.S. Highway 321, Lenoir City

TVA engineers first thought of Fort Loudon Dam and Lake as one of the series of major dams on the Tennessee River designed to improve river navigation and provide flood control, with electrical generation being a secondary priority. But in 1940 the earthen wall, concrete, and steel dam became a wartime priority. Construction often occurred around the clock. Finished in 1943, Fort Loudon Dam is medium-sized compared with other TVA facilities on the Tennessee River. It is 125 feet high, with the steel decking for U.S. Highway 321 riding above the top of the dam. Its length is 4,190 feet; the dam created a reservoir 61 miles long.

Energy from its turbines at first went mostly to Oak Ridge, Alcoa, and other military priorities, but after the war, its electrical power boosted local industries. Lenoir City had been established in the late nineteenth century as a planned industrial town. Despite several investments by eastern capitalists, the place was not much more than a small Appalachian factory town until the arrival of TVA. The Great Depression hit the town hard; 889 families received direct relief in 1934, and the countryside was not much better off. According to a 1935 federal survey, gullying and sheet erosion had damaged at least 70 percent of the farmland in Loudon County. People were leaving the land in droves.

Local boosters refused to give up and turned to modern technology for answers. In 1940 Lenoir City won the competition in Tennessee for a specially

Postcard of Fort Loudon Dam, Loudon County.

commissioned post office mural. *Electrification*, by David Sloane Martin, installed at the Lenoir City post office in 1942, dramatically expressed the local confidence in the power of electricity to transform lives. The dam was closed the next year, and the changes brought about by modern engineering began.

No worker villages were constructed at Fort Loudon; instead, there were large wooden barracks for the construction crews. After all, it was wartime—there was not the time or money to build model construction camps. Nor were funds available for archaeology research, even though some of the state's most important historical archaeological sites were just a few miles away along the Little Tennessee River. In 1942 Dr. Thomas M. N. Lewis prodded TVA into transferring a few thousand dollars for a quick survey of the Little Tennessee, conducted by Chandler Rowe. Due to its military classification, Fort Loudon had no demonstration parks nor major recreation areas. Picnic grounds and overlooks were developed along a scenic drive that led from the highway to the powerhouse at the bottom of the dam. This vantage point provides a compelling visual perspective of the transformation wrought by the authority all along the Tennessee Valley. As R. L. Duffus asserted in TVA's own celebratory *The Valley and its People: A Portrait of TVA* (1946):

> This building of dams and powerhouses, this setting up of transmission lines, with towers that looked like giant models of dressmakers' dummies, this orderly fury of construction, was one of the most marvelous spectacles of its kind that have been seen in this generation on this or any continent.
>
> It was in part a simple triumph of planner, designer, and engineer, of an art and science which has been brought near to perfection in twentieth-century America. In a way it would not have mattered who the employer was. The dams would have looked the same if they had been built by private contract for a private corporation which would presently hold the fate of the Valley and all its people in the hollow of its hand. It wasn't merely an agency created by act of Congress that was at work here. It was the genius of a nation.
>
> But this genius was being expressed in new forms, here in the Valley. For one observer, who saw the task going forward at intervals over a decade, it came in time to have the thrill of the march of an army with banners—and more than that. It was like seeing the pioneers cutting down trees in New England and Ohio. It was like watching the first plows moving across the unbroken land of Kansas. It was like coming on the first wagons moving over the South Pass. It was like history. It was like epic poetry. It was like music.[20]

His words were a powerful expression of faith in the engineered landscape held by TVA, and much of the New Deal. In twelve years, from 1933 to 1945, TVA not only had tamed the river; it had also re-engineered the lives of thousands of displaced families, restructured towns and communities, and had contributed mightily to winning World War II. TVA's words in 1946 proclaimed victory in this new frontier; the men and women who worked there felt they were writing a new chapter in history.

Another writer in 1946, however, mourned the passing of that older frontier, and the people and history that accompanied it. In his first volume on *The Tennessee* (1946), Donald Davidson sadly observed the passing of a great wild river from the pages of history. "Now, at long last, the old wild river is submerged, is lost in its great progeny, the river of the TVA. of all the rivers of the world, [it is] the one mostly deftly chained, the one most thoroughly subdued to main's designing will. The Tennessee is now a civil and obliging stream. One flick of a switch by the tenderest human finger, and the Tennessee is any man's obedient slave, though he be a thousand miles away."[21]

To Davidson and others, TVA was not like history nor like music. It was a denial of history, and the sounds of its construction were hard, dissonant, and loud, like the sounds of the end of the world. In their minds, the engineers did not tame TVA into submission. Instead, they destroyed the river, removed its residents, and replaced it with a technological machine that they could control.

Adjacent to Fort Loudon Dam, on Tennessee Highway 444, is Tellico Dam and Lake. Planning for this project dates to the New Deal era, but actual construction and closing of the dam took place in the 1960s and 1970s, a generation after the New Deal. Tellico was certainly TVA's most controversial project in Tennessee. Its completion in 1979, indicated historians Bruce Wheeler and Michael J. McDonald, "marked the death of the agency as it had been known." Although TVA won a long and costly battle with conservationists, state and local officials, and historic preservationists, its victory "constituted a fitting, if limited, end to the American obsession with technocratic power."[22]

MADISON COUNTY
McKellar Airport (1933–34, 1936–37), Westover Road, Jackson vicinity

McKellar Airport, now named McKellar-Sipes Regional Airport, is located west of Jackson on U.S. Highway 70, which was in the 1930s the state's major east-west highway. It was originally named in honor of U.S. Sen. Kenneth D. McKellar, who was a strong early advocate of New Deal programs. McKellar was also interested in improving aviation in Tennessee. He helped to convince the Civil Works Administration to acquire this property, level the fields, and construct its initial runways during the winter of 1933–34. The WPA expanded the field and constructed additional buildings two years later. Between 1941 and 1945 the U.S. Army improved the field again as it used it for a military aviation training center. After the war, it reverted back to the control of the city and county. Although officials have enlarged the airport and built new structures several times since the depression decade, its location and name still connects the airport to its New Deal origins.

MARSHALL COUNTY
Agricultural Programs and Public Utilities (1934–40), Marshall County Courthouse, Town Square, Lewisburg

The Marshall County Courthouse was built as the Great Depression began in 1929. During the New Deal, it was the administrative center for several federal programs aimed at improving local farm incomes and standards of living.

Agriculture was the county's dominant industry, with dairy production of special importance. Renowned for its Jersey cattle, the county was home to the U.S. Dairy Experiment Station, which had been established in 1929. However, the depression had crushed milk prices and the county found itself in desperate straits by 1932 when it cut funds for its extension agent.

Various federal programs, such as the Agricultural Adjustment Administration, the Tennessee Emergency Relief Administration, the WPA, and the Rural Electrification Administration, began to affect the county significantly in 1934–36. W. T. Pritchett became county extension agent in 1934, and his yearly reports underscore the significance of New Deal programs to agricultural expansion in the depression decade. For example, in 1934 the Marshall County Burley Tobacco Association was organized, as well as similar AAA associations for corn, swine, wheat, and cotton. A part-time cotton extension agent also began work with local cotton farmers.

The year 1935 witnessed further program expansion in the creation of a Soil Erosion Club and a joint private-public program in which a major dairy corporation, Borden Milk, encouraged farmers, with WPA support, to build sanitary milk barns and sheds—over one hundred structures were completed. Soil conservation and home demonstration were major programs in 1936. In that year, farmers created the Marshall County Soil Conservation Association, a county Farm Bureau Cooperative, and a reorganized Dairy Herd Improvement Association. The county's first soil conservation agent was hired, joined by an assistant soil conservationist in 1937. Home Demonstration programs emphasized a Better Homes campaign and pushed for the adoption of rural electrification to improve home life and make life easier for mothers through electrical appliances.

By the end of the thirties, improved soil conservation and the joint efforts of the associations and co-operatives that met at the courthouse had changed the county's rural landscape. Farm families, together with CCC and WPA workers, in 1938 planted six thousand black locust seedlings and two thousand black locust sprouts. The black locust was by far the most common tree planted in New Deal soil-conservation projects. The next year, the number of black locust plantings jumped to twelve thousand. Eighty-five acres of private farmland was terraced, and fifteen hundred tons of lime were spread across hundreds of acres of fields in 1939.

In that same year, public and federal officials dedicated a rare courthouse square monument to a PWA public-utility project. The simple concrete base contains a bronze plaque marking the Lewisburg electrical system as a PWA project completed in 1939. Installing a modern electrical system in the town proved to be more difficult than local officials ever imagined; perhaps that is why they marked the end of their long ordeal with a small monument.

As early as 1935 local voters had approved a bond of fifty-five thousand dollars and received a PWA grant of forty-five thousand dollars to build a city-owned electrical system, which would compete with an existing, but inadequate and expensive, TEPCO system. TEPCO sued the city and the PWA and obtained an injunction that barred any construction from taking place. The case stayed before the courts until 1938, when TEPCO asked for dismissal. The city finally awarded contracts for construction. After TEPCO decided to sell out to TVA in the summer of 1939, the city of Lewisburg bought the TEPCO system for forty thousand dollars and finished the city's electrical project by that November.

MCNAIRY COUNTY
Soil Conservation Projects, Rosecreek community, U.S. Highway 64

CCC Company 1423, known as Camp Joe E. Williams, carried out various soil conservation, reforestation, and fire prevention projects in McNairy County and the surrounding area from 1933 to 1935. The camp stood near the old Rosecreek school, approximately five miles west of Selmer on old highway 64W, and consisted of four long, rectangular frame barracks as well as a mess hall, kitchen-recreation building, bath house, officer quarters, and dining room. "Many of the men who had learned to work" at the camp, observed enrollee Norbett Burgess, "were better prepared for the labor market."[23]

POLK COUNTY
Ocoee No. 3 Dam (1941–42), U.S. Highway 64, Ducktown vicinity

Ocoee No. 3 was the last in a series of four dams built along the Ocoee River from 1910 to 1941. TVA acquired Ocoee No. 1, Ocoee No. 2, and Blue Ridge Dam (the latter in North Carolina) as part of its TEPCO purchase. It then built Ocoee No. 3 as one of its wartime preparation projects. The dam is 110 feet high and 612 feet in length. It was designed for power production, not flood control or navigation, although now it has become an important dam in the regulation of water flow for the Ocoee's internationally recognized white-water rafting course, a site of competition in the 1996 Summer Olympic Games.

The dam was also a major alteration in the landscape of the Ocoee River country. It diverted the river through a concrete mountain tunnel to a powerhouse three miles away. After its construction, noted historian R. E. Barclay in 1946, the "Ocoee Gorge, which was at one time a thing of scenic grandeur, now presents nothing more awe-inspiring than a dry river bed and some silent, mysterious-looking powerhouses."[24] The modernist-styled concrete-and-steel

Ocoee Dam No. 3, Polk County.

powerhouse produces twenty-six megawatts of power—the most of the Ocoee's hydroelectric facilities. When the powerhouse went into production in 1943, a military official proclaimed that "electricity from this station will help turn out the weapons and materials of war to defeat our enemies."[25]

PUTNAM COUNTY
Soil Conservation Projects, Cane Creek Park, C. C. Camp Road, Cookeville

About three miles west of downtown Cookeville on U.S. Highway 70N is C. C. Camp Road, which leads to Cane Creek Park, a municipal recreation area centered around a fifty-six-acre lake. In 1940–41, a CCC company worked here and in other parts of Putnam County on various farm improvement projects, including drainage ditches, terracing, reforestation, and fence construction. The many miles of fences, in fact, gave a new, more ordered appearance to the rural landscape of Putnam County. The first CCC camp in Cookeville dated to the summer of 1933, when Col. Hubert Crawford of the local National Guard unit donated land for Camp Walton, located approximately three miles east of downtown. The company built and improved local roads as it also carried out fire prevention, reclamation, and conservation projects.

Another important public improvement project occurred during the winter of 1933–34, when the CWA worked with local officials and Leonard A. Allen of the Tennessee Highway Department to build the original Cookeville airport. CWA crews leveled the ground, laid out two sod runways, each twenty-five hundred feet in length, and constructed several small buildings for airport operations. The airport was dedicated on May 7, 1934, with elaborate ceremonies and a stunning air show viewed by an estimated ten thousand spectators. The Upper Cumberland Regional Airport, located about halfway between Cookeville and Sparta, now serves local residents.

The projects of 1933 and 1934 were the first of many New Deal public improvement programs in Putnam County. From 1936 to 1938, the federal government spent well over six hundred thousand dollars in the county. "In addition to giving work to the unemployed, the public works programs aided the county in many other ways," reported local historian Mary J. DeLozier. "Employees extended water and sewer lines, giving many town residents running water and indoor toilets for the first time. Workmen improved town streets, built 'farm-to-market' roads in rural areas, and constructed bridges, culverts and retaining walls."[26]

RHEA COUNTY

Watts Bar Dam and Lake (1939–42), Tennessee Highway 68, Spring City vicinity

Watts Bar is the best TVA property in Tennessee to witness the authority's evolution since its creation in 1933. The 112-foot-high dam is only the seventh-highest TVA facility on the Tennessee River, while its 2,960-foot width ranks it at the bottom of TVA dams on the river. But Watts Bar created the second longest reservoir (96 miles) on the Tennessee, meaning that the project affected the lives of thousands of rural residents in Rhea, Meigs, Roane, and Loudon Counties. Then, Watts Bar became the location of the first TVA coal-fired electricity plant, built between 1940 and 1945, and the third TVA nuclear power plant, constructed between 1973 and 1996. It is the only New Deal–era TVA facility in Tennessee to have an adjacent nuclear power plant. Watts Bar, thus, has two impressive visitor centers. The one at the dam control building dates to the New Deal era. It provides an overlook of the dam, the highway bridge that runs across it, and the lake. The one at the nuclear plant is a state-of-the-art educational center, designed for tourists and thousands of school children who visit the center annually; its focus is the nuclear power plant.

Construction at Watts Bar Dam began in July 1939 and at its peak, some 2,680 workers were at the dam site. They poured some 480,200 cubic yards of concrete. Another 500 plus employees worked to remove and relocate

Watts Bar Dam and Highway Bridge, Rhea County.

families and cemeteries and to clear land for the large reservoir. A small model village of modernist-styled homes was constructed. No demonstration parks were located along the lake, but a picnic area was developed facing the powerhouse along the lake's east bank in Meigs County. The total project cost was approximately $38.1 million.

TVA officials originally viewed Watts Bar as another key facility in their plan to provide flood control and better navigation. These themes are still emphasized in the displays at the dam control building's visitor center, which provided tourists a view of the lake, dam, and its controls. Architectural historian Walter Creese interprets the building as evidence of the authority's loss of confidence during the war years. "The building seems more cheap and detached, more solitary and aloof from its landscape," he argues, "than any other Tennessee Valley Authority example."[27]

Power production became more important as war clouds gathered and darkened in 1940. Since the facility already had an electrical switchyard under construction, officials chose Watts Bar for the location of its first coal-fired steam plant to produce additional amounts of electricity. In November 1940, a year before the United States officially entered World War II, federal officials classified Watts Bar as a restricted area and sent in troops to guard the place around the clock. This coal-fired plant, built from 1940 to 1945, operated until 1982.

Watts Bar, viewed by federal and military officials as primarily a power producer, stayed that way after the war. As such, the rambling nature of the engineered landscape at Watts Bar serves as a compelling metaphor for TVA's evolution into little more than an appendage of the industrial-military complex in the United States. Producing electrical power was no longer an incidental mission of the authority; in the eyes of its directors and government leaders, producing power was its only important mission. The construction of the nuclear plant was just another step in TVA's evolution, but one that proved extremely costly, both in terms of money and in popular support for the authority, which was once widespread across Tennessee.

RUTHERFORD COUNTY
City Waterworks (1936–37), College Street, Smyrna

The city of Smyrna, now headquarters of the Nissan Motor Manufacturing Corporation, U.S.A., was a small railroad town in northern Rutherford County in the 1930s. It had few municipal services. Its only public water supply was a pump at Railroad Park next to the passenger depot. The Nashville,

Chattanooga, and St. Louis Railway had installed the pump in the 1920s as a courtesy to its depot employees, travelers, and the general public. Use of the pump was restricted to whites. In November 1936 PWA State Administrator Kenneth Markell announced that the PWA would grant the city twenty-five thousand dollars and loan it another twenty-five thousand dollars for a small city waterworks. Work began in the winter of 1937, with W. L. Haley and Company of Nashville receiving the contract to build wells and a distribution system. Taylor Iron Works and Supply Company of Macon, Georgia, received the contract to build a large steel water tower on College Street. The system served the city until 1954–57, when it was modernized and expanded.

SEVIER COUNTY

Douglas Dam (1942–43), Tennessee Highways 139 at 338, Sevierville vicinity

Although located at the northeast border of Sevier County, most of the impoundment from Douglas Dam flowed eastward into Jefferson County. Here, around the Dandridge area, was some of the best farmland in East Tennessee. Thus, when TVA began planning for the dam's construction as part of its wartime preparation program, authority director Harcourt Morgan voiced a sharp dissent. These farmers, he argued, did not need TVA to uplift them out of poverty; they were actually doing well, compared with other East Tennesseans. But those clamoring for more electricity and more rapid construction, no matter the costs, drowned out Morgan's call for restraint. Director David Lilienthal wanted the dam in the name of national security; he was joined by William S. Knudsen, a former General Motors executive who served as the government's manufacturing czar for its military buildup.

Thus during 1941 a heated controversy over Douglas Dam dominated state newspapers. U.S. Sen. Kenneth McKellar, the Tennessee Farm Bureau Federation, and a plethora of state and local officials came out in public opposition. But Lilienthal and Knudsen prevailed. Congress approved the project on January 30, 1942, although President Roosevelt agreed that a large earth and rock dike would be built on the immediate outskirts of Dandridge to keep this historic county seat from being covered by Douglas Lake. This huge earthen pile, mere steps from the county courthouse, remains a powerful artifact of the political compromise inherent in the construction of Douglas Dam.

Construction of the only TVA dam on the French Broad River began in 1942, with much of the equipment, labor, and prefabricated (and segregated)

Douglas Dam, Sevier County.

housing moving over from the Cherokee project to Douglas. With some 6,000 people working around the clock, it was finished in a mere thirteen months. Its formal dedication, presided over by TVA chair David Lilienthal, took place on March 1, 1943 and its first electricity was produced three weeks later. For the reservoir, TVA personnel removed 525 families—over 2,000 people—in Sevier, Jefferson, Cocke, and Hamblen Counties; rural villages of schools, homes, and businesses were destroyed. As in other TVA projects, personnel relocated cemeteries. TVA also provided a limited amount of funds for archaeological excavations on the French Broad River's Zimmerman Island, a known Middle Mississippian period mound site. Chandler Rowe directed the project from March to June 1942.

From a hillside overlook constructed by TVA on the north side of the French Broad River, Douglas Dam is an architecturally impressive 202-foot-high and 1,705-foot-wide concrete structure. Its streamlined concrete-and-steel powerhouse gantry is similar to those at Cherokee and Watts Bar, two other wartime projects. Roland Wank designed the dam, as he had most other major TVA facilities of the 1930s. The dam, in the words of architectural historian Robbie Jones, "is an expression of Art Moderne–style combined with German Expressionism and, is juxtaposed in stark contrast to the traditional and vernacular architecture of the rural East Tennessee countryside."[28]

Many valley residents detested what this modern machine did to their countryside. In her moving history of the French Broad River, writer Wilma Dykeman told the story of Cousin Fanny Swann, whose home and farm had been buried by the waters of Douglas Lake. Swann had protested the coming of the dam by sending letters and poems to Washington officials. "The land never had a stranger, more earnest, spokesman than this bundle of emotion and determination," Dykeman wrote, "who throughout a sheltered life had grappled with most of the realities of experience."[29] There were hundreds of Cousin Fannys in the way of Douglas Lake, people who had an abiding sense of faith, place, and memory tied to their farms and villages of the valley along the French Broad.

SHELBY COUNTY
Memphis Humane Center (1936), Auction Avenue and Front Streets, Memphis

Due to the political clout of the Crump machine, ably orchestrated in the halls of Washington by Tennessee's senior U.S. senator, Kenneth McKellar, Memphis and Shelby County acquired millions of dollars of federal funds during the New Deal. The short-lived CWA spent two million dollars there. The PWA's *Public Buildings* (1940) highlighted the construction of the Colonial Revival–styled Hyde Park school for African Americans as well as several major public improvement projects: a grain elevator, a fire tower, and an electric distribution center. The PWA alone spent almost $8.5 million in Memphis, including working with the U.S. Army Corps of Engineers to build Riverside Drive and to improve the city's levee system.

In comparison, the WPA spent only $5.2 million in the city, substantially less than the PWA. Historian Roger Biles accounts for the difference, in part, because of the poor administration of WPA projects in Memphis and the control of the agency by the Crump machine. But when Biles totaled up the spending by the various federal relief agencies, some $22 million had been spent in Memphis by 1938. The Flood Control Bill of 1937 eventually would raise that total by another $13 million.

Thus, with millions spent on public improvements in the Bluff City, many different projects exist, but perhaps most illustrative of the largesse that passed to Memphis during the depression decade is the Memphis Humane Shelter. Built in 1936, the animal shelter suggests that no project was too small or inconsequential to receive funding. In addition, the building is architecturally stylish, an example of Art Deco by Memphis architects Furbringer and Ehrman. All of this for a dog shelter in the name of public health—nowhere else in Tennessee but Memphis could such a structure have been constructed in the 1930s.

The New Deal constructed a new urban face in Memphis. But, as Roger Biles has argued in his *Memphis in the Great Depression*, by refusing to challenge its political boss, its racial prejudice, and the power of its commercial and industrial base, all of the new buildings and public improvements represented a mere "cosmetic" change. The soul of Memphis remained as dark as it had been before all of the efforts for New Deal–driven reform.

SHELBY COUNTY

Memphis Municipal Airport (1933–34, 1936–37), Airport Road, Memphis

This municipal airport opened in 1929 with only a sod runway and three small hangars. During 1933–34, the CWA constructed three asphalt diagonal runways along with additional buildings. From 1936 to 1937, the WPA built a new terminal and generally modernized the airport's facilities. As outlined in a state report, the improvements would make Memphis the state's most modern airport. A total of 140 acres of land would be added, and the entire field would be graded "to almost a pool-table level." Other improvements included "installing a complete hard-surface runway system, additional lighting system, augmenting the drainage system, and preparing for the installation of radio and lights used in making instrument landings."[30] The federal Bureau of Air Commerce installed this last, high-tech improvement. It made Memphis the only airport in Tennessee with such a system and one of only twenty across the nation.

From this solid foundation of the 1930s, the Memphis airport would evolve after World War II into an important national, and eventually international, airfield. The original WPA terminal remained in use until 1963, when the city dedicated the present terminal, designed in New Formalism style by architect Roy Harrover.

SULLIVAN COUNTY

Tri-City Airport (1936–37), Tennessee Highway 75, Kingsport vicinity

The development of the Tri-City Airport was part of the WPA's effort to construct modern airfields for the state's major cities. This project, initially named McKellar Field in honor of U.S. Sen. Kenneth McKellar, was placed at a rural location roughly equally distant from Kingsport, Bristol, and Johnson City. Local governments bought in $50,000; the WPA in return offered $400,000. But due to the rocky terrain and the need for additional work, it took approximately $1 million of the WPA's money to finish the airport. The final price tag was set at $1,050.136.

Construction began at the 323-acre site on October 12, 1935. The WPA planned for the airfield to have hard-surfaced runways of approximately 4,000 feet in length, but the airfield's two runways eventually measured only 3,584 feet and 3,150 feet, respectively. The agency also constructed a modernist-styled terminal building, as well as 120-foot-by-115-foot steel-trussed hangar that had a clearance of 22 feet. The facility was well equipped with electrical lighting for night landings. It opened on September 1, 1937, with its formal dedication taking place on November 5, 1937.

WILSON COUNTY

Lebanon Airport (1933–34, 1936–37), 760 Franklin Road, Lebanon

The CWA provided the initial funding for the Lebanon airport, with work beginning in December 1933. The city leased forty-five acres for five years from Haywood Johnson, Dr. R. B. Gaston, and Hugh Chenault. It hired over a hundred men to scrape out a basic sod runway with hand tools. In 1936–37, WPA funds allowed the city to expand the airport's facilities and improve its runways. In 1939 Cumberland University acquired the airport for five thousand dollars in order to establish a Civilian Pilot Training program. It operated this program until World War II, when the U.S. Army Air Force took over control of the field and established its local headquarters at the university's gymnasium (see Wilson County Community House in chapter 4).

Notes

Introduction

1. Wayne C. Moore, comp., *Messages of the Governors of Tennessee. Volume 11: 1933–1945* (Nashville: Tennessee Historical Commission, 1998), 75. Moore's introductions to the administrations of McAlister, Browning, and Cooper are invaluable secondary sources on the New Deal era in Tennessee politics and government.

2. James Olson, *Saving Capitalism: The Reconstruction Finance Corporation and the New Deal, 1933–1940* (Princeton: Princeton Univ. Press, 1988), 227.

3. Jordan A. Schwarz, *The New Dealers: Power Politics in the Age of Roosevelt* (New York: Vantage Books, 1994), xi.

4. James W. Steely, *Parks for Texas: Enduring Landscapes of the New Deal* (Austin: Univ. of Texas Press, 1999), 37.

5. Thomas C. Coode, "Public Works Administration," in *Tennessee Encyclopedia of History and Culture* (Nashville: Tennessee Historical Society, 1998), ed. Carroll Van West, et al., 754.

6. "Kenneth Markwell, State PWA Director, on School Buildings," *Tennessee Teacher* 4 (Oct. 1936): 19.

7. Roger Biles, *The South and the New Deal* (Lexington: Univ. Press of Kentucky, 1994), 44.

8. Forrest A. Walker, *The Civil Works Administration: An Experiment in Federal Work Relief, 1933–1934* (New York: Garland, 1979), 84.

9. John Dean Minton, "The New Deal in Tennessee, 1932–1938," (Ph.D. diss., Vanderbilt Univ., 1959), 93.

10. Quill E. Cope, "A Hot Lunch Program in a Rural County," *Tennessee Teacher* 8(Apr. 1941): 46. See the discussion on school lunch programs in Martha H. Swain, "A New Deal for Southern Women: Gender and Race in Women's Work Relief," Christie Anne Farnham, ed.,*Women of the American South: A Multicultural Reader* (New York: New York Univ. Press, 1997), 252.

11. Dewey W. Grantham, *The South in Modern America: A Region at Odds* (New York: Harper Collins, 1994), 168.

12. George Fort Milton, "Down for the Tennessee Valley," *Review of Reviews* 87 (June 1933): 33–34 and "The South Do Move," *Yale Review* 29 (Sept. 1939): 138–52.

13. Eleanor Roosevelt, *This I Remember* (New York: Harper and Brothers, 1949), 137.

1. State Offices and County Courthouses

1. Lois Craig and the staff of the Federal Architecture Project, *The Federal Presence: Architecture, Politics and Symbols in the United States Government Buildings* (Cambridge, Mass.: MIT Press, 1977), 343.

2. This section is adapted from Lauren Batte, Holly Rine, and Carroll Van West, "Historic County Courthouses in Tennessee, 1865–1945," National Register of Historic Places Multiple Property Nomination, Tennessee Historical Commission, 1995, pp. E-27 to E-36.

3. Anne-Leslie Owens, "Cornwell, Dean," in *Tennessee Encyclopedia of History and Culture*, ed. West, et al., 210.

4. Sue B. Beckham, *Depression Post Office Murals and Southern Culture: A Gentle Reconstruction* (Baton Rouge: Louisiana State Univ. Press, 1989), 287.

5. Mendel-Mesick-Cohen-Waite-Hall Architects, *Tennessee State Capitol: Historic Structure Report* (Nashville: Dept. of General Services, 1986), 74.
6. Franklin County Court Minutes, Minute Book V (1937): 485.
7. Trina Binkley, "Lauderdale County Courthouse," National Register of Historic Places Nomination Form, Tennessee Historical Commission, 1994, 8–11.
8. Remark by Rufus Campbell in Kate Johnson Peters, *Lauderdale County from Earliest Times* (Ripley, Tenn.: Sugar Hill Lauderdale County Library, 1957), 125.
9. *Jackson Sun*, Jan. 4, 1937.
10. Ibid., Mar. 12, 1937.
11. E. A. Marshall, ed., *History of Obion County*. (Union City, Tenn.: The Daily Messenger, 1941), 32.
12. Holly A. Rine, "Obion County Courthouse, Union City, Tennessee," National Register of Historic Places Nomination Form, Tennessee Historical Commission, 1995, 8–10 and 8–11.
13. Marshall, *History of Obion County*, 31.

2. Federal Courthouses and Post Offices

1. Quote from Craig, et al, *The Federal Presence*, 364.
2. Marlene Park and Gerald E. Markowitz, *Democratic Vistas: Post Offices and Public Art in the New Deal* (Philadelphia: Temple Univ. Press, 1984), 5.
3. Ibid., 6.
4. Barbara Melosh, *Engendering Culture: Manhood and Womanhood in New Deal Public Art and Theater* (Washington, D.C.: Smithsonian Institution Press, 1991), 7.
5. Ibid., 122–23, 279n.; Lloyd Nease to Minna Citron, Nov. 1, 1940, cited in Howard Hull, *Tennessee Post Office Murals* (Kingsport, Tenn.: Overmountain Press, 1996), 120; *Survey Graphic* citation from Beckham, *Depression Post Office Murals*, 308.
6. Melosh, *Engendering Culture*, 123.
7. Frank Orr, et al., *Notable Nashville Architecture, 1930–1980* (Nashville: Middle Tennessee Chapter, AIA, 1989), 23.
8. Christopher Hetzel, "Dickson Post Office," National Register of Historic Places Nomination Form, Tennessee Historical Commission, Nashville, 1996, p. 7–1.
9. Edwin Boyd Johnson to Edward B. Rowan, Aug. 18, 1938, National Archives, Record Group 121, Series 133.
10. Edwin Boyd Johnson to Edward B. Rowan, Jan. 3, 1939, and Hugh Reeves to Treasury Department, Jan. 16, 1939, National Archives, Record Group 121, Series 133. A copy is in the Marianne B. Hillenmeyer Collection, Albert Gore Sr. Research Center, Middle Tennessee State Univ.
11. William Zorach to Inslee Hopper, Mar. 20, 1940, National Archives, Record Group 121, Series 133.
12. Melosh, *Engendering Culture*, 123.
13. For more on the building and its arts, see Sara A. Butler, "Federal Building," in *Tennessee Encyclopedia of History and Culture*, ed. West, et al., 304–5; Hull, *Tennessee Post Office Murals*, 18–23.
14. Henry B. Davenport to Ed Rowan, Feb. 19, 1940, cited in Hull, *Tennessee Post Office Murals*, 95.
15. Hull, *Tennessee Post Office Murals*, 124.
16. Beckham, *Depression Post Office Murals*, 306.
17. Park and Markowitz, *Democratic Vistas*, 63.
18. John H. R. Pickett to Ed Rowan, July 26, 1938, National Archives, Record Group 121, Series 133. A copy is in Hillenmeyer Collection, Gore Center.
19. Hull, *Tennessee Post Office Murals*, 114.

20. Park and Markowitz, *Democratic Vistas*, 30.
21. Dayton *Herald News*, June 13, 1939.
22. Dresden Garden Club to Ed Rowan, Oct. 17, 1938, National Archives, Record Group 121, Series 133. A copy is in Hillenmeyer Collection, Gore Center.
23. Quote from Beckham, *Depression Post Office Murals*, 300.

3. Community Buildings and Institutions

1. Swain, "A New Deal for Southern Women," 247.
2. President Franklin D. Roosevelt, "Establishment of the National Youth Administration," Commissioner of Education Files, Group 92, Folder 17, Box 258, Tennessee State Library and Archives.
3. Federal Writers' Project, *The WPA Guide to Tennessee* (1939; reprint, Knoxville: Univ. of Tennessee Press, 1986), 191.
4. Union City *Daily Messenger*, Mar. 10, 1941; R. C. Forrester and Bill Threlkeld, *Roads Less Traveled: Self-Guided Tours to Historic Sites and Scenic Areas in Obion County* (Union City, Tenn.: Lanzer Printing, 1996), 65.
5. Murfreesboro *Daily News Journal*, Feb. 15, 1938.
6. Ibid., Apr. 26, 1942.
7. Ibid.
8. Little historical information about the hospital has been published, but a wealth of material is available from records, photographs, and documents maintained at the York Center Archives in Building No. 9 at the York VA Medical Center.
9. Interview of Willie Higdon by Holly A. Rine, Nov. 16, 1993. Notes in "Dunlap Community Building, Sequatchie County" folder, National Register Files, MTSU Center for Historic Preservation, Murfreesboro, Tenn.
10. Eugene J. Johnson and Robert D. Russell Jr., *Memphis: An Architectural Guide* (Knoxville: Univ. of Tennessee Press, 1990), 325.

4. Schools

1. "Kenneth Markwell, State PWA Director, on School Buildings," *Tennessee Teacher* 4 (Oct. 1936): 19.
2. C. W. Short and R. Stanley-Brown, *Public Buildings* (Washington: Public Works Administration, 1939), xix.
3. W. Burr Cullom, "WPA Builds, Remodels, and Repairs Schools," *Tennessee Teacher* 3 (May 1936): 19.
4. W. Burr Cullom, "Tennessee Schools Get a 'Face Lifting,'" *Tennessee Teacher* 5 (Apr. 1938): 15.
5. W. Burr Cullom, "Schools Are Looking Better," *Tennessee Teacher* 4 (Sept. 1936): 25.
6. Mary S. Hoffschwelle, *Rebuilding the Rural Southern Community: Reformers, Schools, and Homes in Tennessee, 1900–1930* (Knoxville: Univ. of Tennessee Press, 1998).
7. "Nashville's 1938 School Building Program Nears Completion," *Tennessee Teacher* 7 (Mar. 1940): 4.
8. Linda T. Wynn, "Pearl School (1883–1983)," Bobby L. Lovett and Linda T. Wynn, eds., *Profiles of African Americans in Tennessee* (Nashville: private, 1996), 101.
9. Robert Townsend and Mrs. Louise Binkley, "Our Unique Fruit House," *Tennessee Teacher* 9 (Jan. 1942): 29.
10. W. Burr Cullom, "I Sure Enjoyed Your Show, Mister!" *Tennessee Teacher* 6 (Mar. 1939): 24.
11. Union City *Daily Messenger*, Sept. 4, 1936.

12. Milton Hamilton and C. D. Hilliard, "Home and Family Life . . . in Obion County," *Tennessee Teacher* 7(Nov. 1939): 20. Hamilton was the county school superintendent; Hilliard was the county director of education.
13. Ibid., 21.
14. *WPA Guide to Tennessee*, 509.
15. Jeanette Keith, *Country People in the New South: Tennessee's Upper Cumberland* (Chapel Hill: Univ. of North Carolina Press, 1995), 141.
16. Mary J. DeLozier, *Putnam County, Tennessee, 1850–1970* (Cookeville: Putnam County Government, 1979), 228.
17. Wali R. Kharif, "Darwin School and Black Public Education: Cookeville in the Decade of the *Brown* Decision," *Tennessee Historical Quarterly* 56(Spring 1997): 24.
18. H. C. Headden, "The New Springfield High School," *Tennessee Teacher* 6 (May 1939): 12.
19. Ibid., 16.
20. Bruce Overton, "N. Y. A. Projects in Tennessee," *Tennessee Teacher* 7 (Sept. 1939): 27.
21. "Mary Pupil Praises Her New School" first appeared in the 1940 edition of the school annual yearbook, *The Cadmea*. It was reprinted in the *Tennessee Teacher* 8 (Dec. 1940): 9–14.
22. Cited in Park and Markowitz, *Democratic Vistas*, 140.
23. "Community House Near C.U. Campus," newspaper clipping, Stockton Archives, Cumberland Univ. Library, Lebanon.

5. Housing

1. *WPA Guide to Tennessee*, 164, 166.
2. Phoebe Cutler, *The Public Landscape of the New Deal* (New Haven, Conn.: Yale Univ. Press, 1985), 119.
3. Gail Radford to Tom Thurston, NEWDEAL LISTSERV moderator, Oct. 6, 1997. Radford's illuminating study, *Modern Housing for America: Policy Struggles in the New Deal Era* (Chicago: Univ. of Chicago Press, 1996), is highly recommended.
4. William F. Larsen, *New Homes for Old: Publicly Owned Housing in Tennessee* (Knoxville: Univ. of Tennessee Extension Series, 1948), 24–25.
5. Diane Ghirardo, *Building New Communities: New Deal America and Fascist Italy* (Princeton: Princeton Univ. Press, 1989), 126.
6. "A Homesteads Celebration," *Crossville Chronicle*, July 1, 1998, 5.
7. Ibid., 2.
8. Ibid.
9. Ibid., 4
10. Charles S. Johnson, "A Social Study of Negro Families in the Area Selected for the Nashville Negro Federal Housing Project," [1934], Typescript, Nashville Room, Metropolitan Nashville/Davidson County Library, Nashville.
11. The ministers' letter of Nov. 14, 1934, is cited in Minton, "New Deal in Tennessee," 156.
12. *WPA Guide to Tennessee*, 203.
13. Don H. Doyle, *Nashville Since the 1920s* (Knoxville: Univ. of Tennessee Press, 1985), 98–99.
14. *Nashville Tennessean*, Jan. 24, 1937.
15. Interview with Jesse Cannon Sr. cited in Richard A. Couto, *Ain't Gonna Let Nobody Turn Me Round: The Pursuit of Racial Justice in the Rural South* (Philadelphia: Temple Univ. Press, 1991), 28.
16. Interview with Jesse Cannon Jr. in ibid., 29.
17. Ibid., 39.

18. Johnson and Russell, *Memphis: An Architectural Guide*, 126–27.
19. Larsen, *New Homes for Old*, 53.
20. Peter Guralnick, *Last Train to Memphis: The Rise of Elvis Presley* (Boston: Little, Brown, 1994), 33–34.
21. Roger Biles, *Memphis in the Great Depression* (Knoxville: Univ. of Tennessee Press, 1986), 95.
22. Ibid., 96.
23. Ibid., 107.
24. Margaret Ripley Wolfe, *Kingsport: A Planned American City* (Lexington: Univ. Press of Kentucky, 1987), 138.

6. Parks, Memorials, and Museums

1. Bevley R. Coleman, "A History of State Parks in Tennessee," (Ph.D. diss., George Peabody College for Teachers, 1963), 37.
2. Linda F. McClelland, *Presenting Nature: The Historic Landscape Design of the National Park Service* (Washington, D.C.: U.S. Dept. of Interior, 1993), and *Building the National Parks: Historic Landscape Design and Construction* (Baltimore, Md.: Johns Hopkins Univ. Press, 1998), 381.
3. Donald Dale Jackson, "To the CCC: thanks for the memories and monuments," *Smithsonian* 25 (Dec. 1994): 78.
4. Tennessee Valley Authority, *The Norris Project* (Washington, D.C.: Government Printing Office, 1940), 557.
5. Ruth Nichols, "The Civilian Conservation Corps and Tennessee State Parks: 1933–1942," (M.A. thesis, Middle Tennessee State Univ., 1994), 104.
6. *WPA Guide to Tennessee*, 517–18.
7. Durwood Dunn, *Cades Cove: The Life and Death of a Southern Appalachian Community, 1918–1937* (Knoxville: Univ. of Tennessee Press, 1988), 256.
8. Kevin E. Smith, "Mound Bottom," in *Tennessee Encyclopedia of History and Culture*, ed. West, et al., 648.
9. Stuart Neitzel to Carl Kuttruff, Jan. 29, 1974, photocopy in Mound Bottom file, research collection of Kevin Smith, Department of Sociology and Anthropology, Middle Tennessee State Univ.
10. *WPA Guide to Tennessee*, 491.
11. Jackson, "To the CCC," 72.
12. Ibid., 78.
13. Edwin A. Lyon, *A New Deal for Southeastern Archaeology* (Tuscalooa: Univ. of Alabama Press, 1996), 37.
14. Ibid., 141.
15. Tennessee Valley Authority, *Scenic Resources of the Tennessee Valley* (Washington, D.C.: Tennessee Valley Authority, 1938), 184.
16. Ibid., 114.
17. National Park Service, *Park Structures and Facilities* (Washington, D.C.: U.S. Dept. of the Interior, 1935), 171.
18. Claudette Stager, "Pickett State Rustic Park," in *Tennessee Encyclopedia*, ed. West, et al., 733–34.
19. NPS, *Park Structures and Facilities*, 103.
20. Cited in Tennessee Dept. of Agriculture, *Biennial Report, 1935–1936* (Nashville: State of Tennessee, 1936), 102.
21. *The Heritage of Polk County, Tennessee, 1839–1997* (Waynesville, N.C.: Polk County Historical and Genealogical Society and Don Mills, Inc., 1997), 18.

22. Carlos C. Campbell, *Birth of a National Park in the Great Smoky Mountains* (Knoxville: Univ. of Tennessee Press, 1960), 125.
23. Laura Thornborough, *The Great Smoky Mountains* (New York: Thomas Y. Crowell, 1937), 110.
24. Robbie D. Jones, *The Historic Architecture of Sevier County, Tennessee* (Sevierville: Smoky Mountain Historical Society, 1996), 120.
25. Kenneth J. Bindas, *All of This Music Belongs to the Nation: The WPA's Federal Music Project and American Society, 1935–1939* (Knoxville: Univ. of Tennessee Press, 1995), 114.
26. Johnson and Russell, *Memphis: An Architectural Guide*, 206.
27. Tennessee Valley Authority, *Scenic Resources of the Tennessee Valley*, 5.
28. Ibid., 5–6.
29. "Big Ridge State Park," *Tennessee Conservationist* 28 (Nov. 1961): 18.
30. McClelland, *Building the National Parks*, 392.
31. Michael J. McDonald and John Muldowny, *TVA and the Dispossessed: The Resettlement of Population in the Norris Dam Area* (Knoxville: Univ. of Tennessee Press, 1982), 61–62.
32. Ibid., 201.
33. Tennessee Valley Authority, *Scenic Resources of the Tennessee Valley*, 158.
34. Ginger Ramsey and Carroll Van West, "Cedars of Lebanon State Park Historic District," National Register of Historic Places Nomination, Tennessee Historical Commission, Nashville, July 1995, 8–6.

7. Dams to Privies

1. Meeting of National Emergency Council, No. 19 (Dec. 11, 1934), cited in McDonald and Muldowny, *TVA and Dispossessed*, 264.
2. Nancy L. Grant, *TVA and Black Americans: Planning for the Status Quo* (Philadelphia, Pa.: Temple Univ. Press, 1990).
3. Robert H. White, *Tennessee: Its Growth and Progress* (Nashville: Robert H. White, 1936), 290. This book became the Tennessee history textbook for generations of elementary and high school students.
4. *WPA Guide to Tennessee*, 434.
5. Stuart Chase, *Rich Land Poor Land* (London: Whittlesey House, 1936), 286–87.
6. Interview cited in Samuel H. Shannon, "A Study of the Social and Economic History of the Columbia Reservoir Area," vol. 2, 1890–1945: TVA Contract No. TV-60056A, Typescript Report, c. 1985, 82.
7. Donald Davidson, *The Tennessee*, vol. 2: *The New River from Civil War to TVA* (New York: Holt, Rinehart and Winston, 1948), 229–30.
8. Ibid., 230–31.
9. Marian Moffett, "Norris Dam," in *Tennessee Encyclopedia of History and Culture*, ed. West, et al., 694.
10. Walter L. Creese, *TVA's Public Planning: The Vision, the Reality* (Knoxville: Univ. of Tennessee Press, 1990), 182.
11. *WPA Guide to Tennessee*, 166.
12. Cutler, *Public Landscape of the New Deal*, 138.
13. McDonald and Muldowny, *TVA and the Dispossessed*, 235.
14. Robert L. Mason, *History of Cannon County, Tennessee* (Woodbury, Tenn.: Cannon County Historical Society, 1984), 248.
15. Doyle, *Nashville Since the 1920s*, 90.
16. Robert S. Clement, compiled by H. Alan Ragan, *From Mile Post 42 . . . To City of Dickson 1980* (Dickson, Tenn.: H. Alan Ragan and Dickson County Historical Society, 1999), 191.

17. Thomas M. N. Lewis and Madeline D. Kneberg Lewis, *The Prehistory of the Chickamauga Basin in Tennessee*, comp. and ed. Lynne P. Sullivan (Knoxville: Univ. of Tennessee Press, 1995), 1: xvi.

18. Roosevelt's speech was printed in the *Chattanooga Times*, Sept. 3, 1940.

19. Tennessee Aeronautics Commission, *An Analysis of Aviation in Tennessee* (Nashville: Tennessee State Planning Commission, 1936), n.p.

20. R. L. Duffus, *The Valley and its People: A Portrait of TVA* (New York: Knopf, 1946), 78.

21. Donald Davidson, *The Tennessee*, vol. 1: *The Old River: Frontier to Secession* (New York: Holt, Rinehart and Winston, 1946), 17.

22. William Bruce Wheeler and Michael J. McDonald, *TVA and the Tellico Dam, 1936–1979: A Bureaucratic Crisis in Post-Industrial America* (Knoxville: Univ. of Tennessee Press, 1986), x.

23. Burgess is quoted in *Reflections: A History of McNairy County, Tennessee, 1823–1996* (Marceline, Mo: Heritage House Publishing, 1996), 48.

24. R. E. Barclay, *Ducktown: Back in Raht's Time* (Chapel Hill: Univ. of North Carolina Press, 1946), 3.

25. Cited in West, *Tennessee's Historic Landscapes*, 206.

26. Mary J. DeLozier, *Putnam County, Tennessee, 1850–1970* (Cookeville, Tenn.: Putnam County, 1979), 228.

27. Creese, *TVA Public Planning*, 208.

28. Jones, *Historic Architecture of Sevier County*, 140.

29. Wilma Dykeman, *The French Broad* (New York: Holt, Rinehart and Winston, 1954), 338.

30. Tennessee Aeronautics Commission, "Analysis of Aviation in Tennessee," n.p.

A Note on Sources

To identify and interpret significant places in the New Deal landscape of Tennessee, I used a combination of traditional primary sources—local newspapers, interviews, and records and reports from local, state, and federal government agencies. The latter sources, especially the 1930s reports of the Tennessee Valley Authority, the Tennessee Department of Conservation, and the Tennessee State Planning Commission, were invaluable for gaining an understanding of the magnitude of New Deal reform and recovery efforts in Tennessee. Major depositories of these records are at the Tennessee State Library and Archives in Nashville and the TVA Division of Cultural Resources and its Archives at Norris, Tennessee. Other important written sources, more accessible to readers and travelers, were Depression-era books about the New Deal. The Federal Writers' Project's *The WPA Guide to Tennessee* (1939; reprint, Knoxville: Univ. of Tennessee Press, 1986) guided me to the places that WPA writers considered as the most important New Deal projects. The Tennessee Valley Authority's *The Scenic Resources of the Tennessee Valley* (Washington, D.C.: Tennessee Valley Authority, 1938) was similarly important in giving a period description of various conservation areas and projects. C. W. Short's and R. Stanley Brown's *Public Buildings* (Washington, D.C.: Public Works Administration, 1939) highlighted representative buildings and structures as well as providing a useful insight to agency assumptions about architecture and the need for public improvements.

In addition to these written sources, I relied on documentation typically used in the field of historic preservation, such as county architectural surveys, listings in the National Register of Historic Places, and cultural resource management reports by state and federal agencies. Major collections of these records are at the Tennessee Historical Commission, the Tennessee Department of Environment and Conservation, and the Tennessee Department of Transportation in Nashville, as well as the Center for Historic Preservation at Middle Tennessee State University. Particularly important National Register documents included three thematic studies that are defined as multiple property nominations. These nominations were the Tennessee Historical Commission's study of the CCC, WPA, and state parks in Tennessee, the Memphis Landmarks Commission's study of New Deal public housing in Memphis, and the MTSU Center for Historic Preservation's study of Tennessee courthouses built between 1865 and 1940. My fieldwork in all ninety-five counties identified representative properties for each of the chapters. Property owners, county historians, museum professionals, and local librarians greatly assisted my fieldwork, especially state parks personnel and employees at TVA visitor centers.

Fortunately for this study, scholars have shed much light on the state and national contexts of the New Deal landscape. On the concept of a New Deal landscape, Phoebe Cutler's *The Public Landscape of the New Deal* (New Haven, Conn.: Yale Univ. Press, 1985); Walter Creese's *TVA's Public Planning: The Vision, the Reality* (Knoxville: Univ. of Tennessee Press, 1990); and Linda F. McClelland's *Building the National Parks: Historic Landscape Design and Construction* (Baltimore, Md.: Johns Hopkins Univ. Press, 1998) were constant references. How the New Deal fit into traditions of federal architecture is analyzed in Lois Craig, et. al., *The Federal Presence: Architecture, Politics and Symbols in the United States Government Buildings* (Cambridge, Mass.: MIT Press, 1977). A partial state context is provided through the author's *Tennessee's Historic Landscapes: A Traveler's Guide* (Knoxville: Univ. of Tennessee Press, 1995). How other authors studied state parks also informed my research. Susan Flader, ed., *Exploring Missouri's Legacy: State Parks and Historic Sites* (Columbia: Univ. of Missouri Press, 1992), and Rebecca Conard, *Places of Quiet Beauty: Parks, Preserves, and Environmentalism* (Iowa City: Univ. of Iowa Press, 1997), blend environmental history, with some focus on the New Deal era, in their studies of parks in Missouri and Iowa. An extremely useful study, which analyzed the combined impact of New Deal agencies on state park development, is James W. Steely, *Parks for Texas: Enduring Landscapes of the New Deal* (Austin: Univ. of Texas Press, 1999).

To compare the New Deal experience in Tennessee with other southern states, and the nation in general, there are numerous major political studies. A representative sampling would include James C. Cobb and Michael V. Namorato's *The New Deal in the South* (Jackson: Univ. Press of Mississippi, 1984); Roger Biles's *The South and the New Deal* (Lexington: Univ. Press of Kentucky, 1994); George B. Tindall's *The Emergence of the New South, 1913–1945* (Baton Rouge: Louisiana State Univ. Press, 1967); Dewey Grantham's *The South in Modern America* (New York: Harper, 1995); John A. Salmond's *The Civilian Conservation Corps, 1933–1942* (Durham: Duke Univ. Press, 1967); Robert D. Pope's "Senatorial Baron: The Long Political Career of Kenneth D. McKellar," (Ph.D. diss., Yale Univ., 1976); Douglas Smith's *The New Deal in the Urban South* (Baton Rouge: Louisiana State Univ. Press, 1988); William D. Miller's *Mr. Crump of Memphis* (Baton Rouge: Louisiana

State Univ. Press, 1964); and William Majors's *Change and Continuity: Tennessee Politics Since the Civil War* (Macon, Ga.: Mercer Univ. Press, 1986).

The public art of the New Deal has received scholarly attention at national, regional, and state levels. Barbara Melosh's *Engendering Culture: Manhood and Womanhood in New Deal Public Art and Theater* (Washington, D.C.: Smithsonian Institution Press, 1991) is a multidisciplinary analysis of a wide range of arts projects. Marlene Park and Gerald Markowitz's *Democratic Vistas: Post Offices and Public Art in the New Deal* (Philadelphia: Temple Univ. Press, 1984) focuses on the Treasury Department's Section of Fine Arts program, while a southern perspective on that same topic is Sue B. Beckham's *Depression Post Office Murals and Southern Culture: A Gentle Reconstruction* (Baton Rouge: Louisiana State Univ. Press, 1989). Jonathan Harris's *Federal Art and National Culture* (New York: Cambridge Univ. Press, 1995), Michael Denning's *The Cultural Front: The Laboring of American Culture in the Twentieth Century* (New York: Verso, 1996), and Bruce I. Bustard's *A New Deal for the Arts* (Washington, D.C.: National Archives and Records Administration, 1997) address the New Deal contribution to the tradition of federally sponsored arts. University of Tennessee professor Howard Hull has compiled all of the extant Tennessee post office murals in his extremely useful *Tennessee Post Office Murals* (Kingsport, Tenn.: Overmountain Press, 1996). By extensively using the Treasury Department records contained in Record Group 121, Series 133 of the National Archives, Marianne Bevel Hillenmeyer's "Depression Era Art: Tennessee Post Office Murals," (M.A. thesis, Middle Tennessee State Univ., 1995) adds valuable detail on the Tennessee murals. Public art projects in Tennessee outside of the post office murals, however, have not received much scholarly attention.

Once neglected New Deal programs have been the topics of recent book-length studies. Edwin A. Lyon's *A New Deal for Southeastern Archaeology* (Tuscaloosa: Univ. of Alabama Press, 1996) provides context on the key archaeological programs carried out in Tennessee by the CWA, WPA, and TVA. Kenneth H. Bindas's *All of This Music Belongs to the Nation* (Knoxville: Univ. of Tennessee Press, 1995) addresses the Federal Music Project of the WPA, although much work on individual projects in Tennessee remains to be done.

On the significant issue of population displacement, important studies include Michael McDonald and John Muldowny's *TVA and the Dispossessed: the Resettlement of Population in the Norris Dam Area* (Knoxville: Univ. of Tennessee Press, 1982); Durwood Dunn's *Cades Cove: The Life and Death of a Southern Appalachian Community, 1918–1937* (Knoxville: Univ. of Tennessee Press, 1988); Dan Pierce's "The Barbarism of the Huns: Family and

Community Removal in the Establishment of the Great Smoky Mountains National Park," *Tennessee Historical Quarterly* 57 (Spring/Summer 1998): 62–79; Stephen Taylor's "Building the Back of Beyond: Government Authority, Community Life, and Economic Development in the Upper Little Tennessee, 1880–1992," (Ph.D. diss., Univ. of Tennessee, 1996); and Margaret L. Brown's "Power, Privilege, and Tourism: A Revision of the Great Smoky Mountains National Park Story," (M.A. thesis, Univ. of Kentucky, 1990). By comparison, population displacement due to conservation and resettlement projects in Tennessee awaits full scholarly treatment.

Many articles in the *Tennessee Teacher*, the monthly magazine of the Tennessee Education Association, addressed the wide range of New Deal funded or sponsored school programs from 1933 to 1942. Mary S. Hoffschwelle's *Rebuilding the Rural Southern Community: Reformers, Schools, and Homes in Tennessee, 1900–1930* (Knoxville: Univ. of Tennessee Press, 1998) creates an understanding of the impetus and goals of educational reform in Tennessee at the time of the Great Depression; a similar study for the depression decade itself is needed.

The New Deal's role in public housing has received considerable attention recently. Recommended studies include Gail Radford's *Modern Housing for America: Policy Struggles in the New Deal Era* (Chicago: Univ. of Chicago Press, 1996) and Katharine G. Bristol's "Beyond the Pruitt-Igoe Myth: The Development of American High-Rise Public Housing, 1850–1970," (Ph.D. diss., Univ. of California, Berkeley, 1991). Also useful are John F. Bauman's *Public Housing, Race, and Renewal: Urban Planning in Philadelphia, 1920–1974* (Philadelphia: Temple Univ. Press, 1987) and Gwendolyn Wright's classic *Building the Dream: A Social History of Housing in America* (Cambridge, Mass.: MIT Press, 1981). There is ample contextual literature on the resettlement projects, including Paul K. Conkin's pathbreaking study, *Tomorrow a New World: The New Deal Community Program* (Ithaca: Cornell Univ. Press, 1958); Diane Ghirardo's *Building New Communities: New Deal America and Fascist Italy* (Princeton: Princeton Univ. Press, 1989); and Sidney Baldwin's *Poverty and Politics: The Rise and Decline of the Farm Security Administration* (Chapel Hill: Univ. of North Carolina Press, 1968). More study, however, needs to be focused on the Haywood Farms project. The Tennessee Humanities Council in 1998–99 conducted a community history workshop and program with members of the project.

The New Deal transformation of southern agriculture is surveyed in Gilbert C. Fite's *Cotton Fields No More: Southern Agriculture, 1865–1980* (Lexington: Univ. Press of Kentucky, 1984). TVA's rural programs, and other key aspects of the authority's history, are discussed in Edwin C. Hargrove and Paul K. Conkin's *TVA: Fifty Years of Grass-roots Bureaucracy* (Urbana: Univ. of Illinois Press, 1983). An excellent county study that focuses on agricultural change during the depression is Wayne C. Moore's "Farm Communities and Economic Growth in the Lower Tennessee Valley, Humphreys County, Tennessee, 1785–1980," (Ph.D. diss., Univ. of Rochester, 1990). The MTSU Center for Historic Preservation maintains the records of the Tennessee Century Farms Program, many of which were involved in TVA demonstration programs, soil conservation projects, and other activities of New Deal agencies. Land conservation during the New Deal is introduced in Timothy Lehman's *Public Values, Private Lands: Farmland Preservation Policy, 1933–1985* (Chapel Hill: Univ. of North Carolina Press, 1995).

Statewide studies of the New Deal in Tennessee exist but few have been published, or if they were published, they are not in print today. John D. Minton's *The New Deal in Tennessee, 1932–1938* (New York: Garland, 1979) and Bevley R. Coleman's "A History of State Parks in Tennessee" (Ph.D. diss., George Peabody College for Teachers, 1963) remain authoritative. Ruth Nichols's "The Civilian Conservation Corps and Tennessee State Parks: 1933–1942," (M.A. thesis, Middle Tennessee State Univ., 1994) has expanded the Coleman study and added an architectural history perspective on the history of Tennessee's parks. Martha Carver's "A Survey Report of Historic Bridges in Tennessee," a research report for the Tennessee Department of Transportation in 1993, impressively documents historic bridges, bridge companies, and the patterns of bridge building in the state. The recent *Tennessee Encyclopedia of History and Culture* (Nashville: Tennessee Historical Society, 1998), edited by Carroll Van West, Connie L. Lester, Anne-Leslie Owens, and Margaret Binnicker, has many different individual entries on New Deal projects and agencies from architectural historians, social historians, and historic preservationists.

Tennessee urban historians identified significant properties as they also provided a context on the New Deal's impact on the state's cities. Roger Biles's *Memphis in the Great Depression* (Knoxville: Univ. of Tennessee Press, 1986) and Eugene Johnson and Robert Russell Jr.'s *Memphis: An Architectural Guide* (Knoxville: Univ. of Tennessee Press, 1990) are basic sources about the Bluff City. Don H. Doyle's *Nashville Since the 1920s* (Knoxville: Univ. of Tennessee Press, 1985) is especially strong on New Deal developments in the state capitol while the author's *Nashville Architecture: A Guide to the City* (Nashville: Vanderbilt Univ. Press, 2001) identifies and discusses its major New Deal era landmarks. Michael McDonald and Bruce Wheeler's

Knoxville, Tennessee: Continuity and Change in an Appalachian City (Knoxville: Univ. of Tennessee Press, 1983) and Lucille Deaderick's *Heart of the Valley: A History of Knoxville, Tennessee* (Knoxville: East Tennessee Historical Society, 1976) remain basic sources for Knoxville. Margaret Ripley Wolfe's *Kingsport: A Planned American City* (Lexington: Univ. Press of Kentucky, 1987) is a model study of an Appalachian industrial town. James Livingood's *A History of Hamilton County, Tennessee* (Memphis: Memphis State Univ. Press, 1981) devotes an entire chapter to Chickamauga Dam and other New Deal projects in the Chattanooga area.

Local and county histories address the New Deal era in a haphazard fashion. William R. Snell's *"Hard Times Remembered": Bradley County and the Great Depression* (Cleveland, Tenn.: Bradley County Historical Society, 1983) is excellent, but many authors in the Memphis State University Press's county history series of the 1980s said little about the depression decade. Local and county histories produced during the Tennessee bicentennial of 1996 tend to shed more light on the era. A representative example is Robbie Jones's *The Historic Architecture of Sevier County, Tennessee* (Sevierville: Smoky Mountain Historical Society, 1996).

Index

Adult education, 114–16, 120
Agricultural Adjustment Act of 1933, 214
Agricultural Adjustment Act of 1938, 215
Agricultural Adjustment Administration (AAA), 16–17, 175–77, 214–15, 244
Airports, 19, 218, 226–27, 229, 235–36, 243–44, 247, 253–54
Alabama Museum of Natural History, 237
Alcoa, Tenn., 226–27
Alden, John, 234
Alpine, Tenn., 116–17
Alpine Institute, 116–17
American Red Cross, 84
Amphitheaters, 126, 133, 155, 184
Anderson County, 10, 49–50, 153–55, 219–26
Appalachian Club, 194
Appalachian Trail, 189, 193, 203
Archeological projects, 152, 156, 161–62, 174, 178, 181, 187, 199–201, 233–34, 237, 242, 251
Archville, Tenn., 189
Armories, 22, 78–80, 83–84, 85–88, 90, 93–94, 95
Arnold, R. V., 125
Art: CWA projects, 18, 35–36, 198; murals, 32–34, 36, 48–54, 56–72, 74–75, 126–27, 198; Public Works of Art projects, 33–36, 47, 198; sculpture, 32, 35–36, 58, 59–61, 67, 72; Treasury Department projects, 47–54, 56–72, 74–75, 242; WPA Federal Art Project, 20, 47–49, 198
Art Deco style, 40, 42–43, 78, 83, 95, 101, 111–12, 121, 123, 197–98, 252
Ashland City, Tenn., 217
Ashwander et al. v. Tennessee Valley Authority (1936), 10
Athens, Tenn., 78, 215

Auger, Tracy, 223
Austin Homes, Knoxville, 141
Awsumb, George, 143

Baggenstoss, Herman E., 169
Bank of Tennessee, 1
Bankhead-Jones Farm Tenant Act, 129
Barber, Charles, 112, 193–94
Barber, Frank O., 111
Barber and McMurry, 112
Baumann and Baumann, architects, 49, 111–12
Beasley, Shubael T., 94
Beauty Spot Gap, 203
Bedford County, 80, 155–56
Beech Hill, Tenn., 106
Benton, Tenn., 43
Benton County, 50, 175, 217
Berry, Harry S., 19, 168, 229
Berry Field, 229
Biafora, Enea, 58
Big Fiery Gizzard Creek, 169
Big Ridge State Park, 4, 204–8
Billings, Henry, 68–69
Binkley, Louise, 106
Bledsoe County, 157, 208
Blount County, 157–60, 226–27
Board of the National Missions of the Presbyterian Church, USA, 116
Bohannon, C. B., 43
Bohannon Building, Livingston, 21, 43
Bolivar, Tenn., 61
Bonded Construction Company, 62
Booker T. Washington State Park, 171–72
Bradley Academy, 77
Bradley County, 31, 77, 80–81, 188, 213–14
Bridges, 15, 17, 19, 165–66, 193, 218, 223, 234, 236
Bristol, Tenn., 124–26, 201–2, 254
Brock, Hershel, 92

Brooks, Cora Davis, 79
Brooks, T. D., 79
Brooks Memorial Art League, 198
Browning, Gordon, 3, 21–22, 52
Brownsville, Tenn., 62
Brushy Mountain State Prison, 181
Buffalo Springs Wildlife Management Area, 231
Bungalow style, 86–87
Burgess, Norbett, 246
Burnham, Herbert M., 93, 142, 146
Byford, Allen, 14
Byrns, Joseph W., 8

Cades Cove, Tenn., 157–60, 194
Cagle, Tenn., 122
Cahill, Holger, 48
Caldwell and Company, 1
Callicott, Burton, 64, 198
Calloway, Harry M., 66
Camden, Tenn., 50, 156, 217
Cameron, Daniel, 178
Camp Andrew Johnson (CCC), 215, 232
Camp Cleoga (CCC), 189–90
Camp Coie Foster (CCC), 231
Camp Cordell Hull (CCC), 13, 203–4
Camp Gordon Browning (CCC), 156
Camp H. A. Morgan (CCC), 193
Camp Joe E. Williams, 215, 245–46
Camp McCroy (CCC), 189
Camp Old Hickory (CCC), 189
Camp Sam Houston (CCC), 157
Camp Walton (CCC), 247
Campbell, Lloyd, 86
Campbell County, 50–51, 99, 160–61, 223
Cane Creek Falls, 208–9
Cane Creek Park, 247
Cannon, Jesse, Jr., 141
Cannon, Jesse, Sr., 141
Cannon County, 81, 91, 217, 227–28
Carlisle, Louis, 142
Carlton, Nevan, 93
Carroll County, 52, 175
Carter County, 99–100, 203
Carthage, Tenn., 123, 218
Cartwright, Tenn., 122
Caryville, Tenn., 99, 160–61
Cathey, H. B., 218

Cedars of Lebanon State Park, 210–11
Centerville, Tenn., 83–84
Chambellan, Rene, 32
Chambers, Moreau B., 174
Chase, Stuart, 216
Chattanooga, 2, 30, 38, 47, 60–61, 78, 107–9, 130, 138–39, 216–17, 232–36
Chattanooga Housing Authority, 138
Chattanooga Regional History Museum, 47
Cheatham County, 31, 161–62, 217
Cheatham Place public housing, 130, 137–38
Chenault, Hugh, 254
Cherokee National Forest, 12, 13, 25, 188–90, 202–4
Chester County, 31, 128, 163–65
Chickamauga Lake, 171–72, 232–35
Chickasaw State Park and Forest, 163
Child, Charles, 63–64
Chilhowee Mountain, 189
Chucalissa Village Museum, 200–201
Citron, Minna, 52–54
City Federation of Women's Clubs of Knoxville, 84
City halls, 31, 38, 45
Civil Works Administration (CWA), 17–18, 29, 43, 77, 80, 96, 120, 123, 125, 126, 131, 174, 217–18, 243, 247, 252–54
Civilian Conservation Corps (CCC), 4, 11–14, 114, 120, 131, 133, 135, 149–57, 159–66, 169–74, 175–77, 179–80, 182–90, 192–96, 199–209, 211, 213–18, 231–32, 239, 245–46, 247
Claiborne County, 223
Clark, John, 32, 36
Clark, Richard, 137
Clarksville, Tenn., 13, 21, 48, 78, 114
Classical Modern (PWA Modern) style, 30, 32–35, 37, 40–44, 49, 50, 55–56, 58, 60, 67–69, 93, 98, 101–2, 112–15
Classical Revival style, 38, 65, 91, 94, 98, 100, 121
Cleland, G. L., 176
Clement, Robert S., 230
Cleveland, Tenn., 80–81, 188, 214
Cleveland Weekly Herald, 214

INDEX 271

Clinch River, 2, 155, 207, 225–26
Clinch River Bridge Cooperative, 208
Clinton, Tenn., 48, 49–50
Clinton Engineering Works, 50–51
Cluck, Fain, 111
Cocke County, 52–53, 81, 251
Coffee County, 53–54
Coleman, Beley R., 149
College Hill Courts, Chattanooga, 138–39
Collegiate Gothic style, 108, 112
Colley, C. K. and Son, architects, 102
Collierville, Tenn., 123
Colonial Revival style, 36, 45, 46, 49–50, 52–54, 56, 58–59, 61–65, 67, 69–74, 83, 84–85, 91, 97–99, 103–5, 107–9, 111, 113, 124, 126–27, 134, 137–38, 142, 146–48, 177, 193–94, 224
Columbia, Tenn., 67–68, 85–86
Columbia Federal Courthouse, 67–69
Columbia Herald, 151–52
Commonwealth and Southern Company, 233
Commonwealth Fund, 88
Company Paul Lawrence Dunbar, 174
Condon, James, 121
Condra, R. M., Co., 39, 107
Confederate Park, Memphis, 195
Conger, Dixie L., 239–40
Connelly, William B., 179
Cookeville, Tenn., 247
Coolidge, Calvin, 180, 191
Cooper, Hobart S., 181
Cooper, Prentice, 3, 22, 78, 80, 87, 90
Copperhill, Tenn., 190
Cornwell, Dean, 32–33
Corryton, Tenn., 111
Courthouses, county, 29–30, 37–44
Courthouses, federal, 46, 49, 59–61, 67–69
Cove Lake State Park, 99, 160–61
Covey, Margaret, 70–71
Cox, Amy, 133
Cox, E. C., 122
Cox, P. E., 180
Crab Orchard stone, 43, 54, 78, 117, 131–32, 134
Crawford, Hubert, 247

Cret, Paul, 30, 49
Crockett, David, 74
Crossville, Tenn., 24–25, 54, 128, 131–35, 165–66, 228
Crump, Edward H., 1, 8, 21–22, 79, 145, 146, 201, 219, 252–53
Cullom, W. Burr, 97, 114
Cumberland County, 24–25, 54, 128, 131–35, 165–66, 217, 228
Cumberland Homesteads, 24–25, 54, 128, 131–35, 165–66
Cumberland Mountain State Park, 133, 165–66
Cumberland Presbyterian Church, 169
Cumberland University, 127, 254
Cummings, Will, 233

Dailey, Laura Woolsey, 47
Dams: Cherokee, 11, 64, 216, 238–39; Chickamauga, 10, 47, 216, 232–35; Douglas, 11, 216, 250–51; Fort Loudon, 11, 66, 216, 241–43; Great Falls Dam, 10; Kentucky, 11, 156, 216, 237; Norris, 10, 160–61, 216, 219–26; Ocoee No. 3, 11, 216, 246–47; Pickwick, 10, 62, 216, 236–37; South Holston, 126; Tellico, 243; Watts Bar, 11, 216; Wheeler, 236; Wilson, 236
Dancy, Mrs. Alex, 42
Dandridge, Tenn., 216, 250
Darwin, J. Claude, 120
Daugherty and Clements, architects, 127
Davenport, Henry B., 62
Davidson, Donald, 221–22, 243
Davidson, George, 36
Davidson County, 16, 29, 32–36, 55–56, 81–82, 100–105, 130, 136–38, 166–68, 181, 219
Davidson County Public Building and Courthouse, 16, 32–33
Day, Horace, 49
Dayton, Tenn., 71
Decatur County, 98, 128
Decaturville, Tenn., 98
Decherd, Tenn., 58
DeKalb County, 105
Dent, Lucian M., 93
Desoto Park, Memphis, 94

Dickson, Tenn., 56–57, 168–69, 230
Dickson County, 23, 56–57, 77, 168–69, 230
Dickson Resident Work Center, 23, 230
Dillard, John L., 116
Displacement of population, 11, 150, 159–60, 174, 184, 194, 196, 206–8, 211, 226, 233, 237, 239, 251–52
Dixie Highway, 80, 90
Dixie Homes public housing, 130, 142–43
Dixon, Harry, 198
Donaldson, Heloise, 84
Dougherty, Clemmons and Seale, architects, 100
Dougherty, Edward E., 35
Dougherty, Edwin, 168
Douglas Lake, 250–52
Douglass, Willis B., 140
Douglass, Tenn., 140–41
Draper, Earle, 150, 223
Dresden, Tenn., 73–74
Dresden Garden Club, 74
Dresslar, Fletcher B., 98
Dryden, Allen, 109
Dryden, Allen, Sr., 95
Ducktown, Tenn., 190
Dunlap, Tenn., 92–93
Dunlap Community Hall, 92–93
DuPont, William I., Jr., 168
Dyer, Tenn., 96
Dyer County, 217, 219, 231

Eakin, Mrs. John Hill, 101
East Lake Courts, Chattanooga, 138
East Tennessee State University, 48, 126
Edmondson, William, 47
Elizabethton, Tenn., 99–100
Elkmont, Tenn., 194–95
Ellington, Duke, 95
Elliott, Grover, 92
Elmwood Farm, 232
Emergency Conservation Work program, 11–14, 192
Erwin, Tenn., 73, 203–4
Etowah, Tenn., 86–87, 188
Eva site, 156
Everett, Robert A., "Fats" 87
Ewton, James, 93

Fairbanks, Charles, 234
Fall Creek Falls State Park, 208–9
Farley, James A., 67
Farm Security Administration (FSA), 19, 129, 133, 140–41, 166, 176
Fayette County, 105
Fayetteville, Tenn., 240
Fechner, Robert, 14
Federal Emergency Administration of Public Works, 15
Federal Emergency Relief Administration (FERA), 18, 128
Federal Housing Authority (FHA), 147
Federal Music Project, 152–53, 182, 197
Federal Works Agency, 46
Federal Writers' Project, 20
Fentress County, 105
Fire towers, 169, 176, 182, 186, 189, 192, 203, 252
First Baptist Church, Lauderdale, 145
Fish hatcheries, 193, 231
Fisk University, 101, 136
Fisk University Social Settlement, 101
Fiske-Carter Construction Company, 109
Fleming, Bryant, 168
Flood Control Bill of 1937, 219, 252
Flood of 1937, 94–95, 219
Folger, D. F., 133
Foote, W. H., Homes, Memphis, 144–45
Forcum Jones Company, 44
Ford, Henry, 236
Forrest, Nathan B., State Historical Area, 155–56
Fort Dickerson, 178
Fort Loudon Lake, 241–43
Fort Loudoun State Historical Area, 181
Fort Negley, 166–67
Foster, William Dewey, 67
Foster and Creighton, 42
Foster Falls, 170
Franklin County, 37, 58, 218
Franklin County Courthouse, 37
Franks, C. D., 90
Frazier, T. A., 87
Fredonia Lodge Drum and Fife Ensemble, 141
French Broad River, 251–52
Frist Center for Visual Arts, 56

INDEX

Frozen Head State Natural Area, 181–82
Fuller, T. O., 145, 199, 201
Furbringer, Max, 145, 197, 252
Fyfe, John, 50

Gallatin, Tenn., 44
Galloway, Robert, 195
Gardens, community, 77, 81, 85
Gaston, John, Hospital, 79
Gaston, R. B., 254
Gentry school, Putnam County, 18
Gibson County, 58–59, 82, 96–97, 176, 231
Giles County, 106
Gillium, Emma D., 85
Gooch Wildlife Management Area, 231
Gleason, Tenn., 74–75
Good, Albert H., 151, 192
Good, Minnetta, 74
Good and Goodstein, architects, 72
Gore, Albert, Sr., 123
Gore Center Archives, MTSU, 122
Gossage-Blue, Edith, 134
Govan, Gilbert E., 108
Government Rustic style, 89, 151, 154–56, 174, 179, 184–87, 193, 204–6, 211
Grand Junction City Hall, 38
Grain elevator, 252
Grainger County, 223, 231, 239
Great Depression in Tennessee, 1–8
Great Smoky Mountains Conservation Association, 190–91
Great Smoky Mountains National Park, 25, 64, 157–60, 188, 190–95
Green, Arthur, 125
Green, Grafton, 34–35
Greene County, 59–60, 97, 215, 232
Greeneville, Tenn., 49, 59–60
Greeneville Federal Courthouse, 59–60
Greenfield, Tenn., 45
Greenfield City Hall, 45
Greenwood, Grace, 62
Greenwood, Marion, 54
Greer, Susan, 93
Grundy County, 79, 107, 169–71
Grundy County Forest Association, 170
Grundy Forest State Natural Area, 169–70
Grundy Lakes Park, 170–71

Guerry, Alexander, 108
Guild, Jo Conn, Jr., 233
Gymnasiums, 98, 100, 102, 105, 107, 115, 117, 121–22, 123–24, 127

Haley, W. L., and Company, 250
Hamblen County, 5, 22, 31, 38, 79, 238, 251
Hamblen County Jail, 38
Hamilton, Albert ,198
Hamilton County, 38, 60–61, 78, 107–9, 130, 138–39, 171–72, 216–17, 232–36
Hancock County, 83, 109
Handy, W. C., 153
Hanker, William J., 143
Hankins, M. H., 43, 70
Hansen, Anker F., 142, 146
Hardeman County, 38, 61
Hardin County, 61–62, 128, 172–74, 236–37
Harmon, Ray, 93
Harmon, Wiley L., 93
Harrison Bay State Park, 172
Hart, Freeland, and Roberts, architects, 100, 101
Hart and Russell, architects, 40, 121
Hartman, Bertram, 71–72
Hawkins, William H., 226
Hawkins County, 2, 239
Hawks, W. R., 75
Hay, William H., 163
Haywood County, 62, 129, 140–41
Haywood County Farms Project, 129, 140–41
Hazard, James O., 185, 196, 210
Headden, H. C., 121
Heinrich, Christian, 72
Henderson County, 62, 128, 175–77
Henry, James A., Resource Center, 108
Henry County, 11, 78, 215, 217
Hermitage, 91
Hibbs, Henry C., 81, 100, 137
Hickman County, 83–84, 97, 181
Higdon, Willie, 92–93
Higgins, Eugene, 69
Highlander Folk School, 79
Hill Avenue Viaduct, 218
Hine, Lewis, 207

Hirons, Frederic C., 32–33, 36
Historic American Building Survey (HABS), 35, 142
Historic sites, 152, 155–56, 164, 166–67, 169, 178, 180–81
Hoffschwelle, Mary S., 98
Hogue, Jack, 93
Hohenwald, Tenn., 40–41
Holt, Carl, 231
Hoover, Herbert, 2–3
Hopkins, Harry L., 19–29
Horton, Henry, 1
Hoskins, Lynn Wood, 231
Hospitals, 79, 90–92, 94–95
Housing, 128–48
Houston County, 110
Howard, Ebenezer, 223
Howse, Hillary, 103
Hull, Cordell, 8, 123
Hull, Cordell, Bridge, 218
Hull, Howard, 47, 69
Humphreys County, 63, 178, 237–38
Hunt, Reuben H., architects, 38, 43, 60, 107, 109
Huntingdon, Tenn., 2

Ickes, Harold, 35
Infrastructure, federal spending on, 5–8, 9–11, 15–16, 17, 19, 80, 123, 125, 176, 182, 189–90, 193, 212–54
International style, 142
Ipcar, Dahlov, 50–51
Irvin, Marie, 133, 135

J. A. Jones Construction Company, 32
Jacksboro, Tenn., 161
Jackson, Andrew, 34, 74, 91
Jackson, Andrew, Courts public housing, 130, 136–37
Jackson, Arthur, 152, 166
Jackson, Tenn., 41–42, 130, 216, 243–44
Jackson County, 22, 97
Jackson Housing Authority, 130
Jails, 29–31, 38, 41–42
Jamestown, Tenn., 105–6
Jefferson City, Tenn., 63–64, 239
Jefferson County, 63–64, 238–39, 250–51
Jennings, Jesse, 234

Jim Crow segregation, 8
Johnson, Charles S., 61, 101, 136
Johnson, Edwin Boyd, 56–57
Johnson, Haywood, 254
Johnson City, Tenn., 13, 48, 126–27, 254
Johnson County, 110–11, 203
Johnsonville, battle of, 156
Jones, Bascom F., 87
Jones, Dudley E., 142, 145
Jones, Walk, Jr., 93, 143
Jones, Walk, Sr., 93, 142, 146
Jones, Wendell, 126–27
Jonesborough, Tenn., 45, 127

Kahn, Albert, 222
Keeble, Edwin A., 90
Keith, Jeanette, 117
Kenyon, Suzanne, 69
Kerley, Grady, 93
Kingsport, Tenn., 95, 130, 148, 252–54
Kingsport Civic Auditorium, 95
Kingsport Housing Authority, 148
Kinney, Belle, 35–36
Kiwanis Park, 182
Knox County, 2–3, 30, 49, 84, 111–12, 130, 141–42, 178
Knoxville, 2–3, 30, 49, 84, 111–12, 130, 141–42, 178, 216, 218
Knoxville College, 72, 142
Knoxville Housing Authority, 141
Knoxville Journal, 13
Knoxville News-Sentinel, 133
Knudsen, William S., 250
Kuttruff, Carl, 163

LaFollette, Tenn., 50–51
Lake County, 38–39, 84–85, 178–80, 219, 231, 239
Lake County Courthouse, 38–39
Lake Isom National Wildlife Refuge, 179
Lamar Terrace, Memphis, 146
Larsen, William F., 130–31
Lauderdale County, 39–40, 64–65
Lauderdale County Courthouse, 39–40
Lauderdale Courts public housing, 130, 143–44
Lawrence County, 65
Lawrenceburg, Tenn., 65

Lea, Luke, 1
Lebanon, Tenn., 127, 210–11, 254
Lebanon Cedar Forest Project, 210
Leech, Hilton, 60
Leech-Larkins Farm, 230
Lehman, Timothy, 214
LeMoyne College, 94, 146
LeMoyne Gardens, Memphis, 146
Lenoir, W. G., Museum, 155, 226
Lenoir City, Tenn., 65–66, 241–43
LeQuire, Alan, 36
Lester, W. C., 143
Levees, 218–19, 231, 239, 252
Lewis, Madeline Kneberg, 156, 234
Lewis, Meriwether, 180
Lewis, Thomas M. N., 156, 163, 178, 199–201, 234, 242
Lewis County, 40–41, 180–81
Lewis County Courthouse, 40–41
Lewisburg, Tenn., 48, 67, 85, 217, 244–45
Lexington, Tenn., 62
Lexington Progress, 176
Liberty, Tenn., 105
Libraries, 39, 81–85, 92, 108
Lidberg, George, 200, 234
Life magazine, 65–66
Lightfoot, William V., 169, 171
Lilienthal, David, 9, 53, 108, 233, 250–51
Lincoln County, 31, 112–13, 216, 239–40
Lincoln County Electric Membership Corporation, 216, 239–40
Linden, Tenn., 98
Lingerfelt, E. R., 114
Little River Stone Bridge, 193
Livingston, Tenn., 21, 70
Lockhart, Jack, 92
Lodges, scout, 86, 89
Longmire, Evelyn Hill, 207
Loudon County, 29, 65–66, 241–43, 248
Lovell, John E., 235
Lovell Field, 235–36
Loyster, Earl, 234
Luten Bridge Company, 218

Macon County, 6
Madison County, 6, 41–42, 130
Madison County Courthouse, 6, 41–42
Madisonville, Tenn., 97, 113

Manchester, Tenn., 48, 53–54
Marion County, 67, 98
Markwell, Kenneth, 15–16, 96, 250
Marr and Holman, architects, 35, 37, 39, 41–42, 44, 55–56, 87
Marrowbone Lake, 168
Marshall County, 67, 77, 85, 244–45
Marshall County Burley Tobacco Association, 244
Marshall County Dairy Herd Improvement Association, 244
Marshall County Farm Bureau Cooperative, 244
Marshall County Soil Erosion Association, 244
Marshall County Soil Erosion Club, 244
Martin, David Stone, 65–66, 241
Martin, Harley, 93
Martin, Thelma, 70
Maury County, 67–69, 85–86, 113, 181, 214, 218
Maryville, Tenn., 227
Maynard, Paul, 234
McAdams, John B., 45
McAdow, Samuel, 169
McAlister, Hill, 3, 18, 185
McClelland, Linda, 151, 205
McClung Museum, 234
McCullough, Hubert, 90
McEwen, Tenn., 237–38
McGhee Tyson Airport, 226–27
McGuire, H. J., & Co., 38
McKellar, Kenneth D., 8, 46, 50, 124, 233, 243, 250, 252–53
McKellar-Sipes Regional Airport, 243
McKenzie, Tenn., 48, 52
McKissack and McKissack, architects, 102
McMahan, Fred, 72
McMahan Construction Company, 72
McMinn County, 78, 86–87, 188, 215
McMinnville, Tenn., 2
McNairy County, 215, 245–46
McReynolds, Sam, 233
Meeman, Edward J., 195–97
Meeman-Shelby Forest State Park, 195–97
Meharry Medical School, 92, 100
Meigs County, 216, 248–49

Melick, Neal A., 67
Memphis, 2, 8, 16, 79, 93–95, 97, 130–31, 142–47, 195, 197–201, 218–19, 252–53
Memphis Academy of Art, 52
Memphis Brooks Museum of Art, 198
Memphis Commercial Appeal, 146
Memphis Federation of Musicians, 197
Memphis Housing Authority, 144, 146
Memphis Humane Center, 252
Memphis Municipal Airport, 253
Memphis Open Air Theatre, 197
Memphis Pink Palace Museum, 198
Memphis Press-Scimitar, 195–96, 199
Memphis Small House Construction Bureau, 147
Memphis Zoological Garden, 199
Memphis-to-Bristol Highway, 76, 81
Menzler, C. C., 17
Meriwether Lewis National Monument, 180–81
Middle Tennessee Electric Membership Corporation, 216
Middle Tennessee State University, 122
Milan, Tenn., 58
Miller, Irene, 50
Miller, J. P., 50
Mills, grist ,154, 159, 205–6, 221–22
Milton, George Fort, 24
Monroe County, 70, 97, 113, 181, 188
Montgomery County, 21, 114
Montgomery Bell State Park, 168–69
Monument, 156, 161–62
Moore County, 5–6
Morgan, Arthur S., 9, 108, 224
Morgan, Harcourt, 9, 108, 240, 250
Morgan County, 181–82
Morgan County State Forest, 182
Morristown, Tenn., 22, 38, 79, 239
Morristown College, 22
Moses Center, Knoxville, 84
Mound Bottom site, 161–62
Mount Pleasant, Tenn., 69
Mountain City, Tenn., 110
Mulbry, Howell B., 146
Murfreesboro, Tenn., 14–15, 77, 90–92, 121–22, 216
Muscle Shoals, Ala., 9, 213, 221, 236

Museum of Appalachia, 226
Music, 105, 126, 152–53, 182, 197–98

Nash, Charles, 200–201, 234
Nashville, 29, 30, 32–36, 55–56, 81–82, 100–105, 130, 136–38, 166–68, 215, 229
Nashville Allied Architects, 136–37
Nashville Banner, 215
Nashville City Market, 81–82
Nashville Housing Authority, 137
Nashville Tennessean, 1, 55, 138
Natchez Trace Parkway, 180–81
Natchez Trace State Park and Forest, 175–77
National Council of Christians and Jews, 198
National Council of Jewish Women, Memphis section, 94
National Housing Act of 1934, 147
National Industrial Recovery Act, 15, 128
National Ornamental Metal Museum, 94
National Park Service, 13, 35, 149–54, 157–60, 169, 180, 183, 185, 186, 190–97, 200–201, 204–5, 208–9, 231
National Recreation Demonstration Areas, 150, 169, 172, 174, 195, 201, 209
National Register of Historic Places, xiii, 50, 56, 58, 64, 72, 86, 93, 102, 105–7, 109, 112, 114, 122–23, 126–27, 135, 168, 211, 230, 232
National Rolley Hole Marble Competition, 185
National Youth Administration (NYA), 20–21, 22–24, 78, 81–86, 89, 92–93, 97–98, 110–11, 114, 118, 122–23, 126, 152, 161, 230
Neblett, John B., 169
Neitzel, Stuart, 163, 234
Neumann, George K., 163
New, William, 227
New Buffalo, Tenn., 100
New Farmers of America, 141
Newbern, Tenn., 217
Newport, Tenn., 48, 52–53
Nichols, Ruth, 154–55
Nicholson, V. L., Bridge Company, 218
Nolen, John, 129

Norris, George, 9
Norris, Tenn., 10, 128, 153, 221–25
Norris Dam, 219–26
Norris Dam State Park, 153–55
Norris Freeway, 221–22
Norris Lake, 153–55, 206–8, 221, 225–26
Nyquist, Carl, 61

Oak Ridge, Tenn., 50, 241
Oberteuffer, H. Amiard, 52
Oberteuffer, Karl, 52
Obion County, 7, 42–43, 86–89, 114–16, 182
Obion County Courthouse, 42–43, 182
Ocoee River, 246
Office of the Supervising Architect, 46–47, 50, 54, 55–56, 60, 65, 67, 69–75
Ogle, Noah "Bud," 195
O'Kelly, Hoke S., 176
Old Hickory, Tenn., 56
Oliver, John, 159–60
Olmstead Brothers, architects, 192–93
Oneida, Tenn., 6, 97
Orange Mound Civic Club, 94
Osborne, Douglas, 156
Overton, Bruce, 22, 123
Overton, Walter, 145
Overton County, 20, 21, 29, 43, 70–71, 116–18, 183–85
Overton Park, 197–99

Panther Creek State Park, 238
Paris, Tenn., 78, 217
Parks, 149–211; *see also* individual listings
Parksville, Tenn., 188–89
Parksville Lake, 189
Parrotsville, Tenn., 81
Parthenon, 36
Pate Memorial Bridge, 218
Peaveyhouse, Elizabeth, 134–35
Peek, George, 16
Perkins, Frances, 108
Perry County, 98
Petersburg, Tenn., 112–13, 240
Phillips, Edwin B., 142, 143
Pickett, John H. R., 67
Pickett Civilian Conservation Corps Memorial State Park, 185–87

Pickett County, 185–87
Pickwick Landing Lake, 236–37
Pickwick Landing State Park, 172–74
Pikeville, Tenn., 157
Pilot Knob, 155–56
Poe, Charles, 163, 199
Polk County, 12, 43–44, 188–90, 246–47
Polk County Courthouse, 43–44
Poor, Anne, 75
Poor, Henry Varnum, 75
Post offices, 46–76
Presley, Elvis, 95, 143
Presley, Gladys, 143
Presnell, James Henry, 142
Pritchett, W. T., 244
Privies, 81, 88, 217, 230
Pruitt, Pauline, 134–35
Public health projects, 17, 79, 81, 88, 94, 217, 230, 247
Public Works Administration (PWA), 14–16, 29–30, 32–45, 49, 56, 67, 79, 81–82, 87–88, 90–91, 95, 96–97, 99–105, 107–9, 112–16, 121, 123, 126–27, 128–30, 136, 142–43, 169, 216–19, 227–28, 230, 237–38, 240, 245, 250, 252
Pulaski, Tenn., 106
Puncheon, Tenn., 106
Putnam County, 18, 77, 118–20, 247

Race, architecture commissions, 72, 102; daycare for black families, 77, 84, 94; depictions of in public art, 57, 61, 69; historic sites, 166–67; limitations of New Deal reforms to African Americans, 17, 24, 130–31, 137–38, 142–46, 152–53, 155, 213, 225, 235, 252–53; segregated housing 129–31, 136–46, 148, 225; segregated schools, 97, 100, 102–3, 108, 120, 121; segregated parks, 171–72, 199–201; segregation in public facilities, 8, 3, 37, 39, 42, 89, 92, 155, 250–51; support for black artists 47
Radford, Gail, 129–30
Rambo, Frank, 239
Reconstruction Finance Corporation (RFC), 2–5
Reelfoot Lake State Park, 178–80

278 INDEX

Reelfoot National Wildlife Refuge, 179
Reeves, Hugh, 57
Regan and Weller, architects, 95, 142, 143
Relief programs, pre-New Deal, 2–3
Resettlement Administration (RA), 18–19, 129, 133, 150, 163–66, 169, 175–78, 183–84, 196, 201, 208–9, 211, 222
Reynolds, Horace, 92
Rhea County, 71–72, 248–49
Rice, Stanley, 141
Richardson, Jane, 143
Rigby, Kate, 133
Ripley, Tenn., 39–40, 64–65
Riverview Apartments, Kingsport, 148
Roach, Hoyte, 228
Roane County, 29, 72, 248
Roaring Fork Motor Nature Trail, 195
Roberts, Frank H. H., Jr., 174
Robertson County, 78, 120–21
Rock Creek Recreation Area, 204
Rock House Falls, 208
Rockefeller, John D., Jr., 191, 194
Rockefeller, Laura Spellman, 191–93
Rockwood, Tenn., 72
Rogersville, Tenn., 2
Roosevelt, Eleanor, 24–25, 53, 135
Roosevelt, Franklin D., 4–5, 22, 23, 46, 48, 78, 90, 160, 190–92, 210, 212–13, 216, 235, 250
Rosemary Lane Subdivision, Memphis, 147
Rosenwald Fund, 96, 98, 118, 120
Rowan, Edward, 47, 57, 67
Rowe, Chandler, 242, 251
Rutherford County, 14–15, 77, 89–92, 121–22, 249–50
Rural Electrification Administration, 65, 216–17, 230, 239–40, 244–45

Sampson, Ruby Hill, 207
Sanderlin, Jackson, 141
Sardis Model Community, 128
Saturn automobile factory, 113
Saunders, Clarence, 198
Savannah, Tenn., 61–62
Sawyers, Louis, 210
Scholz, Leopold, 36, 61
School lunch programs, 20–21, 81, 85, 106, 109, 120

Schools, 16, 18, 22–24, 80, 84, 96–127, 135, 224, 227
Scott County, 6, 97
Seals, Estel, 93
Sequatchie County, 23, 92–93, 122–23
Sevier, John, 33
Sevier County, 72, 190–95, 250–51
Sevierville, Tenn., 72
Shannon, Samuel H., 218
Shelby County, 8, 16, 79, 93–95, 123, 130–31, 142–47, 195–201, 218, 252–53
Shelby County Negro State Park, 199
Shelby Forest State Park, 195
Shelbyville, Tenn., 80
Shields Creek Ranger Station, 190
Shiloh National Military Park, 174
Shreve, Lamb & Harmon, architects, 60
Signal Mountain, Tenn., 107
Simon, Louis A., 47, 49–50, 54, 56, 58, 61–65, 67, 69–74, 76, 95
Smith, J. Frazier, 142–43, 145–47
Smith, W. R., and Sons, 44
Smith County, 123, 218
Smyrna, Tenn., 249–50
Sneedville, Tenn., 109
Social Security Administration, 30
Soil conservation, 13, 17, 19, 150, 156–57, 163, 169, 176, 184, 185–86, 189–90, 196, 203, 211, 213–16, 231, 244–46, 247
Soil Conservation and Domestic Allotment Act, 214
Solomon Federal Building, 60–61
Somerville, Tenn., 105
South Cumberland State Recreation Area, 169–71
South Pittsburg, Tenn., 67
South West Tennessee Electric Membership Corporation, 216
Southeastern Fox Hunters Association, 165
Southgate, Donald, 103
Spangler, Walter, 93
Sparta, Tenn., 76
Spencer, Tenn., 97
Spring Hill, Tenn., 113
Springfield, Tenn., 120–21
Stadiums, football and track, 100, 103, 115, 120, 122, 125–26

Standing Stone State Park, 20, 183–85
Stanton, William Macy, 133–35
State office buildings, 33–36
Steanes Coal and Lumber Company, 185
Steele Creek Park, 201–2
Steeplechase, 168
Stewart, B. M., 239
Stewart, Tenn., 110
Stewart County, 5, 11
Stokes, Walter, 103
Stone Castle, 125–26
Sullivan, Lynne P., 234–35
Sullivan County, 95, 124–26, 130, 148, 201–22, 253–54
Sumner County, 44
Sumner County Courthouse, 44
Swann, Fanny, 251–52
Swimming beaches, 204, 205, 206
Sycamore Falls, 170

Taylor Iron Works and Supply Company, 250
Tellico Plains, Tenn., 97, 188
Tennessee Coal, Iron, and Railroad Company, 170–71
Tennessee Department of Conservation, 3–4, 163, 211
Tennessee Department of Education, 98
Tennessee Department of Institutions and Public Welfare, 3–4
Tennessee Division of Archaeology, 163
Tennessee Division of Soil Erosion Control, 176
Tennessee Division of State Forests, 14, 165, 176, 187, 209
Tennessee Education Association, 120
Tennessee Electric Power Company, 10, 216, 232–33, 245–46
Tennessee Emergency Relief Administration (TERA), 18, 29, 43, 77, 96, 100, 118–19, 120, 123, 125–26, 131, 175–76, 183–84, 244
Tennessee Farm Bureau Federation, 250
Tennessee Game and Fish Commission, 165, 196
Tennessee Highway Department, 247
Tennessee Historical Quarterly, 79
Tennessee Historical Records Survey, 79
Tennessee Historical Society, xiv
Tennessee Housing Authorities Law, 129–30
Tennessee National Guard, 78, 80, 83, 85–88, 90, 93–95
Tennessee River Folklife Interpretive Center, 156
Tennessee River Museum, 62
Tennessee State Capitol, 29, 35–36
Tennessee State Forests, 157, 163–65, 175–78, 181–82, 185–88, 195–97, 208–11
Tennessee State Library and Archives, 79
Tennessee State Museum, 36
Tennessee State Office Building (John Sevier Building), 29, 33–34
Tennessee State Park and Forestry Commission, 149
Tennessee State Parks, 149–56, 160–61, 163–66, 168–88, 195–97, 199–201, 204–11
Tennessee State Planning Commission, 3–4, 219
Tennessee State Relief Administration, 17, 18, 84
Tennessee State Supreme Court Building, 29, 34–35
Tennessee State University, 103
Tennessee Technological University, 120
Tennessee Valley Authority, xiii, 4, 9–11, 14, 53, 62, 64, 66, 112, 126, 128, 133, 135, 149–51, 153–56, 160–61, 163, 171–74, 204–28, 212–13, 215–16, 219–26, 232–43, 245–52
Tennessee Wildlife Federation, Knox County chapter, 231
Tennessee Wildlife Resources Agency, 177, 231
Theater, 105, 126, 133134, 152, 155, 184, 197
Thomas, H. E., 133
Thornborough, Laura, 193
Tigrett Wildlife Management Area, 231
Tipton County, 6
Tiptonville, Tenn., 38–39, 84–85
Tiptonville Woman's Club, 84–85
Tisdale and Pinson, architects, 101, 114, 136

INDEX

T. O. Fulller State Park, 199–201
Townsend, Robert, 106
Tracy City, Tenn., 107, 169–71
Trails, 155, 170, 173–74, 187, 189, 192–93, 207, 211
Trenton, Tenn., 58–59, 82, 88
Tudor Revival style, 134
Tugwell, Rexford, 18–19
Tull, L. E., 62
Tyner, J. D., 166–67
Tyson, Bettie McGhee, 227
Tyson, Lawrence D., 112, 227
Tyson, McGhee, 227

Unaka Mountain, 203
Unaka National Forest, 202
Unicoi, Tenn., 203–4
Unicoi County, 73, 202–4
Union City, Tenn., 7, 42–43, 79, 86–89, 114–16, 182
Union County, 4, 204–8, 223, 226
University of Chattanooga, 47, 108, 126
University of Memphis (Memphis State University), 201
University of Tennessee, 9, 112, 200, 234
University of Tennessee Agricultural Extension Service, 9, 17, 92, 128, 213–14, 232, 244–45
University of Tennessee Medical Center, 79
University of Tennessee Tobacco Experiment Station, 232
University of Tennessee at Chattanooga, 47, 108
U.S. Army Corps of Engineers, 232, 236, 239, 252
U.S. Bureau of Reclamation, 2, 10, 219, 221–22
U.S. Dairy Experiment Station, 85, 244
U.S. Department of Agriculture, 13, 16–17, 19, 62, 70, 135, 150, 163–65, 175–77, 183–85, 210, 213–15
U.S. Department of Interior, 13, 101, 128–29, 133; *see also* National Park Service
U.S. Forest Service, 150, 153, 188–90, 202–4
U.S. Housing Authority, 130, 138–39, 141–42, 144–46, 148

U.S. Marine Hospital, 79
U.S. Soil Conservation Service, 19,
U.S. Treasury Department, 2, 5, 46–75
U.S. War Department, 180

Van Buren County, 22–23, 97, 208–9
Vance, Fred V., 125
Vanderbilt University, 35
Volunteer Electric Membership Corporation, 216
Vonore, Tenn., 97, 181

Wagner-Steagall Housing Act, 130
Wallace, Joel, 146
Wallenberg, Raoul, Band Shell, Memphis, 197–98
Waller, George D., 122
Wank, Roland, 222, 238, 251
Warfield and Keeble, architects, 78, 80, 83, 85, 90, 136
Warner, Edwin, 167
Warner, Percy, 167
Warner Parks, 167–68
Warren, Susie, 211
Warren County, 10, 18, 29,
Washington County, 45, 126–27
Watauga State Park, 201
Waterworks and sewers, 217, 227–28, 230, 237–38, 247, 249–50
Watkins Institute, 56
Watson, Clarence E., 89
Watson, Forbes, 47
Watts Bar Lake, 248–49
Waugh, Sidney, 67–68
Waverly, Tenn., 63
Wayne County, 180–81
Weakley, Robert, 74
Weakley County, 45, 73–75
Western Heights Homes, Knoxville, 141
White, Clara, 133
White, Robert H., 213
White County, 10, 20–21, 76, 77
White House, Tenn., 78
Whitis, W. H., 45
Whitwell, Tenn., 98
Wilkie, Wendell, 233
Williamson County, 29, 181
Wilson, Woodrow, 188

INDEX 281

Wilson Cedar Forest Project, 210
Wilson County, 127, 210–11, 254
Wilson County Community House, 127, 254
Winchester, Tenn., 38
Wolcott, John W., Jr., 65
Women: arts projects, 47; CWA work programs, 17–18; community gardens, 77, 85; daycare, 77, 84, 94; housing officials, 133, 143; homesteaders, 134–35; NYA projects, 84–85; post office mural artists, 50–54, 62, 64–65, 70–71, 74–75; WPA work programs, 20–21, 80–81, 84, 94
Woodbury, Tenn., 217, 227–28
Woods, Everett, 142, 143, 146
Woolwine, Emmons H., 32–33, 36, 136
Works Progress Administration (WPA), 19–22, 29, 38–39, 42, 43, 45, 49–50, 53, 61–64, 70, 73, 77–85, 90–91, 93–95, 96–97, 100, 103, 105–7, 109–11, 113–14, 116–18, 120–23, 125–27, 131, 149, 152, 163–68, 177–78, 180–84, 196–200, 209, 211, 216–19, 227–30, 232, 234–35, 239–40, 244–45, 252–54
World War II, 127, 146, 211, 227–29, 238–39, 241–44, 246–47, 249, 250–51, 254

Yearwood, Niles, 37
York, Alvin C., 92, 105, 166
York Veterans Administration Medical Center, 14–15, 90–92

Zorach, Marguerite, 50, 64–65
Zorach, William, 50, 59–60
Zorthian, Kirayr H., 36

Tennessee's New Deal Landscape was designed and typeset on a Macintosh computer system using PageMaker software. The text and chapter openings are set in Goudy. This book was designed by Ellen Beeler, typeset by Kimberly Scarbrough, and manufactured by Thomson-Shore, Inc. The paper used in this book is designed for an effective life of at least three hundred years.